DIRECT
ACTION

L.A. Kauffman has spent more than thirty years immersed in radical movements as a participant, strategist, journalist, and observer. She has been called a "virtuoso organizer" by journalist Scott Sherman for her role in saving community gardens and public libraries in New York City from development. Kauffman coordinated the grassroots mobilizing efforts for the huge protests against the Iraq war in 2003–04. Her writings on American radicalism and social movement history have been published in *The Nation*, *n+1*, *The Baffler*, and many other outlets.

DIRECT ACTION

Protest and the Reinvention of American Radicalism

L.A. Kauffman

VERSO
London • New York

First published by Verso 2017
© L.A. Kauffman 2017

All rights reserved

The moral rights of the authors have been asserted

3 5 7 9 10 8 6 4 2

Verso
UK: 6 Meard Street, London W1F 0EG
US: 20 Jay Street, Suite 1010, Brooklyn, NY 11201
versobooks.com

Verso is the imprint of New Left Books

ISBN-13: 978-1-78478-409-6
ISBN-13: 978-1-78478-422-9 (UK EBK)
ISBN-13: 978-1-78478-410-2 (US EBK)

British Library Cataloguing in Publication Data
A catalogue record for this book is available from the British Library

Library of Congress Cataloging-in-Publication Data
A catalog record for this book is available from the Library of Congress

Typeset in Garamond by MJ&N Gavan, Truro, Cornwall
Printed in the US by Maple Press

To the memories of
Armando Perez (1948–1999)
Ray Davis (1963–1999)
Françoise Cachelin (1923–2003)
Brad Will (1970–2006)

Contents

Introduction

What happened to the American left after the sixties? Whole book-shelves groan under the weight of histories of the sixties, and both the Old Left and the New Left have been richly and extensively studied. Yet, while significant waves of activism have punctuated the history of the last forty years, the story of American radicalism in recent decades remains almost untold.

That may be, at least in part, because the story is such a difficult one to tell—not for lack of radical endeavors over this time period, but because of their profusion. It's not simply that there's no single organization or political tendency or leader that could plausibly represent the larger left. The most significant dynamic in American radicalism in the period after the sixties has been a proliferation of movements, causes, and political identities. These are so numerous that listing them all would be tedious: the landscape of the contemporary left includes feminisms of many forms and hues; radical movements for racial justice as varied as the communities of color that have given rise to them; lesbian, gay, bisexual, transgender, and queer radicalisms, evolving and complex; radical forms of environmentalism, from deep ecology to the climate justice movement; labor-based radicalisms and multiple strains of anarchism and socialism. At times, it can seem like the number of recent radicalisms stands in inverse proportion to their overall influence, for on the whole, the period since the 1960s has been inhospitable for the left. In the face of this tangled multiplicity of movements and political initiatives, it's perhaps not surprising that there have been few attempts to survey the post-sixties radical landscape as a whole, to tease out broad historical patterns from the plethora of organizations, mobilizations, and events.

This book represents one telling of the tale, a distillation of more than thirty years of observation, reporting, and organizing on the frontlines of many of these movements. The story of American radicalism is told here through the lens of direct action: the fierce, showy tradition of disruptive protest employed by many of the era's most distinctive and influential movements. Direct action was far from the only approach used by radical movements throughout this era, and there's no claim here that it's always the best or most productive one. It has, though, consistently served as a laboratory for political experimentation and innovation, and as an arena for grappling with many of the big challenges facing progressive movements more generally: how to win meaningful victories and sustain communities of resistance in a rightward-shifting political climate; how to build movements that don't replicate the very power dynamics they seek to challenge, especially in matters of race and gender; how to create effective political alliances that respect the voice and autonomy of all partners; how to inspire vision, hope, and action in hard times.

"Direct action" can refer to a huge variety of efforts to create change outside the established mechanisms of government—it's a slippery and imprecise term, much debated by the movements that use it. Protest marches, boycotts, and strikes all are, or can be, forms of direct action; the same is true of picket lines, sit-ins, and human blockades. The term itself dates back about a century, having first been widely used by the early twentieth-century Industrial Workers of the World (IWW), known colloquially as the Wobblies, the liveliest and most fiercely anti-capitalist labor movement in US history. "The working class and the employing class have nothing in common," the IWW's manifesto began, and the organization always considered the complete abolition of capitalism to be its ultimate goal. Toward that end the Wobblies called for "industrial action directly by, for, and of the workers themselves, without the treacherous aid of labor misleaders or scheming politicians," action that encompassed everything from work slowdowns and factory occupations to industrial sabotage.

It is the black civil rights movement of the 1950s and the 1960s that serves as the most important touchstone for the direct-action movements of recent decades, however. From the Montgomery bus boycott and the Greensboro lunch counter sit-ins to the Freedom Rides and the march over Selma's Edmund Pettus Bridge, the civil rights movement's acts of resistance to racial segregation and white supremacy have become so emblematic of transformative collective action that every major movement since has referenced them in some way. The mythic status acquired by the civil rights movement over time cemented its role as model and inspiration, even as persistent racial divisions on the left complicated claims to its legacy. But the basic vision of direct action outlined by Dr. Martin Luther King Jr. in his letter from Birmingham jail has shaped its use ever since: "Nonviolent direct action seeks to create such a crisis and foster such a tension," King famously wrote, "that a community which has constantly refused to negotiate is forced to confront the issue. It seeks so to dramatize the issue that it can no longer be ignored."

Direct action is most closely associated with movements of the left, but there is no necessary correlation between a movement's use of direct action and its politics: disruptive protest can be employed to further all kinds of agendas, some downright reactionary. Most dramatically, the anti-abortion group Operation Rescue organized a massive and sustained campaign of blockades outside abortion clinics in the late 1980s, involving more than 20,000 arrests. The guide that many of these blockaders used, anti-abortion activist Joseph M. Scheidler's 1985 *Closed: 99 Ways to Stop Abortion*, directly echoed the catalog of protest methods found in political scientist Gene Sharp's 1973 classic *The Politics of Nonviolent Action*, a foundational text of direct-action organizing. But the relative rarity of right-wing direct action is testament to the democratic and anti-authoritarian values that typically pervade the practice: in theory the tactics of direct action might be politically neutral, but in the actual world of grassroots organizing, they have been anything but.

This book, in any case, doesn't try to catalog the variety of ways that direct action has been used in recent decades. Instead, it follows the unfolding of a specific, linked, and messy set of political experiments. The movements profiled in this book embraced a particular set of organizing practices, deeply shaped by feminism and queer radicalism, in response to a broad sense of crisis and retrenchment after the 1960s. Of course they wanted to remake American society, but many concluded that they first had to remake the American left, much of which seemed dispirited and directionless as the grand hopes of the sixties receded. The new movements rejected hierarchical organizational structures, traditional leadership models, and rigid ideologies, and they sought forms of activism and political engagement that could preserve rather than subsume difference and multiplicity. Women, especially queer women, played crucial roles in this process of political reinvention, infusing this new radicalism with feminist practices and values through the very process of movement-building.

Some of the movements chronicled in this account have had enormous impact: ACT UP saved millions of lives by hastening the development of key AIDS medications and expanding access to their use. Others, though, only added a modicum of political friction as policies they opposed moved forward: though they had a variety of important political impacts, the global justice movement and Occupy Wall Street no more stopped the forward march of neoliberalism than the antiwar movement stopped the 2003 invasion of Iraq. Protest actions that felt important and empowering to participants sometimes had few repercussions outside the small world of activism, while others that seemed futile at the time had far-reaching effects that weren't felt for years.

The book begins with an ending and ends with a beginning. It starts with the last major protest against the Vietnam War, which was also the largest and most ambitious direct-action protest in US history: a remarkable yet nearly forgotten attempt by antiwar radicals to shut down the federal government through nonviolent action in May 1971. This protest so badly rattled the Nixon administration that it ordered federal troops to sweep up protesters by the thousands, in the largest mass arrests in US history. This Mayday 1971 protest also pointed the way toward a new style and structure of radical organizing that movement after movement would embrace and adapt in the decades to come. The book concludes with another watershed moment more than forty years later, when protests against the August 2014 police killing of Michael Brown in Ferguson, Missouri grew into a nationwide movement for black lives, animated by disruptive direct action and an intersectional politics rooted in the feminism of queer women of color. Along the way, the book traces deep connections between movements usually viewed in isolation, and considers how activists have grappled with a political landscape divided by race and dominated by the right.

To weave together this story, much has been left out: the labor movement, for instance, mostly embattled and declining over this time period but with interesting pockets of promising insurgency, receives only glancing attention. Race is central to this narrative, but it's largely considered in black and white; important traditions of organizing and resistance in other communities of color, from Native American organizing around land rights, environmental justice, and climate justice to the direct-action immigrant rights movement of recent decades, are only mentioned briefly. All stories are of necessity partial renderings of complex realities, this one especially so.

Those who have taken part in direct action know that it's a profoundly embodied and often personally transformative experience. Organizer Brad Will, a builder of bridges between radical movements until his 2006 murder by right-wing paramilitaries in Mexico, captured it well in a 2000 interview. Direct action, he said, "is like a conduit, like electricity. It moves through you, not just into you. You're not a battery, you're a wire." The movements that have sought to harness this kind of energy in recent decades and channel it into sweeping change have never come close to achieving their full aims. But through direct action, these movements have won more victories and catalyzed more social transformation than one might expect given their relatively modest size. Together they have fashioned a new kind of American radicalism along the way. This is a story about dealing with defeat and marginalization, but its ultimate message—for those who share the values of the movements profiled here—is one of hope: no matter how long the odds, with smart organizing, and the right tools, we can win more than we imagine.

1

Mayday

The largest and most audacious direct action in US history is also among the least remembered, a protest that has slipped into deep historical obscurity. It was a protest against the Vietnam War, but it wasn't part of the storied sixties, having taken place in 1971, a year of nationwide but largely unchronicled ferment. To many, infighting, violence, and police repression had effectively destroyed "the movement" two years earlier in 1969. That year, Students for a Democratic Society (SDS), the totemic organization of the white New Left, had disintegrated into dogmatic and squabbling factions; the Black Panther Party, meanwhile, had been so thoroughly infiltrated and targeted by law enforcement that factionalism and paranoia had come to eclipse its expansive program of revolutionary nationalism. But the war had certainly not ended, and neither had the underlying economic and racial injustices that organizers had sought to address across a long decade of protest politics. If anything, the recent flourishing of heterodox new radicalisms—from the women's and gay liberation movements to radical ecology to militant Native American, Chicano,

Washington
**if the government
won't stop the war
we'll stop the
government**
May Day Movement

Puerto Rican, and Asian-American movements—had given those who dreamed of a world free of war and oppression a sobering new awareness of the range and scale of the challenges they faced.

On May 3, 1971, after nearly two weeks of intense antiwar protest in Washington, DC, ranging from a half-million-person march to large-scale sit-ins outside the Selective Service, Justice Department, and other government agencies, some 25,000 young people set out to do something brash and extraordinary: disrupt the basic functioning of the federal government through nonviolent action. They called themselves the Mayday Tribe, and their slogan was as succinct as it was ambitious: "If the government won't stop the war, we'll stop the government." The slogan was of course hyperbolic— even if Washington, DC were completely paralyzed by protest for a day or week or a month, that would not halt the collection of taxes, the delivery of mail, the dropping of bombs, or countless other government functions—but that made it no less electrifying as a rallying cry, and no less alarming to the Nixon administration (Nixon's White House chief of staff, H.R. Haldeman, called it "potentially a real threat"). An elaborate tactical manual distributed in advance detailed twenty-one key bridges and traffic circles for protesters to block nonviolently, with stalled vehicles, improvised barricades, or their bodies. The immediate goal was to snarl traffic so completely that government employees could not get to their jobs. The larger objective was "to create the spectre of social chaos while maintaining the support or at least toleration of the broad masses of American people."[1]

The protest certainly interfered with business as usual in Washington: traffic was snarled, and many government employees stayed home. Others commuted to their offices before dawn, and three members of Congress even resorted to canoeing across the Potomac to get themselves to Capitol Hill. But most of the planned blockades held only briefly, if at all, because most of the protesters were arrested before they even got into position. Thanks to the detailed tactical manual, the authorities knew exactly where protesters would be deployed. To stop them from paralyzing the city, the Nixon Administration had made the unprecedented decision to sweep them all up, using not just police but actual military forces.

Under direct presidential orders, Attorney General John Mitchell mobilized the National Guard and thousands of troops from the Army and the Marines to join the Washington, DC police in rounding up everyone suspected of participating in the protest. As one protester noted, "Anyone and everyone who looked at all freaky was scooped up off the street." A staggering number of people— more than 7,000—were locked up before the day was over, in what remain the largest mass arrests in US history.[2]

Many observers, including sympathetic ones, called it a rout for the protesters. "It was universally panned as the worst planned, worst executed, most slovenly, strident and obnoxious peace action ever committed," wrote esteemed antiwar journalist Mary McGrory in the *Boston Globe* afterwards. In the *New York Times*, reporter Richard Halloran flatly declared, "The Tribe members failed to achieve their goal. And they appear to have had no discernible impact on President Nixon's policy in Vietnam." Even Rennie Davis, the Chicago 7 defendant and New Left leader who had originally conceived of the Mayday action, announced at a press conference that the protest had failed.[3]

But the government's victory, if you can call it that, came only as a result of measures that turned the workaday bustle of the district's streets into what William H. Rehnquist, the assistant attorney general who would later become chief justice of the Supreme Court, called "qualified martial law." While the government hadn't been stopped, there was a very real sense that it had been placed under siege by its own citizens, with the nation's capital city transformed into "a simulated Saigon," as reporter Nicholas von Hoffman put it in the *Washington Post*. Nixon felt compelled to announce in a press conference, "The Congress is not intimidated, the President is not intimidated, this government is going to go forward," statements that only belied his profound unease. White House aide Jeb Magruder later noted that the protest had "shaken" Nixon and his staff, while CIA director Richard Helms called Mayday "a very damaging kind of event," noting that it was "one of the things that was putting increasing pressure on the administration to try and find some way to get out of the war."[4]

Mayday, the scruffy and forgotten protest that helped speed US withdrawal from Vietnam, changed the course of activist history as well. It came at a time of crisis for the left—indeed, the distress call embedded in the mobilization's name could apply equally well to the state of American radical movements in 1971 as to the conduct of the war they opposed. The last major national protest against the Vietnam War, Mayday was also a crucial first experiment with a new kind of radicalism, one rooted as much in its practices as in its ideas or demands. This quixotic attempt to "stop the government"—so flawed in its execution, yet so unnerving in its effects—was organized in a different manner than any protest before it, in ways that have influenced most American protest movements since.

The history of American radicalism since the sixties, when it's been considered at all, has typically been misunderstood as a succession of disconnected issue- and identity-based movements, erupting into public view and then disappearing, perhaps making headlines and winning fights along the way but adding up to little more. Mayday 1971 provides the perfect starting point for a very different tale, a story about deep political continuities, hidden connections, and lasting influences. It's a story rooted less in radicals' ideas about how the world ought to change than the evolving forms of action they've used to actually change it—whether hastening the end of an unpopular war, blocking the construction of nuclear power plants, revolutionizing the treatment of AIDS, stalling toxic trade deals, or reforming brutally racist police practices. Many movements contributed to this long process of political reinvention, but feminism and queer radicalism played special, central roles, profoundly redefining the practice of activism in ways that have too rarely been acknowledged. And because this is an American story, it's shaped at every level by questions and divisions of race. The story begins with a major racial shift in the practice of disruptive activism, as the direct-action tradition refined by the black civil rights movement in the fifties and sixties to such powerful effect was taken up and transformed by mostly white organizers in the seventies and eighties.

The Mayday direct action took place a year after the Nixon Administration invaded Cambodia, an escalation of the Vietnam War that had provoked angry walk-outs on more than a hundred college and university campuses. At one of these, Ohio's Kent State University, National Guardsmen fired into a crowd of protesters, killing four and wounding nine; ten days later, police killed two students and wounded twelve more at Jackson State University in Mississippi. The deaths sparked strikes at hundreds more campuses and inspired thousands who had never protested before to take to the streets. By the end of May 1970, it's estimated that half the country's student population—perhaps several million youth—took part in antiwar activities, which, in the words of former University of California president Clark Kerr, "seemed to exhaust the entire known repertoire of forms of dissent," including the bombing or burning of nearly one hundred campus buildings with military ties.[5] So many people were radicalized during the spring 1970 uprising that the antiwar movement suddenly swelled with a new wave of organizers spread all throughout the country, many in places that had seen relatively little activism before then.

The tumult of spring 1970 faded by the fall, however, and an air of futility hung over the established antiwar movement. Many of the longtime organizers who had persevered beyond the movement's crisis year of 1969 were now burning out. As one antiwar publication put it in an unsigned piece, for the previous seven years "we have met, discussed, analyzed, lectured, published, lobbied, paraded, sat in, burned draft cards, stopped troop trains, refused induction, marched, trashed, burned and bombed buildings, destroyed induction centers. Yet the war has gotten steadily worse—for the Vietnamese, and, in a very different way, for us." It seemed that everything had been tried, and nothing had worked. "Most everyone I know is tired of demonstrations," wrote New Left leader David Dellinger. "No wonder. If you've seen one or two, you've seen them all ... Good, bad, or in between, they have not stopped the war, or put an end to poverty and racism, or freed all political prisoners."[6]

In this climate of grim frustration, the national antiwar movement split, as long-standing tensions about the political value of civil disobedience divided activists who were planning the antiwar mobilization for spring 1971. A new formation named the National

Peace Action Coalition (NPAC) called for a massive legal march and rally on April 24. This coalition boasted a long and impressive list of endorsers, but was centrally controlled by a Trotskyist organization, the Socialist Workers Party, and its offshoots. NPAC aimed to build a mass mobilization against the war—organizer Fred

A "united front of the masses" (designer unknown; author's collection)

Halstead called it "an authentic united front of the masses"—bringing together the widest possible array of forces. Toward that end, NPAC put forth just one lowest-common-denominator demand: "Out of Vietnam now!"[7]

NPAC also vehemently opposed the use of any tactics that went beyond legally permitted protest. Civil disobedience, the coalition's leadership believed, accomplished little while alienating many from the cause. "In our opinion, small civil disobedience actions—whether in the Gandhi-King tradition or in the vein of violent confrontation—are not effective forms of action," declared the SWP's newspaper, *The Militant*. "While we do not question the commitment and courage of those who deploy such tactics, we feel that they are not oriented toward winning and mobilizing a *mass* movement." The Mayday action came in for special criticism: "When people state that they are purposely and illegally attempting to disrupt the government, as the Mayday Tribe has done, they isolate themselves from the masses of American people."[8]

The other major wing of the antiwar movement ultimately renamed itself the Peoples Coalition for Peace and Justice (PCPJ), and was anchored by pacifist organizations ranging from the Fellowship of Reconciliation to the War Resisters League. PCPJ favored a multi-issue approach to antiwar organizing and worked to build alliances with non-pacifist organizations like the National Welfare Rights Organization, drawing connections between the foreign and domestic policies of the US government. The coalition also felt that stronger tactics than mere marching were called for, and emphatically endorsed civil disobedience. "Massive One-Day Demonstrations Aren't Enough," read the headline of a PCPJ broadsheet issued that spring, "More's Needed to End the War." PCPJ didn't openly discourage people from attending the April 24 NPAC march, but focused its efforts on a multi-day "People's Lobby," which consisted of planned, coordinated sit-ins outside major government buildings.[9]

Into this fractured political landscape came the Mayday Tribe, a new player with a very different approach. The group was launched by Rennie Davis, a white New Left leader who had become nationally famous after the melees outside the Democratic National Convention in 1968, when the federal government prosecuted him and other prominent organizers—the Chicago 7—for conspiracy. In Davis' conception, the Mayday Tribe would bring the most politicized hippies of the time together with the hippest of the hardcore radicals. The word "tribe" itself was a countercultural code word, having been appropriated by whites to signal groovy distance from the dominant culture (the 1967 San Francisco "Be-In" that propelled hippiedom to the national stage, for instance, was known as "A Gathering of the Tribes" despite a notable lack of Native American participation), and Mayday had a long-haired freaky flavor that was decidedly missing from either the Trotskyist or pacifist wings of the antiwar movement. Jerry Coffin, an organizer with the War Resisters League who teamed up with Davis when Mayday was only an idea, recalled it as an attempt "to create a responsible hip alternative" to the Weather Underground: "merging radical politics, Gandhian nonviolence, serious rock and roll, [and] lots of drugs." Many —perhaps most—of the people who took part in the action were relative newcomers to the movement, from the generation that had been radicalized by Cambodia and Kent State.[10]

Davis took the idea of nonviolently blockading the federal government from a bold but ultimately unsuccessful attempt by the Brooklyn chapter of the Congress of Racial Equality (CORE) to paralyze New York City traffic on the opening day of the 1964 World's Fair. CORE was an important interracial civil rights group founded in the 1940s, with pacifist roots and a strong commitment to nonviolent direct action. The organization is best known for the daring Freedom Rides it organized in 1961 to challenge racial segregation on interstate buses in the Deep South. These rides, with small groups of black and white activists defying Jim Crow through the simple act of traveling and sitting together, were met with extreme violence, with one bus firebombed and many Freedom Riders brutally beaten by white mobs. CORE was most active in the North, however, particularly in Chicago where it was founded; there, and in other northern cities, the group used sit-ins and other direct-action tactics as part of a major campaign in the early 1960s against school segregation.

By 1964, many in the civil rights movement were growing impatient at the slow pace of change. The Brooklyn chapter of CORE,

1964 CORE Stall-In leaflet (designer unknown; Elliot Linzer Collection, Queens College Special Collections and Archives, CUNY)

younger and more radical than the organization as a whole, decided to use the occasion of the World's Fair to draw attention to the deep racial inequalities in the event's host city. CORE proposed disrupting the fair's opening day through a "stall-in" at strategic points on the city's highways, with protesters deliberately allowing their cars to run out of fuel so that the vehicles would block the roadways.

"Drive a while for freedom," read a leaflet that organizers distributed throughout Bedford-Stuyvesant and other black neighborhoods. "Take only enough gas to get your car on exhibit on one of these highways." The goal of the planned disruptions was to pressure the city's government to take action on housing, education, police brutality, and other issues of urgent concern to New York City's black and Latino population. But the outcry over this obstructive plan was enormous, with everyone from New York City officials to moderate civil rights leaders to President Lyndon Johnson denouncing the protest as one that would, in Johnson's words, "do the civil rights cause no good." CORE's national director, James Farmer, was so appalled that he suspended the Brooklyn chapter. In the end, very few people went through with the highway action. They almost didn't need to: the controversy had already garnered massive publicity, Fair attendance was a fraction of what had been projected, and civil disobedience protests inside the event led to 300 arrests.[11]

The Mayday protest, with its goal of blockading the nation's capital, echoed the CORE plan in mischievous tone and disorderly intent. The Mayday protest was to entail "action rather than congregation, disruption rather than display." As one Mayday leaflet circulated in advance of the 1971 protests declared, in a clear allusion to the April 24 NPAC event, "Nobody gives a damn how many dumb sheep can flock to Washington demonstrations, which are dull ceremonies of dissent that won't stop the war." Mayday wouldn't be a standard protest rally, where a series of speakers (usually chosen through an acrimonious behind-the-scenes struggle) would lecture to a passive crowd. It wouldn't be a conventional protest march, where demonstrators would trudge along a route that had been pre-arranged with the police, shepherded by movement marshals controlled by the protest leadership. With much antiwar protest having become dreary and routinized ("Should I take pictures, I kept questioning myself, or would photographs from past identical rallies suffice?" asked one radical after April 24), Mayday promised to be novel and unpredictable.[12]

Mayday would also diverge from the traditional form of civil disobedience that PCPJ supported. That type of action, the tactical manual explained, usually "involved a very small group of people engaging in 'moral witness' or action that involved them breaking a specific law, almost always with advance notice to authorities." In a typical civil disobedience protest, participants would sit down at the entrance to a building or inside some official's office and wait until police—who knew ahead of time what the protesters would do—carried them off to jail. If they were attacked or beaten, they would neither fight back nor run away. "Nonviolence in its dynamic condition means conscious suffering," Mohandas Gandhi, the great Indian practitioner of nonviolent resistance, had declared. The philosophy of civil disobedience that he and Dr. Martin Luther King Jr. propounded, and most pacifists embraced, entailed a willingness to accept violence and a refusal to engage in it, even in self-defense.[13]

In the activist climate of the late 1960s and early 1970s, this kind of civil disobedience had acquired an aura of piety and passivity distasteful to many radicals; as Jerry Coffin observed, "very few of [the Mayday protesters] would have identified themselves as being members of a nonviolent movement." The organizers of Mayday had a somewhat difficult sell to make, and the tactical manual emphatically distinguished their disruptive direct-action scenario from conventional nonviolence: "We need to be clear that we are not talking about an exercise in martyrdom; we are not talking about negotiated arrests; we are talking about using a tactic to attain an objective." Explained S.J. Avery, who was working with the Quaker Project on Community Conflict at the time and ran some of the training sessions in nonviolence for Mayday protest, "The kind of nonviolent direct action that we had always been talking about was the very classic, traditional Gandhian sort, where you did your action and then you stayed there and you took your consequences. That was not part of the Mayday rhetoric. People wanted to keep it nonviolent, but I think a lot of people went down there thinking it was going to be pretty much guerrilla action. And that some people would get arrested, and some figured if they could get away, that was great."[14]

The Mayday organizers hoped to tap into the revulsion many felt toward the tactics of the Weather Underground and other violent groups, while steering clear of the submissiveness and sanctimony radicals associated with nonviolence. Explained Maris Cakars, editor of the influential pacifist magazine *WIN*, "The idea of 'we've tried everything, now there's nothing left but violence' was pretty much replaced with the notion that now that violence—trashing, bombing, off the pigging—had failed it was time for a *really* radical

A new take on nonviolence (designer: Markley Morris; courtesy of Markley Morris)

approach: nonviolent civil disobedience." The tactical manual explained that Mayday would be militant in a way "that conforms more with our new life style" and deploys "joy and life against bureaucracy and grim death." An organizing leaflet elaborated: "The overall discipline will be non violent, the tactic disruptive, and the spirit joyous and creative." To underscore their gently irreverent take on the sometime pious tradition of nonviolence, Mayday's planners used witty remixed versions of social-justice artist Ben Shahn's line drawing of Gandhi in their mobilizing materials, sometimes showing a crowd of Gandhis, sometimes rendering him with a raised fist.[15]

The most novel aspect of Mayday, though, was its organizing plan. Unlike any national demonstration before it, this action was to be created through a decentralized structure based on geographic regions. "This means no 'National Organizers,'" the tactical manual explained, in contrast to all the big DC marches and rallies that had come before. "You do the organizing. This means no 'movement generals' making tactical decisions you have to carry out. Your region makes the tactical decisions within the discipline of nonviolent civil disobedience."[16]

This approach reflected a major shift in activist temper over the previous two years or so: a growing disdain for national organizations, movement celebrities, and structured leadership, all of which were felt to stifle creativity and action. "Following the disintegration of SDS," the radical magazine *Liberation* explained, "there were many in the movement who were thoroughly disillusioned with the whole idea of a national political structure. They came to feel that authentic radicalism must grow out of involvement in local or small-group activity, that it cannot flourish within a national organization." The now-defunct SDS certainly came in for special scorn, along with the "movement heavies"—influential or hardline radical men—who so often represented the group to the media. But the criticism also extended to the national antiwar movement in its various organizational guises, which had "really well-known people who were on the letterhead and [acted as] spokespeople for the movement," as Ed Hedemann of the War Resisters League put it.[17]

A pamphlet published by an anonymous group of West Coast activists not long before Mayday (and circulated among anarchists ever since) outlined an underlying critique of the very idea of a national or mass movement. *Anti-Mass: Methods of Organization for Collectives* defined "the mass" as an intrinsically alienating and repressive structure of capitalist society, designed purely to facilitate consumption. Radicals who aspired to create a mass movement— like the Socialist Workers Party with its April 24 NPAC march and rally—were reproducing the very structure they should be challenging. "We don't fight the mass (market) with a mass (movement)," the essay argued. "This form of struggle, no matter how radical its demands, never threatens the basic structure—the mass itself." The antidote to mass society, the pamphlet declared, was a decentralized movement based on small, self-organized collectives.[18]

A related impulse toward decentralization characterized the radical identity-based movements that had emerged between 1966 and 1969—the multihued array of "power" movements (Black Power, Puerto Rican Power, Chicano Power, Yellow Power, Red Power), and the women's and gay liberation movements. A central theme of each was the question of representation: who speaks for whom; who makes decisions, and in whose name. As Stokely Carmichael and Charles V. Hamilton wrote in their influential 1967 manifesto *Black Power: The Politics of Liberation in America,* "Black people must redefine themselves, and only *they* can do that. Throughout this country, vast segments of the black communities are beginning to recognize the need to assert their own definitions, to reclaim their history, their culture; to create their own sense of community and togetherness." By 1971, identity-based movements were fixtures of the radical landscape, whose very existence challenged the idea of an overarching 'capital-m' Movement that could speak with one voice. A mass movement—or, to put it another way, a movement of masses—seemed to drown out difference in the name of unity, something that many activists could no longer accept.[19]

The radical women's liberation movement made this challenge to mass or national organizing explicit. Its signature contribution to radical activism was the assertion that the personal is political, a proposition that was electrifying in its day. Building upon the New

Left project of countering personal alienation by uncovering "the political, social, and economic sources of [one's] private troubles" (to quote from the 1962 Port Huron Statement, the founding document of SDS), the mostly white radical feminists of the late 1960s and early 1970s made consciousness-raising a centerpiece of their politics. This process of self-examination and collective discussion was best suited for small groups, which facilitated greater intimacy and internal democracy than large organizations. By the early 1970s, the small group was the predominant radical feminist form, characterized by "a conscious lack of formal structure, [and] an emphasis on participation by everyone," in the words of organizer and theorist Jo Freeman. Though Mayday could hardly be termed a feminist initiative—there was a women's tent and a women's contingent, but the mobilization was planned and shaped by New Left men—the decentralized and radically democratic organizing principles of the women's liberation movement helped shape the larger political climate that gave rise to the Mayday Tribe.[20]

The Mayday organizers proposed that everyone who wanted to help shut down the federal government organize themselves into "affinity groups." Affinity groups are small assemblages of roughly five to fifteen people who take part in an action jointly, planning their participation collectively. Mayday was the first time they were used in a large-scale national demonstration in the United States, as well as the first time they were used in an explicitly nonviolent context. Affinity groups have been a recurring feature of many large protests since and a defining structure of a great deal of direct-action organizing. Movements with such wide-ranging concerns as nuclear power, US military intervention in Central America, environmental destruction, AIDS, and global trade agreements have organized their actions on the basis of affinity groups; they have been especially important to movements that have explicitly defined themselves as nonviolent. There's an irony there, for these groups began as underground guerrilla cells, and entered US radical circles through the most violent segment of the white New Left.

The term dates back to Spain in the late 1920s and 1930s, when small bands of militants from the Iberian Anarchist Federation (F.A.I.) undertook a series of guerrilla actions: first against the dictatorship of Primo de Rivera; next against real or suspected fascists during the Spanish Republic; and finally, against the fascist regime of Francisco Franco during the Spanish Civil War. They called their underground cells *"grupos de afinidad,"* explained Murray Bookchin, the writer and social ecologist who first introduced the term to the United States, "because people were drawn together not by residence, not even by occupation, but on the basis of affinity: friendship, individual trust, background, history." The groups reflected both anarchist ideals of free association and military needs for security. The stakes were tremendous: a small slip-up could lead to torture and death. Because affinity groups were small and formed only by people who knew each other well, they were difficult to infiltrate or uncover. Because the groups acted autonomously, with no central command, the discovery or destruction of one would not obliterate the underground altogether.[21]

The phrase and structure entered the New Left in the United States around 1967, when some in the movement were beginning to reject the philosophy of strict nonviolence and shifting, as the saying of the time went, "from protest to resistance." Initially, that meant employing "mobile tactics" during demonstrations, notably the fall 1967 Stop the Draft Weeks in Oakland and New York. Sitting down and awaiting arrest increasingly seemed only to invite beatings from the police—and to accomplish little or nothing in the process; nonviolence had come to seem like passivity. Young militants began to experiment with more chaotic and aggressive measures: dragging mailboxes or automobiles into the streets to serve as temporary blockades; blocking traffic; remaining always in motion in order to create "disruptive confrontation."[22]

To pull that off well, you needed some kind of agile, streetwise organization—something, perhaps, like "a street gang with an analysis." That's how Up Against the Wall Motherfuckers, the SDS chapter from Manhattan's Lower East Side, defined the affinity group in a broadside published around 1968. The Motherfuckers, in their own words, were "flower children with thorns," a fierce and disruptive group devoted to creating a "total break [from the present]: cultural, political, social, everything." Ben Morea, the founder of the Motherfuckers, had learned about affinity groups from conversations and debates with Bookchin, who had done extensive research during the 1960s on the Spanish Civil War. "Murray really understood the history of Spain, and he was telling me about the *grupos de afinidad*. And I immediately saw the possibility," remembered Morea. He was intrigued by the idea of "groups of like-minded people that weren't public," the sort of group that was "totally unknown to anyone else." Embracing this clandestine structure, the Motherfuckers engaged in outrageous actions, which ranged from dumping garbage at New York's Lincoln Center on its opening night (its construction having displaced a Puerto Rican neighborhood) to pelting then–Secretary of State Dean Rusk with bags of cow's blood.[23]

The Motherfuckers' conception of affinity groups partly mirrored their Spanish antecedents: "Relying on each other," explained one leaflet, "the individuals in an affinity group increase their potential for action and decrease the dangers of isolation and/or infiltration. The necessity for these relationships should be obvious at this stage of our struggle." But security was not their only purpose. The Motherfuckers viewed affinity groups in grander terms as well. "In the pre-revolutionary period," they wrote, "affinity groups must assemble to project a revolutionary consciousness and to develop forms for particular struggles. In the revolutionary period itself they will emerge as armed cadres at the centers of conflict, and in the post-revolutionary period suggest forms for the new everyday life."[24]

Morea and the Motherfuckers soon introduced the idea of affinity groups as teams for street combat to Weatherman, the faction of SDS that aspired to be a revolutionary fighting force and to "bring the war home" to the United States. It was during the October 1969 Days of Rage, perhaps Weatherman's most notorious action, that affinity groups made their true US debut. Some three hundred of the group's followers converged on Chicago, where they went on what might best be termed a rampage: battling cops, smashing windshields, running through the streets, and creating mayhem. Jeff Jones, one of the founders of Weatherman, explained that as early as 1967, militant members of SDS began debating whether to adopt more violent tactics during street protests. "We had that discussion over and over again," he recalled in a 2000 interview, "and each demonstration that we went to became a little bit more militant, until it was in our heads to organize a demonstration that was entirely street fighting, which we did, in which affinity groups played a very important role."[25]

All the participants in the Days of Rage were organized into the small groups, which Weatherman treated less like egalitarian collectives and more like military platoons. "There was a pretense made of contributions from everyone, but there was really a final yes or no from the top leadership. There would be a representative of the leadership in each affinity group," recalled Judith Karpova of her time in Weatherman. As Shin'ya Ono described the group's preparations on a Weatherman bus heading to Chicago for the Days of Rage, "In order to get to know each other and learn to move as a group, we divided ourselves into several affinity groups of six or seven persons each and did a couple of tasks together," he wrote. "We discussed the functions of the affinity group, what running and fighting together meant, what leadership meant, and why leadership was absolutely necessary in a military situation." Another account of Weather-style affinity-group organizing during that period by Motor City SDS similarly emphasized a paramilitary command structure: "The tactical leadership explains the plans using maps which they have drawn up, and our forces are divided into affinity groups. Each group sticks together, protects each of its members, acts as a fighting unit in case of confrontation, and functions as a work team."[26]

The Days of Rage were widely viewed as a disaster. The tiny turnout was a fraction of what the Weather organizers had expected; the street fighting left most participants injured or jailed or both, with little or nothing to show for their bravado. When mainstream figures like former Supreme Court Justice Arthur J. Goldberg denounced the actions as "vandalism and hooliganism without a program," many on the left agreed. The tactics used, Dave Dellinger of the Chicago 7 later wrote, "proved counterproductive in terms of their results—injuries, military defeat, an unsatisfactory choice at the end of the action between long prison sentences or enforced [time] underground, and unnecessary alienation of a potentially sympathetic public." Some months later, one anonymous Weather sympathizer calling herself "a daughter of the Amerikan Revolution" published an essay on affinity groups in a spring 1970 issue of the radical *Berkeley Tribe*, endorsing their use for armed struggle. "The term 'affinity group' means different things to different people," she explained, "anything from a group of people that run together in a riot to a basic armed unit for the revolution, which is my conception of it." But already by 1970, even some of those who had flirted with street violence were concluding that rioting and armed struggle were dead ends for the movement, relegating activists to a terrain in which they could always be overpowered by the police or the military, while undermining their moral authority in the process. Affinity groups had proven too useful in practical terms to be abandoned—"they are to many people's minds both safer and more politically acceptable than the marshal system for organizing participants at a demonstration," an organizing manual of the period explained—but their significance and function began to change. [27]

"The reason it changed, and went from a violent to more of a nonviolent kind of thing," said Jeff Jones, "is because violent street fighting played itself out kind of quickly. We took it to the max at the Days of Rage, and the price was too high, and everybody knew it." By the time the Mayday Tribe put out its call to protest, the concept of affinity groups had begun to blend with the other small-group forms that were rapidly growing in countercultural popularity: collectives, communes, cooperatives, consciousness-raising groups. Perhaps there was still a slight frisson of clandestinity attached to the use of affinity groups, given the sense among many that "Mayday was sort of the above-ground Weatherpeople," in the words of John Scagliotti, who worked as a full-time staffer in the DC office for the action. And certainly the impulse toward direct physical confrontation with authority would remain a recurring (and constantly debated) element of disruptive protest for decades to come. But on the whole, affinity groups were coming to be seen as more expedient and sociable than paramilitary or insurrectionary. "Affinity groups at Mayday," remembered John Froines, another Chicago 7 defendant centrally involved in the action, "were both a tactical approach in terms of the street and also something more, connected to people's linkages to one another." [28]

That said, there was a haphazard quality to the Mayday organizing; a lot of the action was put together on the fly. "We had no organization, so we made a virtue out of our weakness, which was what guerrillas had always done," Jerry Coffin explained. "If you've got no organization, what do you do? You create something where no organization is a virtue, and that was the whole affinity group thing we'd been promoting." Much of the initial outreach was done in conjunction with the speaking tours of Rennie Davis and John Froines to campuses throughout the United States. Much of the rest was done by mail, thanks to a resourceful activist who had figured out a do-it-yourself way to reset postage meters. "There was the notion," Froines recalled, "that people from University of Wisconsin or Florida State or Smith College or wherever would come, and they would have encampments of their own, and they would develop tactical approaches to what they were doing."[29]

This decentralized structure, organizers hoped, would also help them avoid the legal entanglements they had faced after the 1968 Chicago Democratic Convention protests. At first glance, Mayday might look "like an engraved invitation to a conspiracy trial," as one activist told *Time*, but it would be virtually impossible for the government to pin responsibility on one or more individual organizers. *Everyone* was responsible. As one participant from Richmond College in Staten Island explained afterwards, "As affinity groups you have to make your own decisions and be fully responsible. You're not simply following a leadership up at the head of a march ... Rather than one conspiracy, it was thousands of conspiracies."[30]

The lack of formal organization, however, tended to undermine the ideal of egalitarian participation as a result of what radical feminist Jo Freeman famously called "the tyranny of structurelessness," in one of the most influential essays of the time. Drawing on her experiences in the women's liberation movement, where collectives and consciousness-raising groups had flourished, Freeman described how the lack of formal structures and decision-making procedures—so democratic in intent and appearance—in fact allowed informal and unaccountable power dynamics to flourish. Structurelessness, she wrote, "becomes a way of masking power," for decisions were always being made in a group: "As long as the structure of the group is informal, the rules of how decisions are made are known only to a few."[31]

That was exactly the character of the Mayday organizing. Local affinity groups might choose their own targets and tactics, but a small group of men around Rennie Davis wrote the organizing materials, controlled the finances, called the press conferences, did the big-picture planning, and spoke for the action as a whole. Scagliotti remarked, "While Rennie and all these guys were the leaders, most of the people in the affinity groups didn't know that, they didn't know who the leaders were. They were just being organized in their local whatever to come to this thing." The looseness of the overall structure gave considerable autonomy to local groups, but it also meant there was no transparency or accountability, no way for affinity groups to have input into the overall decision-making or to dispute what the informal leadership was doing.

The DC office for the actions was largely staffed by a small circle of organizers who called themselves the Gay Mayday Tribe. "Once the Mayday thing started happening, I joined the Mayday collective and lived in the Mayday commune," remembered Scagliotti, who later produced the acclaimed *Before Stonewall* and *After Stonewall* documentaries. "There were about five of us who were gay, and we sort of ran the office. We immediately became very close and out of that was Gay Mayday."

Gay Mayday was an intriguing political experiment in fusing the new gay radicalism with the radicalism of the antiwar movement. (It was also very much a sex-and-drugs party scene.) Since the Stonewall rebellion of June 1969—when patrons of a Greenwich Village gay and transgender bar fought back against police during an attempted raid, an act of proud defiance that sparked the gay liberation movement—some gay activists had worked to play a visible role in the movement against the Vietnam War. "Through a lot of 1970, I remember I must have gone to at least six different antiwar marches where we [gay people] were all joining hands and marching up Fifth Avenue or marching in the park," noted Perry Brass, a Gay Mayday participant who was part of the collective that produced *Come Out!*, one of the few gay newspapers in existence at that time.[32]

There were two major gay liberation groups in 1971, the Gay Liberation Front (GLF), created shortly after Stonewall, and the Gay Activists Alliance (GAA), a more moderate group that broke away just a few months later. Brass and most of the hundred or so other Gay Mayday radicals gravitated to the GLF, whose name intentionally echoed that of the Vietnamese National Liberation Front. GLFers very much viewed themselves as part of the broader radical land-scape of the time. "GLF differs from other gay groups because we realize that homosexual oppression is part of all oppression," explained a leaflet circulated by the group in New York. "The current system denies us our

Gay Liberation Front button, early 1970s (designer unknown; courtesy Lesbian Herstory Archives)

basic humanity in much the same way as it is denied to blacks, women and other oppressed minorities; and the grounds are just as irrational. Therefore, our liberation is tied to the liberation of all peoples." Two of their chants made light of these linkages: "Ho, ho, homosexual, the ruling class is ineffectual!" and the memorable "Up the ass of the ruling class!" But the more emblematic GLF slogan was "No revolution without us!"—expressing the desire to be part of the often homophobic New Left, a desire that partly motivated Gay Mayday. Brass recalled, "A lot of the people in that contingent were very happy to be included in something like [Mayday]. We felt, well, this is our sign that we've been accepted as radicals ... We've just got to prove that we are willing to go in there, get our heads clobbered and arrested and beaten up, prove that we can do this."[33]

The GLF—a primarily gay male organization with few lesbian members, as well as predominantly white in its membership base (characteristics it shared with GAA)—also saw itself as both inspired and shaped by radical feminism. The women's liberation analysis of the linkages between personal and political concerns res-onated with the experiences of these gay radicals, many if not most of whom were newly out of the closet, and their organizing focused most strongly on the inward-looking work of consciousness-raising and community building. "A lot of [GLF activism] was sensitivity groups, tea groups: meeting in church basements and storefronts and people's homes to look at the ways we had been injured in a homophobic, racist, heterosexist, classist society," remembered Warren J. Blumenfeld, who was part of the Washington, DC Gay Liberation Front and helped organize the Mayday action. The radical feminist influence was also felt in the GLF's "structureless" organizational form, comprised of decentralized collectives (called, in this case, "cells") with no formal decision-making process, membership requirements, or bylaws. "GLFers chose the rocky road of fluid cellular organization," explained activist Lois Hart, "rather than perpetuate older, oppressive structures of Follow the Leader and passive participation by voting."[34]

The Gay Activists Alliance was far more conventional in its organization and politics, and more focused on trying to achieve specific reforms than on exploring consciousness and identity. The group adopted a constitution, elected officers, and operated according to Robert's Rules of Order. It defined itself as a "one-issue organization," "exclusively devoted to the liberation of homosexuals," objecting to the GLF's activism on behalf of other radical causes. Elected officials were major targets of the GAA, which sought to influence policy and legislation by mobilizing gays as a political constituency whose interests could not be ignored. This approach seemed hopelessly establishment and uninspiring to some radicals of the time, and especially to the GLF. But GAA was consistently innovative in the means it used to seek reform, and its clever tactics and techniques were later embraced by the AIDS activist group ACT UP and its many offshoots. Borrowing from the Yippies, the late-sixties band of hippie pranksters led by Abbie Hoffman and Jerry Rubin, the GAA specialized in "zaps," boisterous and disruptive small-scale direct actions: sneaking into political events and interrupting them with well-timed harangues; occupying the office of a magazine (*Harper's*) to protest homophobic content; throwing an "engagement party" in the office of the New York City clerk after he bad-mouthed unofficial marriage services being performed in a gay church. One of the founders of the GAA, Arthur Evans, described the zap as "a unique tactic of confrontation politics, combining the somber principles of *realpolitik* with the theatrics of high camp," and designed "to rouse closet gays from their apathy, direct gay anger toward oppressive straight institutions, and create a widespread feeling of gay identity." The speed, flamboyance, and wit of zap activism would become hallmarks of highly effective direct-action movements to come.[35]

The Gay Mayday Tribe viewed its participation in the 1971 antiwar action as more than just a matter of mobilizing gays as a constituency or contingent along the lines of "schoolteachers against the war" or "physicians for peace." Instead, it sought to draw connections between militarism and social constructions of gender. One Gay Mayday leaflet called the Vietnam War "a straight man's game," created by "men who need to gain their masculine identity through the killing of women, children, and their own brothers." A call to participation elaborated, "We know that the men running the country are very deeply sexist—they relate to each other and to situations in an uptight straight male way. These men make decisions in order to satisfy their male egos and their needs for competition with other men." The Gay Mayday Tribe offered up an expansive vision, in which gay liberation could not only transform laws or lifestyles, but also undermine the very foundations of war. For, they promised, "an army of lovers would not fight."[36]

As it happened, the central role of Gay Mayday in logistics and planning for the action brought an unexpected practical benefit. At a time when government surveillance and disruption of radical movements were both routine and highly damaging, the exuberant eroticism of the Gay Mayday Tribe doubled as a form of protection. Investigative journalist Angus Mackenzie would later reveal that the CIA had planted an agent in the center of the DC radical scene to feed information on Rennie Davis and the Mayday plans directly to the White House, but the spy, a young man named Salvatore Ferrera, wasn't able to report anything more useful than that "Davis said Mayday is the most disorganized demonstration he's ever seen." To learn much more, Ferrera would have needed to go a whole lot deeper undercover: "They couldn't infiltrate [the office], because we were all sleeping with each other," recalled John Scagliotti with a laugh. "And we were doing a tremendous amount of illegal things that they could have gotten us all for," including the postage theft. At one point in spring 1971, after the Weather Underground (the name Weatherman took after turning to clandestine action) set off a bomb in the US Capitol, the Mayday office collective was raided. Said Scagliotti, "I remember being woken up by the FBI one morning and the guy saying, 'And what's her name?'—and it was just a hippie guy with long hair [in bed with me]. They were very freaked out by that experience and left us alone." Indeed, after the protest, *Newsweek* reported that "the government's most serious problem was faulty intelligence."[37]

In the days before the action, the Mayday Tribe set up "movement centers" throughout the city where newly arriving protesters could connect with others from their region, get information about nonviolence trainings, and obtain medical advice about possible exposure to tear gas or mace. The organizers had also obtained a permit for an encampment in West Potomac Park from the time of the mass April 24 march and rally through May 3, the Monday morning when the shutdown was to take place. Perry Brass remembered the scene as one of "high hippieism": "People were dropping acid all over the place, smoking marijuana all over the place, just having a wonderful time with a political context to it." John Scagliotti recalled, "It was so romantic: everybody around campfires, all these revolutionaries in their affinity groups, talking and planning their last-minute strategies."[38]

As the action date approached, however, the atmosphere grew more alienating for some activists, especially women, who found little structure or opportunity for participation. "My first night at the camp, I attended an open meeting of almost the entire camp," one woman wrote afterwards. "People from the crowd got up to the microphone and said what was on their minds—sexism seemed to be on the minds of both women and gay men. As the camp grew, however, the open meetings ceased, and were replaced by announcements made over the loudspeaker system by a male voice." The women had hoped for something quite different, something more in the small-group spirit of participatory democracy. "What the women's movement has done as I've seen it in the past year or two," explained one feminist to a camera crew from the radical Videofreex film collective, "it has brought a whole new understanding about leadership and about people relating to each other, that is now going into the whole movement in this country ... It's about people being people; it's getting rid of the old heavy rhetoric kind of politics."[39]

That Saturday, the Mayday Collective threw a rock concert and festival (featuring "Free music! Free dope! Free food!"), which swelled the encampment to something like 45,000 people. Reports of sexual harassment and even assault grew with the crowd: a Liberation News Service account of the day claimed that six rapes had occurred, though they were only mentioned in passing. Fed up by the rowdy atmosphere and the constant sexual advances by stoned hippie men, a group of women, mainly lesbians, stormed the stage along with a handful of gay male allies and tried to turn the concert into a consciousness-raising session. "There's a lot of men and straight women around here who really come down on the gay women when they realize that we're gay," one lesbian activist declared, in footage of the event captured by the Videofreex. "The straight women automatically assume that we're going to rape them all—that's bullshit. And the straight men automatically assume that they're going to cure us—which is bullshit. And I would appreciate it if people would speak to me as a human being and not a freak object."[40]

It's not clear that this action had any measurable impact on the concertgoers or the protests, but the women and gay men's disaffection highlighted the extent to which Mayday, for all its innovations, remained rooted in the male-dominated, old-school habits of the 1960s left. The decentralized, affinity-group-based direct-action techniques championed by the Mayday Tribe would only begin to reach their organizing potential after they were more fully fused with feminist practices—and after women, especially lesbians, reshaped movement culture. Lesbian activists may have had to take over the stage at Mayday to say their piece, but they would become primary transmitters of the direct-action tradition in the decades to come. Time and again from the late 1970s until the present day, women organizers of all races, and especially queer women organizers, would form the key bridges linking one direct-action movement to the next: from anti-nuclear activism to Central American solidarity work, and from there to reproductive rights and AIDS organizing, to the global justice movement and Occupy Wall Street to the Movement for Black Lives. They weren't the only ones to do this connective work, of course, but they did it to a striking degree, weaving feminist and queer sensibilities—and ultimately, what would be called intersectional politics—into radical activism whether or not the issues being addressed were of specific interest to women or LGBTQ people. This role was perfectly captured in the title of one of the most influential texts of women of color feminism, the classic 1981 anthology *This Bridge Called My Back,* edited by Cherríe Moraga and Gloria Anzaldúa. But as Moraga wrote in the book's preface, citing a comment made by black feminist pioneer Barbara Smith, "A bridge gets walked over." The centrality of women, especially queer women, to the reinvention of American radicalism after the sixties was all too often invisible and unrecognized.[41]

Before dawn on Sunday, the morning after the rock concert, the government made its first move. Police descended on West Potomac Park and shut down the encampment, evicting the groggy radicals en masse and arresting those who refused to leave. Additional officers were stationed at other parks throughout the city, to prevent protesters from regrouping. Many affinity groups were able to reassemble at the movement centers, but the government's action had the intended effect: thousands of people—notably those who had been drawn more by the rock concert than the radicalism—decided just to go home, cutting the protesters' ranks by a half or more.[42]

Early on Monday morning, the 25,000 or so remaining members of the Mayday Tribe began moving into Washington to block their designated targets. The government was ready, having mobilized a combined force of 10,000 police, National Guard, and federal troops, with at least 4,000 more troops available on reserve. Their orders were to arrest every demonstrator on sight. (Attorney General John Mitchell explained to Nixon during a White House meeting to plan the government's response to the protests, "I know

MAYDAY TARGETS

1)* Key Bridge, Virginia side. Rosslyn Plaza.
2) Key Bridge, D.C. side. M St., 34th St., 35th St.
3) Theordore Roosevelt Bridge, Virginia side. Route 66
4) Theordore Roosevelt Bridge, D.C. side. Rock Creek Parkway
5) Arlington Memorial Bridge, Virginia side. Memorial Drive, Arlington Ridge Road (Rt. 110).
6) Arlington Memorial Bridge, D.C. side. Rock Creek Parkway, Ohio Drive south.
7)* Washington Blvd. Highway 110
8) Traffic Loop just west of Pentagon. Washington Blvd., Columbia Pike, Shirley Hwy.
9)* Shirley Hwy just south of the Pentagon.

Tactical map for Mayday 1971 (designer unknown; author's collection)

they want to be arrested but, Mr. President, I don't think that's any reason for not arresting them.")[43]

"Small battles raged all over the city as demonstrators would build crude barricades, disperse when the police came and then regroup to rebuild the dismantled obstructions," one underground paper reported. The protesters' nonviolence pledge did not preclude building barricades; nobody felt "that because we will be nonviolent that we could not also be militant and creative." The barricades were indeed inventive: "We threw everything available into the streets," one participant wrote afterwards in the *Berkeley Tribe*, "garbage cans, parked cars, broken glass, nails, large rocks, and ourselves. To add to the confusion, we lifted hoods of cars stopped for lights and let air out of tires." Some of these obstacles—like the one in Georgetown that was constructed by overturning a tractor trailer—were even effective in stopping traffic for relatively long periods of time.[44]

But ultimately, the government had the upper hand on the streets, thanks to a military operation that, in *Newsweek*'s words, "seemed more appropriate to Saigon in wartime than Washington in the spring." Waves of helicopters landed alongside the Washington Monument, ferrying Marines into the city, and federal troops lined the Key Bridge. A Marine battalion was stationed at Dupont Circle; Ann Northrop, who was working as a journalist at the time and went on to play a major role in ACT UP, recalled "tanks around the rim pointing out toward the street with their big guns." The city was effectively under military occupation. "The scene was midway between that of a sham battle and a war of death," one protester wrote afterwards. "Police vans careened around corners, frantic to discharge their human load and return for another. Helicopters chopping overhead made us aware that the ground troops had surveillance of all of our movements."[45]

Remembered Perry Brass, "There were people just running through the streets, there were cops running after them. Any time you stood still you'd be arrested, so you had to keep moving." There was more order to the protest chaos than there seemed to be, thanks to the affinity groups and a sophisticated communications system. "We had all these very expensive radios," explained Jerry Coffin, "thousands and thousands of dollars' worth of radios. And every major group that had a target had a radio and was in communication with our base."[46]

But all the planning and organization counted for little in the face of the government's sweep arrests: there's not a whole lot that nonviolent protesters can do when the government decides to send thousands of troops to round them up. Many of the 7,000 arrestees caught in the dragnet that first day were people with no connection to the protest, who just happened to be where sweeps were taking place. Others were demonstrators who were arrested preemptively, having not yet committed illegal acts. To transport the mass of prisoners, the police had to commandeer city buses; when even that wasn't enough, they hired Hertz and Avis rent-a-trucks. Another

6,000 were arrested over three more days, most of them for block-ading the Justice Department and the US Capitol.[47]

The city jail quickly filled, even though the police crammed as many as twenty people into two-person cells. Another 1,500 were packed into the jail's recreation yard. That still left thousands of prisoners, whom the police herded into an outdoor practice field next to RFK Stadium. Conditions were awful, with next to no sanitary facilities, blankets, or food. One anarchist wag made a sign proclaiming the football field "Smash the State Concentration Camp #1." People who had strongly disapproved of the Mayday Tribe's shutdown plan were appalled by the flagrant violation of civil liberties, and upset to see the nation's capital under military occupation. But the government was clearly more concerned with maintaining control than with maintaining public sympathy, as would prove to be the case time and again—during the Seattle WTO blockades; at an array of Occupy encampments across the country; in Ferguson, Missouri—when direct-action protests threatened public order.

Local residents, especially African Americans, almost immediately began supporting the imprisoned Mayday protesters by bringing food, blankets, and notes of encouragement to the football field and throwing them over the fence. Within a day, leaders of the district's black community, predominantly from the civil rights generation of the 1950s and early 1960s and representing more than fifty organizations, organized a large-scale food drive for the crowd of arrestees, delivering the supplies in a twelve-car caravan. "We've been through all the head beatings and open compounds and we're not going to do it again. But we did want to help them," veteran civil rights activist Mary Treadwell said to the press. "We gave them food so they could put their bodies on the line and disrupt the government," she explained, noting that anything that "can upset the oppressive machinery of the government will help black people."[48]

In retrospect, the moment seems rich in symbolism, like a passing of the direct-action torch. The black civil rights movement of Treadwell's generation had made extraordinary use of nonviolent direct action in the United States to challenge segregation and racial inequality, from the pioneering Montgomery bus boycott to the legendary Southern lunch counter sit-ins to the daring Freedom Rides and even the abortive "stall-in" plan. But white resistance to change, and the unrelenting violence directed toward the movement, had propelled many organizers toward very different approaches. Over the course of the 1960s, black radicals increasingly rejected even militant nonviolence to advocate in favor of self-defense and, if necessary, armed revolution. As Black Power pioneer Stokely Carmichael put it in a 1966 essay, "We cannot be expected any longer to march and have our heads broken in order to say to whites: come on, you're nice guys. For you are not nice guys. We have found you out." Malcolm X had made the point even more forcefully in his famous 1963 "Message to the Grassroots": "There's no such *thing* as a nonviolent revolution," he said. "Whoever heard of a revolution where they lock arms ... singing 'We Shall Over-come'? Just tell me. You don't do that in a revolution. You don't do any singing; you're too busy swinging."⁴⁹

But taking up the gun, literally or metaphorically, had only provided the white power structure with new justification for vio-lently targeting black movements. As longstanding organizer Kai Lumumba Barrow recalled, "There was a major shift in the political expression of the black liberation movement in the mid sixties." Barrow was raised in a radical black nationalist family and played a key role in the revival of direct action in movements of color at the turn of the millennium. The Black Panther Party and other black nationalist groups, she explained, "took the position that nonviolent direct action placed us in a very passive position," and came to view it as a tactic for the privileged. "But what we did," she continued, "was we went to the extreme and started engaging in armed struggle or at least self-defense, and we didn't have enough experience with that perhaps, or we didn't have enough support for that, and we were beat. We were beat pretty badly." Terry Marshall, an activist who was deeply involved in a range of direct-action projects in the 1990s and onward, beginning with the Student Liberation Action Movement and continuing into Black Lives Matter, recalled, "I remember being little, I remember I thought everyone must be dead—Malcolm X was killed, Martin Luther King was killed, I was like, Angela Davis must be dead, all the Black Panthers must be dead." He continued, "The movement was defeated because of internal weaknesses, but it was also militarily defeated."[50]

In the wake of all the repression, recalled Rev. Osagyefo Sekou, an organizer and radical theologian who led direct-action trainings in Ferguson after the 2014 police killing of Michael Brown, "There was a shudder. They say a wounded lion won't fight. It makes sense, it was a shudder," a pulling back from confrontational tactics more generally and from direct action specifically. Black-led movements in particular would not pursue direct action as a strategy to any significant degree until the anti-apartheid upsurge of the mid 1980s, and even then they would employ it in very different ways than their white counterparts; it would not be until the mid-to-late 1990s that movements of color would really begin to embrace and adapt direct action again on a significant scale. The movements that built on the innovations of Mayday to create a new direct-action tradition in the 1970s and 1980s were overwhelmingly white in composition and generally unsuccessful—sometimes spectacularly so—in addressing race.[51]

Mayday wasn't the last antiwar protest by a long shot, but it was the last big national one, and the last major one with ties to the fading New Left. "The white 'New Left' movement of the 1960s is dead and gone," one radical wrote in *Space City!*, a Houston underground paper, soon after the action. "Although government repression had something to do with its demise, the main cause of its death was its failure to confront honestly [the] problems of sexism, racism and ego-tripping in general." For all the efforts to create a decentralized action without "movement generals," Mayday was criticized as too centralized and dominated by Davis and his circle. It was, one activist observed, "hate-the-heavies time," and the complaints about Mayday revealed how dramatically the radical landscape was shifting. Another participant declared, "There were a lot of things about Mayday that were totally wrong. It was a mass mobilization, a national mobilization. It was elitistly organized, mostly by males. It was going to Washington." As Scagliotti put it, "[Mayday was] the end of that sort of male radical leadership, the Rennie Davises, the Chicago 7, all those guys, the whole world of the counterculture mixed with radical street politics."[52]

An acrimonious follow-up conference in Atlanta that August revealed the fissures within the Mayday Tribe. There were separate gay and women's gatherings beforehand, which set a consciousness-raising and identity-focused tone for the conference as a whole. Activists from these groups challenged the rest of the Tribe to examine and overcome their own internal chauvinisms; many participants were left feeling defensive and attacked. "No one seemed to think the conference was functioning to resolve any political problems or effectively to plan any future actions," one attendee reported. "Yet most stayed to engage in the personal struggle with the questions of sexism and elitism in the Movement in general, in Mayday, and in themselves." The heavies didn't show, infuriating everyone else and underscoring in many people's minds the problem of "macho tripping within the movement." Straight white men, including more traditional leftists, just found the whole situation mystifying and uncomfortable. "Gays Dominate Mayday Meeting in Atlanta," the left-wing paper *The Guardian* disapprovingly headlined its post-conference report.[53]

A number of the women and gay participants, however, were energized by the gathering. Or rather—in a sign of the separatism, personalism, and inward focus that would characterize identity politics for much of the seventies—they were energized by the time they spent among themselves. "For a number of us, gay and straight, the women's part of the conference was getting to know one another through dancing, swimming, making music together, singing, rapping in small groups, in twos and threes, digging on each other," one woman wrote in Atlanta's underground paper. "We blew each other's minds by our beauty, our strength. We grew by loving each other." A gay man similarly described the gay caucuses as "really a high for me ... I'd forgotten about the atmosphere of total personal openness, openness about one's deepest confusions, that is so lacking in straight-dominated meetings."[54]

The Mayday Tribe ceased to exist soon afterwards. But in May 1972, when Nixon announced the mining of seven Vietnamese harbors, the underlying political shifts that had shaped Mayday were dramatically on display. Demonstrators all around the country quickly organized themselves and blocked highways, key intersections, and railroad tracks. The sites were mainly not notorious hotbeds of radicalism: they included Minneapolis, Albuquerque, Boulder, and Gainesville; Evanston, Illinois; East Lansing, Michigan; Oxford, Ohio. Protesters blocked the New York State Thruway and Chicago's Eisenhower Expressway; others shut down Santa Barbara's airport by occupying its runways. In Davis, California, demonstrators sat down on Southern Pacific tracks; still more did the same on the Penn Central commuter line in New Brunswick, New Jersey. In St. Louis, the local chapter of Vietnam Veterans Against the War occupied the top of the Gateway Arch, while another group of radicals took over the decommissioned mine sweeper *USS Inaugural*, saying they wanted to repair it and take it to Vietnam to clear the harbor of Nixon's mines. It was nationwide mayhem, neither coordinated nor led by anyone. Longtime activist Leslie Cagan, one of the participants in the mine sweeper action, who would later go on to coordinate many of the largest protests of subsequent decades, from the million-person 1982 anti-nuclear protest in Central Park to the enormous 2003 protests against the Iraq War, recalled that there wasn't "any kind of national organization or network that put out a call for these kinds of bolder actions. It was just one of those moments where a lot of people were on the same wavelength."[55]

The Mayday Tribe hadn't succeeded in its stated goal—"If the government won't stop the war, the people will stop the government"—and its singular experiment in nonviolent obstruction was soon forgotten, too messy or perhaps too unsettling to be part of popular understandings of the Vietnam War and the movements that opposed it. But the daring action had in fact achieved its most important aim: pressuring the Nixon Administration to hasten the end of the hated war. While neither activists nor anyone else would remember this unpopular protest for the outsized impact that it had, the political innovations of Mayday would quietly and steadily influence grassroots activism for decades to come, laying the groundwork for a new kind of radicalism: decentralized, multi-vocal, ideologically diverse, and propelled by direct action. As one participant observed in the protest's immediate aftermath, "Twenty thousand freaks carry the seeds now, and they've been blown to every corner of the land."[56]

Seeds, of course, are small, and only sprout and grow after a period of dormancy. A new era of political retrenchment was beginning, and many of those who dreamed of fundamentally reshaping American society and politics were trying to put down new roots, as the first act in a long process of radical reinvention.

2

Small Change

As late as spring 1971, when radical activists organized the Mayday direct action against the Vietnam War, it remained possible to believe—without too much self-delusion—that the United States was on the verge of a revolution and "the System" was nearing collapse. What collapsed instead, with stunning speed, was any sense that a grand transformation of the existing political and economic order was possible. "I don't know whether it happened in 1969 or 1972, but somewhere along the line the 1960s ended and the 1970s began," mused Roberta Lynch, a longtime feminist and left-labor organizer, in 1977. "When the activists of the '60s perceived that the system was not infinitely elastic and that there was often massive indifference to their goals, naiveté gave way to cynicism."[1]

To be sure, small insurrectionary pockets remained active across the decade of the 1970s, still trumpeting the goal of revolution; but the ways they pursued it only confirmed—and increased—their political isolation. The remnants of the Weather Underground continued to bomb corporate and military targets, using "Hard

Times Are Fighting Times" as the slogan for their 1976 organizing conference, and groups including the Black Liberation Army, the Symbionese Liberation Army, and the May 19 Communist Organization embraced the idea of armed struggle, adopting tactics like kidnapping and bank robbery and the goal of overthrowing the government by force. As they claimed the mantle of revolution, these groups—and their unarmed counterparts in the "party-building" left of the 1970s and 1980s, that squabbling world of Marxist-Leninist and Maoist grouplets, shrill and dreary in tone and obsessed with refining a correct political line—mostly just discredited it for everyone else.[2]

The massive economic crisis that began in 1973, combining deep recession with steep inflation, undercut even middle-class activists' ability to devote most or all of their energies to organizing: it was simply no longer possible, as it had been throughout the sixties, to comfortably skate by with minimal income. Many drifted away from organizing altogether to raise a family, pursue a career, or continue their education. Some of these people shifted rightward in their political views, but more simply scaled back or ceased political action. "The *Los Angeles Times* recently cited the figure of 2 to 3 million erstwhile activists who retain their radical allegiance, though they may lack a cause to which they can pledge it," wrote onetime Weather Underground militant and *Ramparts* editor Bo Burlingham in 1976. "Even if the numbers are accurate, I told myself, there is a difference between 3 million former activists with radical notions, and radical activity. The former is just a statistic; the latter is a political force. And political force, at least for most of my friends and myself, hasn't been a compelling preoccupation in the last couple of years."[3]

The end of the Vietnam War demobilized the ranks of protesters and activists as surely as it did the ranks of the armed forces. The last US troops pulled out in 1973, and the war was finally over in 1975, when the North Vietnamese overtook the capital of South Vietnam. Just ten days after the fall of Saigon, the War Resisters League and other groups organized a celebration in New York's Central Park, featuring performances by such movement luminaries as Pete Seeger and Odetta; some 50,000 people attended. But however much grassroots activism had hastened the conflict's end, too many people had died—combatants and civilians, Americans and Vietnamese—to make it feel like the movement had prevailed in any meaningful way, and the jubilation was tinged with melancholy. "I'd say we won," reflected WRL organizer Ed Hedemann in a 1999 interview, "but not in the cleanest, nicest, best sense, because it just wasn't a simple victory. There was a lot of pain and agony."[4]

For those who had hoped for a more profound change in the existing order, there was disappointment, too, at the movement's lost momentum, a realization that a time of retrenchment was setting in. "There was a tremendous sense of not only relief that the war was ending but also [pride] that we had made some contribution to ending it," remembered veteran organizer Leslie Cagan. "But there was also a tremendous frustration: seeing how quickly any kind of antiwar movement collapsed, disappeared, just wasn't there any more ... Somehow we weren't able to translate it into an ongoing movement beyond the crisis of the war."[5]

The temptation was to look inward when searching for the causes of this collapse—to blame infighting, bad strategic decisions, flawed organizational structures, rhetorical excesses, or any of the other faults that the movements of the sixties might have had. But a series of dramatic revelations across the decade of the 1970s showed that the government had also very actively done its part to bring the movements down. A small group of antiwar activists who suspected their movements were being infiltrated broke into the FBI field office in Media, Pennsylvania in March of 1971, stealing all the files. The documents they released to the press revealed a huge network of paid informants and a concerted plan, in the FBI's words, to "enhance the paranoia endemic in [activist] circles." Over the next few years, Congressional hearings, journalistic investigations, and activist lawsuits filled out these disclosures, revealing vast FBI efforts under its COINTELPRO program to "expose, disrupt, and otherwise neutralize the activists of the 'New Left' by counterintelligence methods," to quote one memo from the Bureau. These and similar inquiries also uncovered a massive and illegal parallel program of domestic surveillance and infiltration by the CIA known as MH/CHAOS.[6]

How much of the left's shrinkage was due to its own failings, or to changing political winds, and how much to government disruption? It would never be possible to say. Certainly the FBI operations against black movements in the 1960s had been especially vicious and far-reaching, with J. Edgar Hoover naming them "hate groups" across the board, targeting them for systematic disruption, and going so far as to sanction the murder of black leaders. The FBI notoriously tried to hound Martin Luther King Jr. into killing himself, and helped the Chicago police assassinate nineteen-year-old Black Panther leader Fred Hampton in a middle-of-the-night 1969 raid, supplying the police with a map showing where Hampton would be sleeping and having an informant drug him with secobarbital to ensure he wouldn't wake up before being shot point-blank in the head. Files released in 2012 by the FBI in response to a lawsuit by scholar Seth Rosenfeld strongly suggest that the man who first supplied guns to the Panthers, Bay Area radical Richard Aoki, was a longtime FBI informant. But the disclosure raised as many questions as it answered: Was it Aoki's idea to arm the Panthers, or the FBI's? Was the FBI guiding Aoki's actions, or was he merely providing them with reports? Might the Panthers have embraced armed self-defense anyway, even without the initial arsenal provided by Aoki? Barring some huge new release of documents from the FBI, no one will likely ever know.[7]

Many of the efforts to investigate grassroots activists, though, were stunningly inept. Despite all its illegal wiretaps and hundreds of break-ins to activist homes and offices, the FBI never tracked down the peace activists who had burgled its offices in 1971, even after these activists directly thumbed their noses at the Bureau. (While the investigation was in its most intense phase, burglary ringleader William Davidon helped organize a "Your FBI in Action" street fair in his Philadelphia neighborhood, where he posed with a large cut-out of Hoover and local children assembled puzzles with photos of the FBI agents assigned to the case.) Nor did the FBI ever solve any of the dozens of Weather Underground bombing cases, though there may of course have been reasons why they didn't want to solve those. Much of the so-called intelligence the FBI gathered through its vast network of informants was routine information with no special strategic value. Overall, though, COINTELPRO and MH/CHAOS played a significant role in amplifying divisions within movements—especially black radical movements, which were targeted the most heavily, followed by the militant wings of other movements of color, including the American Indian Movement, the Young Lords, and the Puerto Rican independence movement. Government operatives also clearly pushed radicals to adopt more extreme tactics and rhetoric than they would have without paid provocateurs within their midst, which in turn marginalized and destabilized their movements.[8]

Learning about the extent of this political sabotage, however, didn't make dealing with the diminished present any easier. The alternative press was filled with the introspective writings of activists trying to adjust to the changed reality. In the radical feminist newspaper *off our backs*, organizer Carol Anne Douglas entitled her 1977 reflections, "What If the Revolution Isn't Tomorrow?" Activists, she wrote, "need to appreciate that resistance in periods of reaction is perhaps even more difficult and important than participating in the high points, the moments when revolution seems just around the corner ... The struggle is going to take all of our lives, not just a few exciting, hectic years."[9]

Many American radicals responded to the new political climate by focusing on the small, on what affected them immediately: the local and the particular, single issues, questions of identity, politics on a manageable scale. This tendency built upon the critique of the mass—and the move toward affinity groups, collectives, and communes—that had shaped activism in the earliest years of the 1970s. It also reflected the feminist embrace of the small group, as a way of safeguarding radical ideals of participation, egalitarianism, and self-expression. The identity-politics exhortation to "organize around your own oppression" and the emerging logic of radical ecology, with its small-is-beautiful search for sustainability, further reinforced radicals' inclination to pursue their broadly transformative goals on a modest and manageable scale.

The catch-phrase for this approach, now something of a cliché, was "think globally, act locally." The slogan was coined by the scientist and Pulitzer Prize–winning writer René Dubos, on the occasion of the 1972 United Nations Conference on the Human Environment. By it, Dubos meant to convey that uniform solutions to global environmental problems were unworkable; policymakers needed to take the cultural and ecological characteristics of distinct locales into account. But as the phrase gained in popularity, adorning bumper stickers and buttons or working its way into newsletters and speeches, its meanings multiplied, as so often happens. To some activists in groups like Citizen Action (founded in 1979), it was a call to neighborhood organizing, canvassing door-to-door for financial and political support (a technique first developed in the early 1970s). Other activists understood the slogan as advocating radical municipalism: taking over the local government in sympathetic cities, as the Progressive Coalition did in Burlington, Vermont in 1980, electing socialist Bernie Sanders as mayor the next year. For still others, the exhortation to think globally and act locally implied using community organizing to grapple with far-reaching problems that had arrived in their backyards, as did, for example, the member organizations of the Citizens' Clearinghouse on Hazardous Wastes, founded in 1981.[10]

Substantial numbers of former radicals began to work inside or alongside the institutions of power during this period. A significant number of African-American organizers, for example, shifted to the mainstream electoral arena. While blacks remained dramatically underrepresented in elective offices, the number of black elected officials tripled between 1969 and 1977.[11] Other activists chose to ally themselves with large liberal organizations, pursuing a species of legislative and electoral politics that tied their fate to the simultaneously declining and rightward-drifting Democratic Party. These groups included the National Organization for Women, which devoted much of its energies throughout the 1970s and early 1980s in an ultimately unsuccessful campaign for an Equal Rights Amendment to the US Constitution; the National Gay Task Force, founded in 1973 (and later renamed the National Gay and Lesbian Task Force), which worked to abolish sodomy laws, establish legal protections for gays and lesbians, and support gay-friendly candidates; and environmental organizations such as the National Resources Defense Council and the Sierra Club, which combined lobbying with litigation to promote an environmental agenda. Circumscribed though their political vision might have been from a radical perspective, many of these organizations thrived in the seventies and eighties, expanding their membership, mastering the art of direct-mail fundraising, and honing their Beltway-insider skills.

Other progressives established alternative educational institutions, from independent Chicano colleges on the West Coast to a school for Marxist education in New York City. Many moved into the academy, where from within established colleges and universities they promoted ethnic and women's studies: roughly 600 college and universities offered black studies courses by 1972; five years later, when the National Women's Studies Association was created, there were 276 women's studies programs in the country.

But above all, the sense of hunkering down for the long haul prompted many to turn their energies toward building alternative, community-based, and counter-institutions, acting to create change at a more modest scale in their immediate surroundings. Environmentalists opened local ecology centers, set up recycling projects, and organized food cooperatives, some of which still exist to this day, such as the Park Slope Food Coop (founded in 1973). Feminists, and especially lesbian-feminists, built a nationwide network of cultural institutions including women's cafes and bookstores and events like the Michigan Womyn's Music Festival, which ran annually from 1976 to 2015; they also created battered women's shelters, feminist health clinics, and self-defense classes with a feminist bent. The period from the mid 1970s to the mid 1980s could be called the age of progressive institution-building: it saw the founding of long-lived, influential infrastructure, such as a movement-oriented advertising agency (the Public Media Center, 1974–2009), a radical philanthropic network (the Funding Exchange, operating between 1979–2013), a training institute for activists of color (the Center for Third World Organizing, founded in 1980), and an annual gathering of left intellectuals (the Socialist Scholars Conference, founded in 1983, renamed the Left Forum in 2005).[12]

A whole wave of activists, particularly from the identity-based movements, focused on the production and distribution of alternative media during this period. "There was this passion for getting information out," recalled Carol Seajay, one of the founders of the Feminist Bookstore Network and the longtime publisher of *Feminist Bookstore News,* which remained in operation until 2000. Most of the underground papers of the sixties had died by the mid seventies, but new publications took their place—along with new publishing houses, and new bookstores to disseminate it all. A certain number of these media institutions were left or broadly radical: Modern Times Bookstore in San Francisco and Midnight Special Bookstore in Santa Monica (both founded in 1971; Midnight Special closed in 2004); *Mother Jones* magazine and the socialist weekly *In These Times* (both founded in 1976); the Center for Investigative Reporting (founded in 1977); the book publishers South End Press (1977–2014) and New Society Publishers (founded in 1982). But the biggest areas of growth were within the identity-based subcultures, most notably the feminist and gay movements. By 1976, there were enough gay newspapers to hold a gay press convention: staff members from nine East Coast papers, with a combined circulation of over 100,000, gathered at the offices of *Gay Community News* (1973–1992) in Boston to discuss common concerns. Later that year, more than 125 women—representing eighty feminist bookstores, periodicals, and publishing houses—gathered at a Camp Fire Girls Camp in Omaha, Nebraska for the first Women in Print Conference; by that point, there were an estimated 150 feminist presses and periodicals in existence.[13]

These institutions prided themselves on their independence, and saw their mission as explicitly political. "Control of our own voices and words is just as important as control of our bodies," explained June Arnold, co-founder of the feminist publishing house Daughters, Inc., in 1976. Ed Hermance, the manager of Giovanni's Room in Philadelphia, which opened in 1973 as one of the country's first gay bookstores, offered a similar rationale. "When the store first opened, there were fewer than 100 titles that anybody could identify that might possibly be of interest to gays and lesbians," he recalled. "The store was just about the only public space that people could go to. That's what it did, was be a public space for lesbians and gay men."[14]

Much about the radical/progressive political landscape in the United States was slowly but decisively shifting in this period of activist introspection. Movements might be smaller and weaker than they had been a decade earlier, but there were more of them, speaking in a greater array of voices. The idea of a single, unitary "left" was always more myth than reality, but that myth was becoming increasingly out of line with reality on the ground. First and foremost, the radical identity-based movements were here to stay; with the late sixties' flush of street militancy behind them, some were turned inward, focused on self-exploration and cultural work, but they would remain fiercely committed to autonomy and self-representation. Issue-based movements and activist projects multiplied alongside them. "We've had a tremendous increase in both the number of demonstrations and the spectrum of issues," the director of Washington, DC's Mayoral Command Center noted in 1978. Where a handful of large mobilizations might have taken place in the nation's capital in any given year a decade or so before, now there was a constant stream of protests, by groups that, in the *Washington Post*'s lively tally, included "farmers, American Indians, religious fundamentalists, Marxists, Maoists, anarchists, anti-abortionists, pro-abortionists, women's libbers, anti–women's libbers, gays, senior citizens, marijuana advocates [and] ban-the-bombers."[15]

Not everyone on the left celebrated this growing diversity of causes and voices, feeling that some sense of shared political purpose had been lost amid the new radical cacophony. Journalist Andrew Kopkind wrote with sadness of "the sense of isolation that pervades the American left since the disappearance of a cohesive movement sensibility," in a 1978 essay entitled, "What to Do Till the Movement Arrives." He continued, "Some important social movements built around specific issues—minority rights, nuclear power, and sexual liberation—have deepened in recent years, but by and large they exclude those who deviate from the narrow genetic, preferential, or topical definitions of the movements, and provide little day-to-day work for ... activists of a leftist or socialist cast." This characterization of the new movements as "narrow," and the related claim that they were fragmenting rather than augmenting the larger radical project, would be a recurring refrain for the next forty years. "The left"—the broad more-or-less socialist political tendency that saw economic relations as fundamental—might now be only one radical subculture among many, and one whose appeal was dwindling rather than expanding, but it would too often continue to view itself as broader and more universal than all the rest. ("When many people think of leftists," quipped Black Lives Matter co-founder Alicia Garza in a 2014 interview with journalist Julia Wong, "they think of white men selling newspapers who are going to tell you what you should think and how you should make revolution happen now.")[16]

There were interesting efforts to bridge the traditional left and what some were now calling the "new social movements," including the journal *Socialist Revolution* (founded in 1970, renamed *Socialist Review* in 1978, folded in 2006) and the multi-issue New American Movement (founded in 1971), which merged with another left formation in 1982 to create Democratic Socialists of America, but none of these had wide impact or electrified a large following. That part of the left that called itself "the left" too often preferred to stay stubbornly unreconstructed, particularly in regard to gender. Well into the new millennium, many institutions of the socialist left, from conferences to publishing houses, remained overwhelmingly male-dominated, lagging far behind mainstream society. This dramatic underrepresentation of women—over decades in which women organizers, and the theory and practice of identity politics, were steadily reshaping much of the radical activist landscape—only served to give an anachronistic feel to certain segments of the socialist left and limit their relevance to movements on the ground. There was a nice irony in the fact that the biggest revival for socialist ideas after the sixties came through the Occupy movement of 2011, whose organizing practices were profoundly shaped by feminism and anarchism: political traditions are, after all, often renewed from the outside.[17]

And indeed, the closer one looks at the more radical of the "single-issue" movements of the early 1970s onward, the less single-minded or narrow they appear. Some or even many of the people who attended a given movement's mass rallies or marches might be interested only in the issue at hand, but the core organizers invariably had a broader vision and critique. Anti-nuclear activists, for instance, weren't simply concerned with the health and safety risks posed by nuclear power plants; they viewed the push toward nuclear power as an outgrowth of a toxic ideology of "progress" and "growth"—one which the traditional left too often shared. The committed organizers who most shaped the new wave of movements tended, moreover, to migrate from one movement to the next, creating deep political, tactical, and strategic continuities between what superficially appeared as disconnected issue-oriented campaigns.

The charges of narrowness and fragmentation were lodged most frequently against the identity-based movements. But during this same period, some were laying the foundation for a new critical approach to structures of power, one that focused heavily on the relations between different systems of domination and in the process fundamentally challenged older views of what was "universal" and what was "particular." The group most often credited with coining the phrase "identity politics," the Boston-based black lesbian and feminist Combahee River Collective (founded in 1974) paved the way. The collective was anchored by the writer and activist Barbara Smith, whose work throughout the 1980s as publisher of Kitchen Table: Women of Color Press would be enormously influential, and her twin sister Beverly, a public health specialist who had been part of the early staff of *Ms.* magazine. It also included acclaimed poets Audre Lorde and Cheryl Clarke within its shifting membership, as well as the writer and political activist Chirlane McCray, who became the first lady of New York City in 2014. The Smith sisters had both been active in CORE in Cleveland during the 1960s, and the civil rights movement had a deep influence on both their theoretical and organizing work. "I always say that's the movement that shaped my politics, because it was the first movement I was involved in, but also because of the values of the civil rights movement, particularly the nonviolence," Barbara Smith recalled in a 2016 interview. That embrace of the civil rights tradition was one factor that set her and her collaborators apart from many black nationalist contemporaries in the seventies; gender politics divided them even more dramatically. "Black women were supposed to walk seven steps behind and have babies for the nation," Smith explained. "I'm not saying that everybody who was a black nationalist had those reductive, misogynistic views of women, but there was enough that it definitely affected people like me."[18]

Combahee tackled an array of local organizing projects that involved questions of race, gender, and sexuality, such as mobilizing support for Kenneth Edelin, a black doctor who was charged and convicted of manslaughter after performing a legal abortion, and defending Ella Mae Ellison, a black woman who was falsely convicted of first-degree murder of a police officer. They organized a major feminist response to a series of murders of black women in Boston that had been largely ignored by authorities and the mainstream media. Some black community leaders—male leaders—had viewed the murders in strictly racial terms and suggested that women should protect themselves by only going out accompanied by male companions. "It's true that the victims were all Black and that Black people have always been targets of racist violence in this society, but they were also *all women,*" explained a pamphlet that the Combahee Collective produced about the murders. "Our sisters died *because* they were women just as surely as they died because they were Black." The pamphlet, originally entitled "Six Black Women, Why Did They Die?" offered self-protection tips and lists of both organizing projects and resources for support, and went into printing after printing as the number of murders grew; according to Barbara Smith, who drafted the initial text, the collective distributed some 40,000 copies.[19]

It was the Combahee River Collective's 1977 manifesto, though, that had the greatest and most lasting political impact. "We believe that the most profound and potentially the most radical politics come directly out of our own identity," the Combahee River Collective statement read. "We are actively committed to struggling against racial, sexual, heterosexual, and class oppression and see as our particular task the development of integrated analysis and practice based upon the fact that the major systems of oppression

Combahee River
Collective leaflet,
circa 1979 (designer:
Urban Planning Aid;
courtesy Lesbian
Herstory Archives)

are interlocking. The synthesis of these oppressions creates the conditions of our lives." This analysis offered a profound shift in perspective. Rather than viewing those, like black lesbians, who simultaneously experienced multiple forms of oppression as representing a narrow constituency, as classic interest-group politics might do, the collective argued that their unique vantage point gave them a broader, deeper, and more nuanced view of the complex workings of power and domination. This vision of identity was rooted in a socialist-feminist framework: "We are socialists because we believe that work must be organized for the collective benefit of those who do the work and create the products, and not for the profit of the bosses," the Collective wrote, with the manifesto first appearing in a collection entitled *Capitalist Patriarchy and the Case for Socialist Feminism.* "We are not convinced, however, that a socialist revolution that is not also a feminist and anti-racist revolution will guarantee our liberation." This influence, all too rarely acknowledged, provided the liveliest and most consequential legacy of the socialist tradition in this period. The women of color feminism created by the Combahee River Collective and others in the late 1970s and 1980s laid the foundation for what would later be termed intersectionality, a focus on the ways systems of power and domination combine and overlap that has been a defining influence on the Movement for Black Lives and the activism of the Millennial generation more broadly.[20]

But while the charges of narrowness and fragmentation lodged against identity politics rather missed the point, there was undoubtedly a general tendency toward localism, introspection, and small-scale organizing throughout this period of contraction and restructuring. With all the focus on community-based projects and institution-building, large mobilizations with large ambitions were few. There was great pragmatism in this shift but a sense of resignation as well—a recognition that acting on a scale larger than the local had become very difficult indeed. Rudy Perkins, an activist with the Clamshell Alliance and later the Coalition for Direct Action at Seabrook, remembers reading in an anarchist journal of the time a "lovely little poem drawing an analogy of tidal pools on the beach, that the wave had receded and now all that was left was little bits of active life in little pools scattered around. And that's how it felt." It was a far cry from the revolutionary dreams of just a few years before. But in some of those little pools Perkins spoke of, activists would experiment—with varying degrees of success—with making their ambitions larger, and direct action would be their primary method.

On August 1, 1976, fourteen men and four women carrying sleeping bags, oak and sugar maple saplings, and small corn plants marched down the railroad tracks leading into the construction site for the Seabrook Nuclear Station, located within an ecologically fragile tidal marsh on the New Hampshire coast. Earlier that summer, despite vocal public opposition throughout New England, the Nuclear Regulatory Commission had issued a permit for the Seabrook facility. In response, several dozen anti-nuclear campaigners, assisted by two seasoned organizers from the Boston-area office of the American Friends Service Committee (AFSC), the Quaker pacifist organization, met and decided to push their fight to a new level. The time had come, they felt, for "direct, nonviolent action such as one-to-one dialogue, public prayer and fasting, public demonstrations, site occupation and other means which put life before property." In an allusion to the mollusks that environmental researchers said would be harmed by the Seabrook nuclear plant, they named their new organization the Clamshell Alliance.[21]

The founders of the Clam (as the group was colloquially known) took much of their inspiration from an extraordinary anti-nuclear direct action that had taken place the previous year in Wyhl, West Germany. After police brutally evicted a modest encampment of 150 protesters from a nuclear construction site there, some 28,000 people, ranging from conservative local farmers to counterculture radicals, swarmed the site and took it over. Thousands stayed and held the space for nearly a year, ultimately forcing the German government to abandon the project. The Wyhl encampment, and the West German anti-nuclear movement more generally, would repeatedly serve as touchstones for direct-action organizers in the United States.[22]

The eighteen people who marched to the Seabrook plant had no illusions that their small group could replicate the Wyhl experience, but the items they carried onto the site gestured toward the ideal of permanently reclaiming the site. They brought the young trees in "a symbolic attempt to reforest the area there," explained one of the protesters, Rennie Cushing, in an interview just before the action; the corn was "a symbol of the native people that once inhabited this land." There was a Native American burial ground on the nuclear site, testimony to that historic habitation, which inspired a small but significant Native American presence in anti-Seabrook organizing. Cushing continued, "Also, the corn shows our intention to be here in the fall to harvest it and the trees show our intention to be here at a later date and view them at maturity with our children and our grandchildren."[23]

The group of eighteen barely managed to get the corn and saplings into the ground before they were arrested for trespassing and hauled away by the police. But they achieved what they wanted: their act of civil disobedience was prominently covered by the local media. Three weeks later, in an escalation that had been carefully planned from the start, 180 people were arrested in an even more widely publicized second occupation attempt. Though activists around the country had long rallied, gathered petitions, attended hearings, and lobbied politicians in opposition to nuclear power, nobody working on the issue had organized anything remotely like civil disobedience on this scale before. "This is the shot heard round the world for the anti-nuclear movement," declared author and activist Harvey Wasserman at the pre-action rally, which drew more than 600 participants. "[We] are moving from the stage of debate into the stage of direct action."[24]

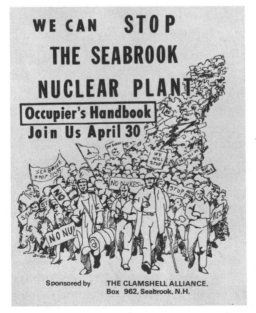

Clamshell Alliance direct-action manual (designer unknown; courtesy Ed Hedemann)

The Seabrook campaign was a historical watershed in several respects. As its organizers hoped, it inspired people throughout the country to form their own groups and engage in direct action against nuclear power plants in their area. This wave of protest, which swelled still further after the partial meltdown of a nuclear reactor at Pennsylvania's Three Mile Island in 1979, contributed greatly to curtailing the spread of nuclear power in the United States for decades to come; over 100 planned projects were canceled over the course of the 1970s and 1980s. The Seabrook activists ultimately lost their fight—the Seabrook Nuclear Plant did eventually begin operation, although not until 1990—but ground was not broken on another new nuclear reactor in the United States until 2013.

As important as the Clamshell Alliance was in helping forestall nuclear plant construction in the United States, its most striking legacy was in consolidating and promoting what became the dominant model for large-scale direct-action organizing for the next forty years, used to powerful effect time and time again. From Seabrook, the prefigurative direct-action model first spread to other anti-nuclear groups around the country, including the Abalone Alliance, which organized a series of large actions against the Diablo Canyon Nuclear Plant. It was picked up by the Livermore Action Group, a California group working against nuclear weapons in the early 1980s, and by the Pledge of Resistance, a nationwide network of groups organizing against US policy in Central America throughout the decade. Some 1,500 protesters used the Clamshell model in an effort to shut down the headquarters of the Central Intelligence Agency in the spring of 1987, in protest against US policy in both Central America and South Africa; hundreds more employed it that fall in a civil disobedience action to protest the Supreme Court's anti-gay *Bowers* v. *Hardwick* sodomy decision. The AIDS activist group ACT UP used a version of this model when it organized bold takeovers of the headquarters of the Food and Drug Administration in 1988 and the National Institutes of Health in 1990, to pressure both institutions to take swifter action toward approving experimental AIDS medications. The radical environmental group Earth First! used it for its 1990 Redwood Summer, a Northern California mobilization to protect old-growth forests from logging. The model was carried forward by the global justice movement to blockade the meetings of the World Trade Organization in Seattle in 1999, and for a series of subsequent trade summit protests. Having been used by anti-nuclear activists seeking to shut down the Stock Exchange in 1979 and radical environmentalists seeking to reclaim Earth Day in 1990, a version of the model was also adopted by Occupy Wall Street and the many Occupy groups that sprang up around the country in 2011.

It's worth pausing a moment to consider the cultural context in which this influential blueprint for action arose, for it would shape the ways it was adopted, modified, and critiqued over the decades to come. The Clamshell Alliance was about as white as it was possible for an American movement to be, bringing together white rural New Hampshire Seacoast residents with white radicals from around New England, advised by white Quakers. The AFSC of course had a longstanding commitment to racial justice and many within the organization had significant direct experience with multiracial organizing; the same was true of some other seasoned activists within the Clam. But many, maybe most, of the people who participated in the direct actions at Seabrook were white people with little or no background in dealing with race, and the Clamshell Alliance devoted little time or energy to addressing the question. The group's manuals and other organizing materials made little or no mention of race, racism, or people of color. "In principle, the common denominator of nuclear protest should attract support from diverse groups of people," wrote longtime activist Marty Jezer in the midst of the Seabrook fight, "for the dangers of nuclear power cut across class, race, sex and ethnic lines, but in practice Clamshell politics and style of organizing excludes people."[25]

By 1979, when anti-nuclear activists including many Clamshell veterans organized a direct action on Wall Street to mark the fiftieth anniversary of the stock market crash and highlight the role of corporate power in the nuclear industry, the movement, though no less white than it had been before, had begun taking some first halting steps toward addressing race directly. After considerable internal debate, the mobilizing materials for Wall Street cited the exploitation of Native Americans and black South Africans as key reasons for the protest and the action manual included a section on racism, sexism, and heterosexism. The text dedicated to questions of race, though, seemed to criticize African Americans rather than the anti-nuclear movement for the movement's whiteness: "Despite the growing awareness in this country of the dangers of nuclear proliferation, blacks are largely silent on this issue. Perhaps it is because nuclear power and weapons seem such a remote idea, far removed from the everyday lives of blacks in this nation," the manual suggested. "There is no issue more overwhelming and all-embracing than nuclear militarism and power," the section continued. "All issues are encompassed in the struggle against those who have pushed and continue to push for nuclear weapons and power."[26] It was an awfully weak beginning—condescending and dismissive, for starters. Though the movements that embraced the direct-action model created at Seabrook would do a significantly better job at addressing race over time, it was a slow process. By the mid 1980s, explicit anti-racism began to be a regular part of direct-action manuals and action trainings, even if the movements themselves remained preponderantly white. But there would be lasting consequences to the fact that the particular model of direct action used in so many large mobilizations from the 1970s onward came out of a cultural context that was at once so white and so lacking in self-awareness about that fact.

The two Boston AFSC staff people who helped get the Clamshell Alliance off the ground, Sukie Rice and Elizabeth Boardman, were instrumental in creating the new model. Rice remembered getting a call from the New Hampshire AFSC staff person in mid 1976, before the construction permit for Seabrook was issued. Rice recalled, "She said, 'There are some people up here who are very concerned about a nuclear plant that might be built, and most of them come out of SDS, and I'm trying to talk to them about nonviolence and they don't know anything about it, and they think it's stupid. They don't want anything to do with it. Would you please come up and talk with them and give them an idea of what it entails?'" Rice was a longtime peace activist and nonviolence trainer. She had done some of the trainings for Mayday 1971, but skipped the action because she felt it wouldn't be strictly nonviolent. She came up to New Hampshire and did a series of role-playing exercises with the soon-to-be Clams, acting out various possible protest scenarios, some involving angry confrontations, others calm and quiet sit-ins. She asked some of the participants to play the part of average New Hampshire citizens watching the events unfold on TV, and to tell the others how each option came across. "People realized," Rice says, "that the only way to reach extremely conservative New Hampshire was through nonviolence, no matter what they had believed in their past political acts of life." When the Seabrook construction permit was approved and the Clamshell Alliance was formally created, nonviolence became one of its central tenets.[27]

Rice was invited back up to New Hampshire for the initial meetings of the Clamshell Alliance and brought Boardman with her. When it came time for the group to make its first decisions, Boardman suggested that, instead of voting, they try using the Quaker method of decision-making. For more than three hundred years, the Society of Friends has employed a practice of "voteless decision-making," which involves determining the "sense of the meeting" through extensive and respectful discussion. The goal is to come up with a decision that everyone can agree to, creating group unity without overriding the objections of a dissenting minority. As Quaker historian Howard Brinton describes it, "The synthesis of a variety of elements is often obtained by a kind of cross-fertilization, and the final result is not therefore, or at least ought not to be, a compromise. Given time and the proper conditions, a group idea, which is not the arithmetical sum of individual contributions nor their greatest common divisor but a new creation or mutation, finally evolves." The foundation for this practice is the religious belief that the group's deliberations are a process of seeking God's will, and that unity will be achieved once it is found. In Brinton's words, "The principle of corporate guidance, according to which the Spirit can inspire the group as a whole, is central. Since there is but one Truth, its Spirit, if followed will produce unity." As another scholar, A. Paul Hare, described it, "Ideally [the group's] consensus is not simply 'unanimity,' or an opinion on which all members happen to agree, but a 'unity': a higher truth which grows from the consideration of divergent opinions and unites them all." If the group cannot reach agreement, it takes no action.[28]

Consensus decision-making was immediately appealing to the Clam, for reasons that had nothing to do with religion. "Friends consider it a waiting upon the Spirit, that you pray that you will do God's will, and that wasn't there in the Clam," remembered Sukie Rice. "The Clam used it as a decision-making process that was consistent with nonviolence." The reason, Rice explained, is "that you are always taking into consideration the heart and soul of each member of the group." Its participatory spirit was a welcome antidote to what Marty Jezer, the Clamshell activist who had drawn attention to the group's weakness on race, called "the structureless-ness in which a hierarchical leadership planned demonstrations and people attended more or less as drones to be added to the body count." Consensus seemed much more consistent with the shifting movement culture of the time—especially, and crucially, consis-tent with feminism, to such a degree that some called it "feminist process." "Many people had felt a sense of alienation and mar-ginalization in mass meetings of various kinds, of SDS and other major political organizations. The developing idea of democracy was that there had to be a way for everybody to be heard," recalled Ynestra King, who was active with the Clamshell Alliance and later a key figure in the Women's Pentagon Actions of 1980 and 1981. "Women had separated out of those organizations and had set themselves up in smaller groups, and had set up situations [like consciousness-raising groups] in which everyone was expected to speak, and everyone was expected to listen respectfully." When the Clamshell Alliance was created, she says, "Certain forms that had been learned from feminism were just naturally introduced into the situation, and a certain ethos of respect, which was reinforced by the Quaker tradition."[29]

The Clamshell Alliance adopted the process in its purest form. "*Under consensus, the group takes no action that is not consented to by all group members,*" explained a Clamshell action manual, using italics to underscore the centrality of this point. The idea was to ensure that no one's voice was silenced, that there was no division between leaders and followers; everyone would decide, and everyone would agree with every decision. That meant, of course, to quote the manual further, that "any one person can state opposition to the proposal and this will block the group's adoption of that proposal." Aware that this put an extraordinary amount of power in the hands of potentially disruptive (or unbalanced) individuals, the manual specified that "the power to object and block consensus should only be used responsibly and sparingly. Block consensus only for serious, principled objections; when possible, object in ways that do not block consensus."[30]

The use of affinity groups also resonated with feminist concerns of the time, although Rice, who had brought the idea to the Clamshell Alliance, suggested them for more pragmatic reasons. Rice had encountered affinity groups at Mayday 1971 and later through the Movement for a New Society, a radical Quaker group espousing "revolutionary nonviolence" that promoted the practice through trainings they conducted from the early 1970s onward. In one of Rice's trainings for the second, 180-person Seabrook action, she explained that forming affinity groups in advance of the action ensured that "people will have a feeling for at least some of the folks that they'll be very close to, will be able to be especially supportive of each other, will be able to care for each other." The other practical reason, beyond mutual support, was to guard against the infiltration and disruption that activists now knew were standard techniques in the government's playbook. As Ynestra King explained, "There were a lot of people who had a lot of awareness about provocateurs from the New Left, and so the feeling was very strong that people should be organized into groups that were in some way accountable to each other."[31] Affinity groups' street-fighting origins had been pretty well forgotten by this point; they were viewed in the Clam "as a source of support for their members, and thereby [as] a concrete reminder of our solidarity," as well as key structures for decision-making.[32]

Longtime action trainer and organizer Joanne Sheehan later noted, "While nonviolence training, doing actions in small groups, and agreeing to a set of nonviolence guidelines were not new, it was new to blend them in combination with a commitment to consensus decision-making and a non-hierarchical structure."[33] The structure that linked the affinity groups together and coordinated overall decisions was called a "spokescouncil," made up of representatives, or "spokes," from each affinity group. These were supposed to shuttle back and forth between the overall decision-making body and their individual affinity groups, to ensure a constant process of consultation. The idea was that the spokescouncil would not exercise decision-making power over the affinity groups but rather would function in such close coordination with them that decisions would be made non-hierarchically. There were important anarchist lineages behind these practices, but on the whole the influence of anarchism in this period was more diffuse than doctrinal, disseminated less through works of theory than through principles of organizing and action.

The movements that created and refined the new model of direct action, from the anti-nuclear movement onward, weren't just seeking to create change through their protest activity; they sought to model, or prefigure, the world they hoped to create through the manner in which they organized. Prefigurative movements dedicate themselves to "forming the structure of the new society within the shell of the old," as the revolutionary Industrial Workers of the World (IWW), the most radical of the early twentieth-century labor movements, famously expressed it in the preamble to their 1908 constitution.[34] To the extent that prefigurative radicalism is a utopian project, it stands within a long American tradition, stretching back at least to the early nineteenth century. The communes of that time, inspired by the ideas of Robert Owen and Charles Fourier, expressed a nearly boundless optimism. They were based on the belief that human nature is the product of social structure, rather than the other way around—a belief with far-reaching ramifications. For if it were true, creating an ideal society would be a fairly straightforward matter of redesigning the structures that regulate people's relationships with one another and the world: replacing monogamous sexual relationships and the nuclear family with group marriage and collective child-rearing, as the members of New York's Oneida Community did, for instance, or collectivizing labor through practices like "time money" and "time stores," as in Owen's New Harmony community. With enough tinkering, perfection was presumably within reach. The utopian communities were invariably small and often isolated—havens, really—but their creators saw them as laboratories for all humankind. For if they succeeded in their mission, they reasoned, surely others would be inspired to imitate them. Personal fulfillment and social harmony could prevail through the force of example and nonviolent persuasion; there was no need for a bloody revolution, or even for bitter conflict.

The prefigurative direct-action movements of the 1970s and 1980s contained traces of all these communitarian views. And like the Wobblies (as the radicals of the IWW were known), they gave them an activist spin. Not content simply to build alternative communities or institutions, they believed in directly challenging the old society at the same time that they created a model of the new. Even so, there was a strangely circumscribed and inward-looking quality to their activism, which set them apart from these predecessors. While the utopians and the Wobblies had different strategies, they shared an assurance that they could remake the world. The prefigurative movements of the seventies and eighties were the products of an awkward and liminal time, and it showed. The organizers of these movements couldn't be as confident and expansive in their utopianism as the New Left and counterculture before them once had been: the lessons of the recent past were too sobering; there had been too many setbacks and too many defeats. Yet the prefigurative radicals hadn't given themselves over to dystopianism either, the way many of their successors in the late eighties and nineties would, movements like ACT UP and Queer Nation, whose fierce sensibility was deeply marked by the punk rock prophesy of "no future." The prefigurative radicals were caught between hope and despair, dreaming of dramatic transformations in what they knew was an age of limits. Without realizing it, they devised a form of activism that neatly counterbalanced these conditions. It enabled them to carry on as activists—organizing protests, fighting for change, putting their bodies on the line—at a time when the left was dwindling and the right ascendant, but in a way that frequently seemed to focus their attention less on the external changes they hoped to see than on the inner workings of their groups and movements.

Because the new prefigurative activism represented such a departure from conventional forms of organizing and thinking, a great deal of political education for individuals, affinity groups, and the movement as a whole was required to propagate the model. Where, in the free-for-all atmosphere of the big sixties mobilizations, a person had only to show up at a demonstration to participate in it, the new direct-action model required extensive advance preparation. At Seabrook, participants needed to belong to an affinity group, and they were required to participate in training sessions lasting five to seven hours in order to be part of the action: specially colored arm bands were distributed to those who had met this latter requirement, and marshals ensured that no one without them took part in the occupation. Organizers created detailed handbooks explaining the new structures, roles, and expectations, nearly all of which would be unfamiliar to newcomers to the movement; as the movement grew, the handbooks grew longer and more involved. A packet created in advance of the planned June 1978 Seabrook occupation dedicated five pages to discussions of the possible roles one could assume in an affinity group, from the discussion facilitator to the "'vibes watcher'—a person who will pay attention to the emotional climate and energy level of the attendees." Participating in the new style of direct-action mobilization entailed both a major time commitment and full immersion in an alternative world with its own culture, lingo, and practices: "An AG 'spoke' is the group's communication liaison to the spokes' meeting or to the cluster," read one definition in the orientation packet, notable for how much prior knowledge it assumed. Everything about this remove from mainstream culture and conventional practices was intentional. In the words of ecofeminist and neo-pagan writer and activist Starhawk, who played an important role in the West Coast anti-nuclear movement and many other direct-action movements of later years, including the 1999 Seattle mobilization against the WTO, "We can change consciousness, we can transform our inner landscape, tell new stories, dream visions in new thought-forms. But to change culture we need to bond in new ways, to change the structures of our organizations and communities."[35]

It was a bold experiment in a new form of direct democracy, and it captured the imagination of thousands. Privileging participation over efficiency, it was challenging work, and it could be excruciatingly slow. Ynestra King remembered the consensus process as "torturous": "The meetings would go on for just days—you'd have even sometimes one or even two people block consensus," meaning the group would have to keep talking—and talking—until that person was satisfied. She continued, "The idea of trying to listen and talk something through until you reached the complete end of the conversation and everybody was with you, that was completely new. That was completely new, and doing it on that scale was new—not with just five or ten people, but when you have hundreds and hundreds of people in an auditorium in a little college in Vermont or something trying to actually reach consensus over where to do an action, what tactics will be used, even a political statement about it."

Exhausting though the debates and discussions often were, the experience was exhilarating and empowering to some—especially those who were used to not having their views heard or issues acknowledged in other settings. Dave Drolet, who described himself as one of few openly gay people at the 1977 Seabrook occupation, credited the consensus process with making him feel actively respected in a situation that might have been alienating. "Its effect is that the majority and minority bodies on any particular issue are reminded of their responsibility to the other's needs and desires," he wrote. "This has great implications for gay people, members of a distinct and possibly permanent minority. Often I found myself not having to introduce the gay aspect of a particular question because my straight brother and sister clams would bring it up for me in a supportive way."[36]

The model worked much less well, though, when the Clam was forced to make strategic decisions, and quite poorly when the group needed to make decisions under pressure. During the 1977 occupation, WRL's Ed Hedemann reported, "Decision-making on the site broke down because there were *continual* meetings of the DMB [Decision-Making Body, or spokescouncil] spending an inordinate amount of time discussing what to name the site, how to send off departing occupiers, how to respond to a possible visit of the governor, what sort of greeting to give the support rally a few miles away, etc. It wasn't until just before we got the order to clear the site, that discussion had begun on the various proposals of what we should do besides simply occupying the parking lot."[37] Recognizing these problems, the group decided to modify its process for its next planned site occupation in June 1978, having several clusters of affinity groups make decisions autonomously rather than have a single decision-making body for the whole action. But a much more serious breakdown in the process occurred before they ever had a chance to test the plan out.

Tensions had already been building in and around the movement over how to define nonviolence and whether it was okay for occupiers to cut through fences in order to reach the site. Some

Hard Rain poster, late 1970s (designer unknown; author's collection)

Clams, including members of the Boston-based Hard Rain affinity group, believed that nonviolence "is best expressed in practice by placing human life first, above property," and argued that the ten-point action guidelines, which specifically prohibited damage to Seabrook property, should be modified to allow occupiers to breach the fences. "Because we have lost our trust for the courts, corporations, government agencies, media, and legislature, we have to take *direct action*," they wrote. "That is, we are not asking the authorities' approval, we are blocking the plant's construction *ourselves*."[38]

Though the Hard Rain proposal did not pass, Clams based in the New Hampshire Seacoast, meanwhile, were growing increasingly worried as the June occupation date approached that some participants in the action would cut through the fence, alienating locals and undermining the cause. Just weeks before the planned direct action, the attorney general of New Hampshire offered demonstrators an alternative location near the Seabrook construction site where they would be allowed to camp out and hold a legal rally if they promised to leave of their own accord at the end of the weekend. Rather than go through a cumbersome process of consultation with affinity groups, the coordinating committee, influenced strongly by Seacoast Clams, simply decided for everyone. They accepted the attorney general's proposal, thereby calling off the blockade, a decision they were not empowered to make under the process which the group had so painstakingly created. Even Clams who agreed with the decision to cancel the direct action were shocked and angry that local affinity groups hadn't been included in the process. What was the point of all those guidelines and meetings and procedures and endless discussion, if a small group of leaders were going to make the crucial decisions by themselves once the pressure was on?[39]

In the spirit of solidarity, most Clams didn't publicly air their objections to this betrayal of the group process, but the campaign to stop the Seabrook plant was marked by splits and internal rancor from that point forward. A number of activists who supported the idea of cutting the fences around the construction site to facilitate a Wyhl-style occupation soon created a new organization, the Coalition for Direct Action at Seabrook (CDAS), in which the Hard Rain affinity group played an important role. The new coalition had a much more literal interpretation of direct action, envisioning a scenario where they would prevent the plant's construction through their direct physical presence. They vowed "to close the Seabrook plant by nonviolently, physically stopping construction. Our aim," they wrote, "is to nonviolently enter the Seabrook nuclear site, and to prevent construction by staying there." Activist Billy Nessen, who worked on the manual for the action and was part of an affinity group called One Love, explained, "We saw direct action versus civil disobedience—when you call it civil disobedience, the point is to get arrested to make a statement. Our thing was to get in the way, to actually stop it. Of course, we knew we'd get moved out, but maybe that was part of our symbolism, that we were saying to everybody, we are definitely going to get in the way and you're going to have to move us out by force."[40]

With the recent Three Mile Island nuclear accident having increased the sense of urgency among many in the movement, CDAS brought some 2,500 occupiers to the site for this purpose in October 1979, outfitted with bolt cutters, crowbars, gas masks, ladders, and other gear. It was a substantial showing for a militant action (much larger than the Days of Rage a decade earlier, for instance), but the numbers were less than half of what the group had hoped to mobilize, and all their army-surplus gear was no match for actual militarized police. They did manage to cut the fence in several places and to pull down one section, but the protest rapidly degenerated into skirmishes with authorities, which the police of course ultimately won. "This is the most ragtag army you've ever seen," one participant sighed, as rain and tides turned the area into a muddy bog, and police tear gas and water hoses drove the protesters away from the site. Looking back on the action many years later, Rudy Perkins of Hard Rain concluded, "We made a big mistake, partly just out of political immaturity. We elevated direct action to a politics instead of just a tactical choice."[41]

The direct-action anti-nuclear movement had created a new model for large-scale actions, one intended not just to reflect the movement's values in the practice of its organizing but to embody a new way of living and acting. The model resonated so strongly with so many activists that it spread and endured for decades. To be

sure, there were numerous problems with how it worked in practice from the first big Seabrook occupation onward, and activists in
subsequent movements would continually tweak various aspects of
its structure and methodology. But the model's lasting appeal had
less to do with practicalities than with its promise. Participating in
actions organized with the prefigurative model was a way to feel like
you were working to build a new world in the moment, whatever
concrete impact your action had. When used for a strategic action
as part of a well-planned campaign—as in the anti-nuclear power
movement—the combination could be powerful, sustaining the
hopes of movement participants even as it mobilized them to create
change. It's noteworthy that the prefigurative model spread at a
time when change was becoming harder to make, though, and the
dreams of a different world harder to sustain. Prefigurative organizing could also be very inward-looking, focusing activists' attention
on the small worlds they were creating, and inwardness was proving
to have a strong hold on activist culture as the country lurched
further and further to the right.

In November 1980, two weeks after Ronald Reagan's election, some
1,500 women gathered in Washington to take a bold stance against
militarism, sexism, environmental destruction, and much else
besides. The Women's Pentagon Action, initiated in part by women
who had been part of the Clamshell Alliance, was a theatrical
protest at the headquarters of the country's military establishment;
not a prankish event, like the infamous attempt by Abbie Hoffman,
Jerry Rubin, and the Yippies to levitate the Pentagon thirteen years
earlier, but earnest and deeply solemn. A silent morning march
through the long rows of graves at Arlington National Cemetery
set the tone of the main event, in which the assembled women
encircled the Pentagon. The demonstration was elaborately choreographed, with four distinct stages, each symbolized by a large
puppet: black for mourning, red for anger, golden for empowerment, and white for defiance. Amid chanting and singing, some
women engaged in civil disobedience by blocking the doors to the
building; meanwhile, in the words of Tacie Dejanikus and Stella
Dawson, two feminist reporters who attended the event on behalf

of the feminist publication *off our backs*, "fearsome painted faces expressed anger and grief, drums beat, bundles of rushes were brandished like broomsticks to sweep the steps of the Pentagon clean, and endlessly women twisted and turned yarn through the railings to spin and spell and weave the doors of the Pentagon shut."[42]

For three months leading up to the demonstration, affinity groups had labored to perfect a consensual "unity statement," conveying the action's intent, working from an initial draft written by poet and activist Grace Paley. The completed document was sweeping in its scope, a gesture toward a new kind of political synthesis. At its core was an attempt to bring together feminism, pacifism, and environmentalism. "We women are gathering because life on the precipice is intolerable," the statement declared in urgent tones. "We want to know what anger in these men, what fear which can only be satisfied by destruction, what coldness of heart and ambition drives their days. We want to know because we do not want that dominance which is exploitative and murderous in international relations, and so dangerous to women and children at home—we do not want that sickness transferred by the violent society through the fathers to the sons." In a notable advance over the anti-nuclear movement's messaging in the previous years, the statement repeatedly referenced racial injustice and included a call "to see the pathology of racism ended in our time."[43]

These women believed that femaleness, as they understood it, could function as a radical force for social transformation, supplanting masculine values of competition and aggression in favor of egalitarianism and a spirit of nurturing. "We understand all is connectedness," the unity statement continued. "The Earth nourishes us as we with our bodies will eventually feed it. Through us, our mothers connected the human past to the human future." The event's complex iconography was intended to capture and communicate this political spirit. The four puppets, for instance, represented the participatory ideal, since they took the place of human leaders—the group deliberately did not feature any individual participants as spokespeople in their press work or outreach. By looping yarn through the Pentagon's doorways, the women saw themselves as symbolically engaged in "reweaving the web of life," a female-coded act of healing and creation. The idea was explicitly prefigurative: "We cannot expect to wait until society is healed in order for us to begin living in a healthier way," explained Gina Foglia and Dorit Wolffberg, two women who took part in the event. "Therefore, we attempt to practice in our own lives an elimination of unnecessary waste and destruction of resources, a way of relating to all people that encourages cooperation and tolerance, a sensitivity to the needs and fears of others, and the understanding that our methods are as important as our goals, if not more so."[44]

The timing of the preparatory work and the action itself were noteworthy: the months of discussion and planning exactly overlapped with the final months of the 1980 presidential election campaign. Ronald Reagan would of course win the election in a landslide, smiling past opponent Jimmy Carter's efforts to portray him as a right-wing extremist and rallying erstwhile Democrats, especially from the white working class, with his sunny promise of "a new day in America." Reagan's victory represented a major political realignment that would make every aspiration of the women gathered at the Pentagon harder to achieve; among other things, he would oversee the largest peacetime military build-up in US history and saber-rattle his way into what came to be called the Second Cold War, awakening new fears of nuclear apocalypse. But the women of the Women's Pentagon Action treated the election almost like a non-event, leaving it unmentioned in their mobilizing materials. Part of the point of their action was to have it take place irrespective of who was elected: "We weren't happy with what Jimmy Carter was doing about the MX missile and rearmament," Ynestra King told the *Washington Post* by way of explanation.[45]

Participants described the event as moving and transformative, and their main frame of reference seemed to be how the organizing choices represented an evolution beyond other activist mobilizations of the past. "We observed an exciting cross fertilization of ideas from different movements," reported Dejanikus and Dawson, the two participant-journalists from *off our backs*. "The tactic of civil disobedience came from the black civil rights and anti-nuke movements; guerrilla theater, used by the Yippees and 1960s feminists;

collective process and decentralized organization, developed by feminists and anarchists; a commitment to working with women and discussions about the politics of lesbianism, originated with the feminist and lesbian-feminist movement; and affinity groups, associated with the anti-nuclear movement."[46]

It was indeed a remarkable new synthesis of many strains of movement culture. It was also completely baffling to outside observers. The *New York Times* allotted several perfunctory paragraphs to the action in a news brief, noting without elaboration that it was a protest against "the arms race, militarism, and violence against women." The *Washington Post* gave it longer but more dismissive play, lazily terming it a "60s-Style Protest," while quoting an unnamed Navy official: "I guess they're having fun," he mused. "I bet these chicks don't even know why they're here." Some participants openly mocked the "uncomprehending men" who couldn't puzzle out the action's meaning, but communicating to outsiders wasn't especially one of the action's goals. "There was a whole discussion within the organization about who are we doing this for," recalled King. "And basically we really believed that we were doing it for ourselves, and that in that sense it was a ritualistic enactment." Explained one participant, Susan Pines, who received a thirty-day federal jail sentence for blocking one of the Pentagon's doors, "It was an action by, and for, women."[47]

By, and for, a particular subset of women, it must be noted. As reporters Dejanikus and Dawson noted afterwards, "The action itself raised many questions that we could not answer. I.e., Why were almost all the demonstrators young and white? What did it mean to us that almost all the cops were male and black? How can the struggles against racism, sexism, and militarism be most effectively combined?"[48] Writer and activist Sarah Schulman, then a young journalist covering the event for *Womanews,* was appalled by the participants' seeming myopia on race. "While many women are doing all they can to stay out of the racist American 'justice' system, these white women did all they could to go to jail … In general police looked cold and bored during the hours the women spent on the steps of the Pentagon singing 'We Shall Overcome' to the black officers."[49]

Far from being discouraged by the insularity of their action, the activists largely felt energized by the experience and analysis they had created together, and they returned to the Pentagon in even larger numbers the following year. They added Spanish to their buttons in a gesture of cultural inclusion and changed the color of the mourning puppet from black to white in response to criticisms that it was racist; once at the site, they did a much more thorough job weaving the entrances shut with yarn. The coverage was, if anything, more uncomprehending: "The protesters, most of them women, represented several causes," read the entire Associated Press account of the action, a brief photo caption published in the *New York Times*. "At the Second Pentagon Action," recalled King, "I remember asking, just how is it that we think we're having an effect on these issues? What is it about what we're doing that we think is actually making a difference? What concrete impact do we think we're having? I think people were always able to answer more assuredly that we were building a movement and building a community—take-the-long-view kinds of answers—than we were able to say, oh, Congress voted this way or that way because of what we did."[50] To their credit, the activists of the Women's Pentagon Action realized the project had problems, and that race was central among them. They decided to disband rather than continue as a virtually all-white group.

Women's Pentagon Action button, 1981 (designer unknown; author's collection)

But with the Reagan administration now in the White House and enjoying a broad popular mandate, how exactly could activists hope to have an impact on such massive problems as militarism and sexism? Weaving yarn across the doorways of the Pentagon wasn't going to stop the war machine, but what could? And what were activists who wanted much more—a radically different society— to do in a period of such reaction? It's not surprising that a good number turned inward—the Women's Pentagon Action was far

from the only activist undertaking of the period to have this character. "It was a difficult and strange moment in the beginning of the
eighties," remembered Leslie Cagan. "A lot of people were feeling
like, *Ronald Reagan? What happened? What's going on here?* It was
kind of a wake-up call to the left and to progressive activists. [The
Right] had moved in a way that—not that we necessarily wanted
to model how they worked—but they had been very strategic in
planning, and thoughtful in fundraising, and had assembled their
mailing lists, and where was the left?"[51] Mostly, the left was struggling. But one movement of this challenging time, at least, was
being quite strategic in its planning—and direct action would be a
crucial part of how it would win.

One day in late 1984, three prominent critics of South African
apartheid—Randall Robinson, director of the advocacy group
TransAfrica; Mary Frances Berry, of the US Civil Rights Commission; and Washington, DC Congressional delegate Walter
Fauntroy—met with the South African ambassador to present a list
of demands. They vowed to stay at the embassy until the demands
were met, and the ambassador promptly had them arrested.
Robinson later said that they hadn't expected to be arrested that day,
and certainly had not at that point planned on mounting a sustained
campaign of civil disobedience, but they quickly pulled together a
response. More apartheid critics showed up at the embassy the next
weekday afternoon, and were arrested. The same thing happened
the next day, and the day after that, with organizers vowing that
the protests would become a daily occurrence. The campaign, now
called the Free South Africa Movement, rapidly gathered momentum. Celebrities like Harry Belafonte and Stevie Wonder came and
were arrested; so were veteran civil rights leaders like Coretta Scott
King and the Rev. Jesse Jackson. Almost two dozen members of
Congress took part, and large numbers of ordinary people, as the
actions continued month after month.[52]

A routine developed early in the campaign. An account in the
Christian Science Monitor explained:

At 4:30 p.m. the loaded buses lumber up the avenue to the embassy, stop, and discharge passengers. The two dozen police begin to look more alert. Protesters form loose ranks and dispatch a delegation to the embassy door. The delegation rings; as always, there is no answer.

Then the ranks begin to sing. It is this act that actually breaks the law, as it is illegal to demonstrate within 500 feet of an embassy. A policeman with a bullhorn asks them three times to stop, as is obligatory. They sing louder. The arrests begin …

In fact it is only technically an arrest. Protesters are rubber-stamped through booking back at the station and are released on their own recognizance. The US Attorney will refuse to press charges. For each protester, there will be no police record of the affair, says a law-enforcement source.[53]

As an action model, it was pretty much the antithesis of the organizing style of Mayday 1971 and Seabrook and its successors. The Free South Africa Movement had a clear and explicit leadership structure which designed and coordinated every aspect of the protests. Participants joined the action; they didn't plan it. The whole thing was closely choreographed, with the arrests unfolding like a theatrical performance. The Clamshell occupations had also featured cooperation with the police, but not quite to this extent, and certainly not with so few repercussions for arrestees. Some direct action proponents found it a deeply unsatisfying model. "It has some strengths in terms of media attention, in terms of ensuring to some degree, as much as you can ensure, a level of safety for the participants," said longtime organizer Kai Lumumba Barrow in a 2000 interview. "But I think as a direct action, it's not valuable. I think it contradicts the whole theory of direct action … which to me is to become empowered, taking an issue in your hands and saying you're going to change it."[54]

But by nearly any standard, in this case, it worked brilliantly. The steady stream of actions brought sustained media attention to the issue, focused pressure on both the South African regime and the US Congress, and catalyzed a larger anti-apartheid movement in the United States. An impressive number of people participated:

there were nearly 3,000 arrests in the first year, and many thousands more came and rallied alongside them in support. This black-led movement certainly drew supporters of all races, including a noteworthy number of white people, but there was special meaning to the way it mobilized large numbers of African Americans to take part in civil disobedience for the first time in many years. The arrests were ritualized, but that didn't mean it wasn't a big step for people—and especially black people—to put themselves in a position where they would be handcuffed and led away by police. Though it would be years before the trend was named and contested, the long march toward mass incarceration of African Americans—what scholar Michelle Alexander famously called "the new Jim Crow"—was already well underway. As John Ehrlichman, one of Nixon's top domestic advisers, admitted years afterwards, "The Nixon campaign in 1968, and the Nixon White House after that, had two enemies: the antiwar left and black people ... We knew we couldn't make it illegal to be either against the war or black, but by getting the public to associate the hippies with marijuana and blacks with heroin, and then criminalizing both heavily, we could disrupt those communities." Over time, though, it wasn't weed-smoking white hippies who would bear the brunt of anti-drug policies; it was black Americans. Prison populations began to climb significantly by 1980, with major racial disparities in sentencing. Reagan announced his War on Drugs in 1982, and spending on antidrug law enforcement that mostly targeted black communities quickly skyrocketed. Tame and perfunctory though the black-led embassy arrests in 1984 might seem to those who preferred even stronger tactics, their significance was weighty in context.[55]

As the crisis in South Africa worsened, the political space opened up by the Free South Africa Movement's embassy protests helped create the biggest movement on college campuses in a generation. The movement took an issue of racial injustice thousands of miles away and turned it into one with concrete and immediate stakes, by focusing on university investments in firms doing business with South Africa. In the words of Josh Nessen, a staff organizer with the American Committee on Africa, which worked to support and coordinate the campus actions, the university provided "a local and visible target on which to focus energy and easily see the impact and results."[56] The divestment strategy was a savvy and ultimately highly effective way to connect the global and the local. And at one campus after another, direct action played a major role in pressuring reluctant officials to sever financial ties with the regime.

The actions began at Columbia University, where there had been an active anti-apartheid movement for years, although its impact had been modest to that point. Frustrated at the lack of progress, the campus Coalition for a Free South Africa, strongly shaped by activists from the Black Student Organization and with a mostly black steering committee, decided to blockade the university's Hamilton Hall in the spring of 1985, some months after the embassy protests began. The plans were closely held. Remembered Rob Jones, one of the main organizers, "Outside the steering committee, there were probably eight people who knew. But those people knew they were not to tell their lovers, their friends; they were not to tell their mothers. The only reason they knew was because we needed them to do X, Y and Z on the day of the blockade." During a publicly announced demonstration, the blockaders quietly moved into place, then chained the doors shut. Jones recalled, "We were deathly afraid the blockade was going to be twenty-five people, and that people were going to think this was the stupidest thing anybody had ever suggested and it would last, like, three hours." But substantial numbers of students and other sympathizers joined the blockade, with as many as 200 camping out on the building steps night after night. One daytime rally drew 2,000 people, and the blockade proved electrifying: by the time the student leadership of the action decided to disband it after three weeks, it had inspired similar actions at campuses including Cornell, Rutgers, UC Santa Cruz, and the University of Massachusetts, as well as solidarity protests at many more.[57]

On the surface, it was not just a remarkable surge of protest, but a remarkable advance in cross-racial organizing, with students of all backgrounds joining in events like the big rally at Columbia. Behind the scenes, things were much messier. The black-led character of the Columbia blockade was the exception rather than the rule, and the organizers faced criticism from various quarters that their steering-committee structure was undemocratic. Anti-apartheid campaigns on most campuses, especially those with wide-open organizing structures, tended to be steered by whites. As Tony Vellela wrote in a 1988 book about student activism of the time, "Divestment campaigns on campus were often led by white-dominated student groups. Many ignored the existing black student organizations. As campaigns evolved, so did divisions. Misunderstandings, territorialism, different styles and other pressures often magnified small rifts and mistrust."[58]

Nowhere were racial divides in organizing styles and philosophies more pronounced than at UC Berkeley, which came the closest of all the campus campaigns to having truly multiracial participation. Two major players in the university's anti-apartheid movement found themselves at odds: United People of Color (UPC) and the Campaign Against Apartheid (CAA). UPC had just been formed in the fall of 1984. It was the era of Jesse Jackson's multiracial Rainbow Coalition, and as organizer Howard Pinderhughes recalled, "There was a feeling that a lot of the student of color organizations were very nationalistic in their focus—you had the African Students Union, and you had MeCha [the Movimiento Chicano Estudiantil de Aztlan], and you had the Asian Students Union, and they dealt specifically with issues that they identified as important to those narrowly defined groups, and we felt like it was important to have an organization that brought those different groups together." Pinderhughes had actually been part of the big 1977 occupation of Seabrook when he was an undergraduate at Williams College, and his experience there as one of very few black participants had a deep impact on his views about tactics and strategy. Rather than taking him to the Armory where the 1,400 or so other arrestees were being held, the police drove him out into the middle of a field, beat him, threatened him with menacing and racist language, and left him there all alone. After that experience, Pinderhughes recalled, "I told myself, I'm not antagonizing no cops. It's one thing if you want to have armed revolution, and try your best not to get hurt. But the idea that I would put myself in the way of a baton—I'm not doing that. I'm happy that there's white people who are willing to do it. And more power to them, because I think they will get less hurt, and that's fundamentally true. But they didn't understand that. They didn't understand the ramifications of it for us."[59]

CAA, the other major anti-apartheid group at UC Berkeley, was predominantly white and influenced by the more militant wing of the prefigurative direct-action world—one key organizer was Billy Nessen, who had been closely involved in the Coalition for Direct Action at Seabrook's messy 1979 occupation attempt. "It's hard to pigeonhole this exuberant, creative group," read a sympathetic profile of CAA in a radical weekly newspaper of the time. "Its organizational process is one of consensus, akin to that of women's peace camps. Tendencies represented include anti-imperialists, Central American activists, anarchists, punks, radical lesbians and gays, pacifists and libertarian Marxists." CAA was sincere in its commitment to ending apartheid, but also very wedded to its own activist style and inexperienced with multiracial organizing work. In the words of Pedro Noguera of UPC, "The tensions with Campaign Against Apartheid were not really racial, they were more ideological. They had a racial character because Campaign Against Apartheid was a white organization."[60]

About a week after the Columbia blockade began, CAA organized a big general meeting, at which participants decided to begin occupying the steps outside the administration building. UPC was not part of the meeting or the decision—they supported the idea of an action, but wanted it to happen at a later date with more planning. CAA, meanwhile, was eager to act. The culture of the occupation they launched was, not surprisingly, firmly theirs, and UPC kept its distance. "Here was the most participatory activity, political activity, in many, many years," CAA organizer Nessen recalled afterwards, somewhat ruefully, in an interview for the 1988 documentary film *From Soweto to Berkeley*, "hundreds, hundreds of people, thousands even, involved, with 400, 500 people on the steps at night, Sproul Hall steps at night, deciding what we were going to do the next day, and the Third World group on campus saying, wait a second, we think that this whole environment excludes us. You call it participatory, but we have a hard time participating in it."[61]

As Pinderhughes put it, "The culture of the steps was not a culture of people of color. There was a handful at best—I think maybe three or four, all of them men, no women of color. Not a single woman of color on those steps." The process that CAA viewed as so participatory—consensus decision-making—proved specifically alienating to the student activists of color, particularly because of the large time commitment it required. Patricia Vattuone of UPC explained, "We felt it was undemocratic to have these long meetings—four hours, eight hours—when … other students are not only active in their own organizations, but can't spend hours and hours and hours on Sproul, and that was the only way you could have input or provide leadership." Pinderhughes echoed, "Basically it was decision by attrition. They had five-hour meetings, and the only people who could attend them were people who didn't have a job, didn't have somewhere to go, and didn't have studying to do."[62]

The encampment on the steps was soon faced with other problems, quite similar to ones that Occupy Wall Street would face some twenty-five years later. The free food and convivial atmosphere drew lots of hangers on, from homeless people looking for a good meal to activists unconnected to the campus looking for a good fight. Sanitation became an issue, as did safety, particularly for women; there were multiple reports of sexual harassment and even assault, much as there had been at Mayday 1971 and would be again at Occupy Wall Street. "As UPC we sat down and we said, we've got a decision to make," remembered Pinderhughes. On the sixth day of the sit-in, rather than letting the occupation continue to degenerate, they rallied several hundred people of color to march over and announce their full support. This major display of public unity quite clearly unnerved the campus administration. In the pre-dawn hours of the next morning, the chancellor sent in the police, evicting the encampment and arresting more than 150 demonstrators.[63]

For the rest of that spring, there was an uneasy peace between the two activist groups. The Sproul occupation was quickly reestablished, while UPC worked closely with another campus group, the UC Divestment Coalition, a mostly white organization that had focused much of its work on research and education, to organize a series of daily sit-ins in front of the doors at nearby University Hall, modeled on the Free South Africa Movement embassy protests. The university regents weren't swayed by any of it; after classes ended for the year, they voted not to divest, setting the stage for renewed conflict the following academic year.[64]

Beginning that fall, a creative new tactic—the construction of mock shantytowns to dramatize the dire living conditions of South Africa's black population—served as a flashpoint at campuses around the country. The first protest shanties were built at Cornell University in spring 1985, and were soon copied elsewhere. Everywhere they were erected, they provoked strong responses from administration officials and, in some cases, from other students. Administrators objected on aesthetic and public safety grounds; one Cornell official called that school's shantytown "a dangerous and sprawling collection of scrap and waste in the center of campus." Students responded with a sign reading, "Apartheid Isn't Pretty Either." The most notorious incident came when right-wing students at Dartmouth took some direct action of their own, demolishing four shanties on their campus with sledgehammers one winter night in early 1986.[65]

When the Campaign Against Apartheid at Berkeley decided to follow the lead of other campuses and construct eight shanties in front of their chancellor's office in April 1986, they were acting out of a classic direct-action playbook: create a crisis that can't be ignored. Organizer Rita Himes explained, "Either they were going to have to divest, take some action toward divestment, or they were going to have to tear down the shantytown. It was intended to force a confrontation." Some within UPC strongly supported the tactic. Pinderhughes called building the shanties "a brilliant thing" and praised the shantytown for "visually making a connection to South Africa that I thought was very good … It was different and engaging and a way to both protest as well as symbolically educate."

But when police knocked the shantytown down, arresting sixty protesters, UPC was less enthusiastic about CAA's immediate decision to rebuild. "We weren't interested in confrontation with the police," remembered Noguera. "We didn't think we were prepared for it, we just thought we would get hurt and get arrested and didn't necessarily see that as being advantageous." But CAA felt a sense of urgency. "The message from South Africa was one of anger," said

Anti-apartheid shanties at UC Berkeley, 1986 (photo: © Ron Riesterer)

Nessen, "it was one of, we are going to do it, at the cost of being beat up, at the cost of being shot, and I think people really identified with that." He didn't specify *which* people, but when police again moved in, it was mainly white protesters who tried to stop the demolition with their bodies, chanting "Just like South Africa!" as police dragged them away.[66]

Two months later, the UC Board of Regents voted to divest from companies doing business in South Africa, as, ultimately, did officials at more than 150 colleges and universities across the United States. They had felt many kinds of pressure, from petitions, rallies, and public forums as well as from marches, sit-ins, and shantytowns. It would be a stretch to credit direct action alone with any of the victories. But as Bradford Martin, a scholar of the movement, wrote in a 2011 study, "At campuses where protest occurred, 60 percent of those institutions divested at least partially, as compared with less than 3 percent at the schools where no protest occurred." Taken together, the many local campus fights across the United States made a tangible contribution toward hastening the end of the apartheid system, a process that began in earnest four years later when African National Congress leader Nelson Mandela was released from prison in South Africa. Mandela himself, in an extraordinary 1990 speech to a crowd of nearly 60,000 in the Oakland Coliseum, gave substantial credit to US anti-apartheid movement for its work: "It is clear beyond any reasonable doubt that the unbanning [of] our organization came as a result of the pressures exerted upon the apartheid regime by yourselves. By yourselves, as part of the international community, as part of the determined actions of our struggling people. You have inspired us beyond imagination." Everyone who had taken part in the movement could feel they had contributed to a world-historic moral and political victory. That was quite a sense of accomplishment, in a period when radical and progressive activists far more often found themselves losing—or pouring their energies into projects with no measurable impact outside their small activist circles.[67]

It was of course ironic and uncomfortable that so much of the organizing had been led by whites, and that where the campus movements were more truly multiracial, relations between black and brown organizers and their white counterparts were often strained. Even in the rare pockets of relative racial harmony, there was a sense that when it came to tactics and strategy, black and white activists were worlds apart. White activists had the luxury of romanticism about the civil rights movement and the nobility of risking arrest for a cause; black activists, attuned to the heightened risks they faced, were generally much more cautious. Sean Carter, an organizer with the DC Student Coalition Against Apartheid and Racism (DC-SCAR), a group that stood out at the time for its solidly multiracial character, remembered his first arrest, at a mid eighties anti-apartheid protest. He and Ray Davis, both black activists, had gone to the South African embassy with two white women who were also active in the group. "We didn't go there necessarily with the idea of being arrested. We were out there with picket signs and Joanie went and sat down on the steps. And I was like, nah— we're not here to do this today, this wasn't the plan. And then Robin went and sat down beside her—*what are you doing?* We didn't come here to do this today." Carter continued, "And I looked over at Ray Davis, and I said, it's going to look kind of funny to have two white women getting arrested, we need some color. I walked over there, and Ray was like, Let me go put my stuff in the truck." Carter and Davis reluctantly joined the two women on the steps, and soon they all got hauled off to jail. "They put me and Ray in a cell together, and Joanie and Robin in a cell together, and we were sitting there talking and they're in the other cell singing freedom songs. I was like, Ray, we weren't supposed to do this today, was we?"[68]

The take-away from the anti-apartheid movement for many activists of color was that they needed to focus their energies more squarely on racism, as deeply entrenched on college campuses —and, arguably, within the white left—as it was in society at large. Over the next few years, anti-racist student movements across the country would tackle issues ranging from student and faculty diversity to curriculum reform. White activists did not rally to support these efforts with the same energy they brought to the anti-apartheid struggle, which only increased the sense of a racial gulf. In a 1988 essay, Matthew Countryman, an influential student and youth organizer of the time, described a widespread sense of disillusionment among black activists and a fatigue with multi-racial work: "As black students, we found it impossible to work with those who were willing to challenge racism only from 5,000 miles away."[69]

White activists who had taken part in the anti-apartheid movement were by and large less troubled by its contradictions; they took from it a strong sense that wisely targeted action could produce concrete results. As an advance toward creating a multiracial progressive movement in the United States, the anti-apartheid movement was not especially a success. But as a step toward learning how to deploy the direct-action techniques of recent decades to win tangible victories against long odds, it marked a real step forward. Soon a new set of movements responding to crises at once local and global—most notably, environmental destruction and the AIDS epidemic—would build on this knowledge and launch a whole wave of attention-grabbing and politically potent direct action.

3

In Your Face

If party conventions are among the greatest rituals of US electoral politics, protesting outside those conventions has become, since 1968, one of the most habitual gestures of US radical politics. There have been some notable protests outside Republican conventions, especially in 2000 and 2004, but by and large, it has been protests outside Democratic conventions that have had the strongest pull, irrespective of whether or not the party held the White House or had a chance of electing its candidate that year. Convention protests predate the 1960s: over 4,000 suffragists brandishing yellow parasols held a silent protest at the 1916 St. Louis Democratic convention; Jane Addams and a caravan of "peace paraders" showed up in Chicago in 1932 to demand that the Democrats work to abolish war; and civil rights activists led by Martin Luther King Jr., A. Philip Randolph, and Roger Wilkins led a 5,000-person strong march in Los Angeles in 1960 in the hope of securing a civil rights plank in the party platform. But after the televised police riot in Chicago in 1968, where antiwar protesters were beaten on live TV for the world to see, targeting the Democrats every four years became something of an ingrained radical habit.[1]

The protests sometimes seemed to happen only because convention protests have happened before, not for any clear strategic reason in the present other than the perennial desire to manifest a wider array of political alternatives than would be showcased inside the convention hall. Though in most cases their impact on American politics has been questionable at best, the quadrennial convention protests have served as a useful kind of movement check-in in an era of multiplicity—a moment when activists from varied issue- and identity-based movements were corralled in the same police pens and could exchange ideas, tactics, and contact information, as well as an opportunity to gauge the temper and character of grass-roots organizing.

From a strategic point of view, the 1984 Democratic National Convention held in San Francisco seems, in retrospect, like a particularly purposeless occasion for protest. Progressives of all sorts had been stunned when Ronald Reagan swept into office in 1980, along with the first Republican majority in the Senate for twenty-five years, and had watched with horror as Reagan cut taxes for the rich and social services for the poor, eliminating more than 200 domestic programs in the 1981 budget alone. The new Republican administration encouraged logging, mining, and ranching on public lands; poured vast public resources into a massive military build-up; came to the aid of authoritarian regimes in El Salvador and Guatemala; and sponsored the contra war against Nicaragua's revolutionary Sandinista government. Reagan opposed most civil rights legislation, supported limits on women's right to choose abortion, and ushered in a long period of crisis and decline for the labor movement after he personally fired more than 10,000 members of the Professional Air Traffic Controllers Organization (PATCO) when they went on illegal strike in 1981. In those surreal first years of the eighties, radicals looked up from the many worlds they had built for themselves on the margins of American life and discovered, most disturbingly of all, that this new reactionary politics enjoyed broad popular support. When the 1984 convention season rolled around, the Democrats didn't have a prayer of electing their candidate in the coming presidential election; Walter Mondale would go on to suffer one of the most overwhelming defeats of the twentieth century. In the rightward-shifting landscape of the time, the exercise of protesting against the Democrats had a quality of the inconsequential confronting the ineffectual. Even so, there were more rallies and protests at the 1984 convention than at any other party convention between 1968 and 2000: what progressives lacked in political power, they more than made up for in persistence. The AFL-CIO and mainstream gay and lesbian organizations mounted especially large marches, each gathering more than 100,000 supporters to show solidarity with the Democratic Party and push it to support their agendas with greater vigor.[2]

Radicals had something very different in mind. "We are here to say that the attitudes which are expressed in Democratic Party politics are the same as those of the Republicans: attitudes of war," declared the anti-nuclear Livermore Action Group (LAG) at one of the numerous protest events held during the convention week, echoing the Women's Pentagon Action's stance toward Reagan's election in 1980. Radicals took to the streets not so much to influence the Democratic Party as to reject the two-party system as narrow, undemocratic, and corrupted by moneyed influence. David Solnit, a central organizer of some of the week's most significant protests, called it "voting with your feet at the altar of the electoral ritual": "Our strength comes from the pressure on and opposition to militarism that we generate, from the creation of an independent movement, and from our direct action, and voting is no substitute for these tasks."[3]

If there was a huge gulf between the political worldviews of those who marched in hopes of influencing the Democrats and those who marched solely to condemn them, a no less significant divide—"a basic conflict in styles of dissent," according to Jack Roush, an activist who covered the convention for the anti-nuclear Abalone Alliance's newspaper—separated the latter into two distinct camps. The first group included traditionally left organizations like the Committee in Solidarity with the People of El Salvador (CISPES), an American group that was tightly allied with one of the five factions in El Salvador's rebel Farabundo Martí National Liberation

Front (FMLN), the insurgent force then fighting to topple the country's brutally repressive government, which was backed by the Reagan administration. CISPES and its allies had come under criticism from activists with a more anarchist bent for cooperating with the police at an April San Francisco protest against Reagan's secretary of defense, Caspar Weinberger; San Francisco police inspector John Hennessy had praised the protesters, saying "It's better for everybody if demonstrators monitor and control their own people instead of us having to do it." Though there were many stylistic and political differences between CISPES and LAG, it too was beginning to face criticism for the scripted character of some of its protests, and especially for orchestrating civil disobedience arrests with the police. LAG had taken the spirit and structure of the Clamshell Alliance and organized a colorful and creative series of early-1980s protests against the nuclear weapons research and development at Livermore National Laboratory; by 1984, though, the group's energies were waning, and some radicals were looking for a new approach.[4]

It was impossible to miss the members of the second camp, a large assemblage of flamboyantly angry punks, whose presence dominated the action outside the convention. They were the ones blocking traffic with impromptu die-ins, running wildly through the streets, occasionally scuffling with the police, and evading arrest whenever possible. Solnit, who was nineteen at the time and would go on to become one of the most influential grassroots strategists of his generation, initiating the call to blockade the Seattle WTO meetings in 1999 among many other accomplishments, played a key role in bringing the punks out into the streets for what organizers called the "War Chest Tours," intended to focus street-level rage at militarism, corporate power, and the two-party system. Solnit later described the actions as "a living critique of the left's forms of protest: monitors controlling and moving people like cattle, tactical leaders with bullhorns repeating monotonous chants, and even anti-nuclear, sit-down-and-wait-for-the-police-to-arrest-you civil disobedience that felt too much on the terms of the police."[5]

To publicize the War Chest Tours, Solnit and his collaborators went outside the usual activist circles to tap into the Bay Area's

Punks outside the 1984 Democratic National Convention
(photo: © Keith Holmes)

hardcore punk music scene. They were partly inspired by a raucous "Stop the City" demonstration held in London earlier that year, mounted by what a reporter for the *Times* of London described as an "unprecedented alliance of punks, anarchists, anti-nuclear protesters and cyclists, and animal liberation, anti-apartheid, and gay rights groups." San Francisco's punk underground was sizable but until that point had been mostly apolitical. Nationally, there had been some prior attempts to bring politics to punk rock, but these had been modest in their scale and impact: beginning in 1979, the Yippies organized regular Rock Against Racism concerts throughout the United States, designed—like the UK concerts on which they were based—to counteract the influence of racist skinheads in the punk rock scene. *Maximum RockNRoll*, the subculture's flagship publication from its inception in 1982, also worked to foster "positive punk" and political awareness among its readership.[6]

For the 1984 Democratic National Convention, activist Jim Martin recalled, "I made fliers with hostage-note headlines to make the demonstration look like a show. David [Solnit] went to shows and passed out fliers to the people waiting in line." The plan was to bring punks and radicals together for a roving protest through San Francisco's financial district, stopping in front of pre-selected corporate targets like Standard Oil of California and the Bank of America: "Explode the myth of the Democrats as the party of peace and the working man as you explore with your guide the crimes of the multi-nationals and their ties to the Democrats," explained the tactical manual. "The location for the action," in Martin's words, "would be at the intersection of mechanical death and lunch time," interrupting ordinary workaday routines to expose corporate malfeasance. At each stop, the protesters were encouraged to engage in various direct-action tactics, including die-ins ("At 'ground zero' everyone screams and collapses in the street as if nuked."), blockades ("Study the terrain of the city—what can be readily converted into a street obstacle?"), and spray-painting ("This artistic vandalism really spoils a businessman's day and also the unity of his bourgeois aesthetic.").[7]

Solnit had a broad political vision for the tours, seeing this type of disruptive protest as one of the "ways we empower ourselves to change the root causes and underlying attitudes in the old system and begin to create a new system." A lot of the people who joined the action, though, were simply pissed off: "We're trying to wake up the sleepwalkers," one punk, who gave his name simply as Peter, told the *Oakland Tribune*. "We're trying to wake America up from its narcotic sleep." The protests did not unfold quite as hoped— the police, knowing the details of the demonstration in advance, swooped in and broke up the first War Chest Tour with preemptive arrests before it had really gotten started. But the Tours had clearly tapped into a cultural current, and punks formed a loud and unruly presence at demonstrations throughout the convention week, dragging newspaper boxes and benches into the streets, shouting obscenities, and obstructing traffic.[8]

Prefigurative direct actionists might at times be maddeningly vague on matters of strategy and goals, as they had been during the two Women's Pentagon Actions; many of the punk demonstrators at the Democratic convention simply paid no heed to either. Theirs was a politics of pure expression, carrying forward something of the Motherfucker ethos into the grim climate of the 1980s. "We were just doing the only thing we could have—using the spectacle of the DemCon to try to wake America up from her Orwellian nightmare," explained an unsigned report in *Overthrow,* a Yippie newspaper of the 1980s. The punks weren't building or prefiguring anything; at most, they hoped to grab the nation's attention. Their contribution to the political discourse of the week was summed up by Jello Biafra of the Dead Kennedys, who led a crowd of thousands at a Rock Against Reagan concert in chanting "Fuck you" to the Democratic Party delegates as they exited the convention hall.[9]

It was not what you'd call constructive, but in the political climate of the mid eighties it had an undeniable, visceral appeal: if you can't beat them, scream at the top of your lungs. As a blueprint for change, this stance was virtually useless, making prefigurative radicalism, with its unwieldy process and utopian aims, seem like a model of pragmatism and efficiency by comparison. But it wasn't intended to be a blueprint for change. This style of protest was primarily about disruption, breaking with the polite complacency of a conservative era and with the politeness of scripted dissent. An exuberant action, of course, isn't necessarily an effective one, and expressive activism can be its own dead end. As Jim Martin wrote afterwards about the summer's events, "Direct action becomes a drug for the dissident, an addiction to the surge of blood and adrenaline." But there were two respects in which this cathartic approach amounted to a productive step forward, out of the cul-de-sac where many radicals found themselves during the 1970s and early 1980s. The punks at the 1984 convention were even further out on the fringe of American society than prefigurative activists like the women at the Pentagon (and proud of it, too), but, crucially, their gaze was directed firmly at the established order they despised, not inward at the workings of their group or consciousness. They made no attempt to evade or ignore how grim the country's political life had become, how outnumbered they were, and how small the prospects were for progressive change. Acutely aware of their powerlessness, the punks used their place on the margins as a platform from which to howl their discontent.

The significance of the 1984 Democratic convention protests, in any case, was not that they brought radical politics to punk rock, an enterprise of uncertain value, but that they showed how punk sensibility could and would be fused to radical politics. Punk was the self-conscious product of an age with "no more heroes anymore," to quote a 1977 single by The Stranglers, and it supplied something that radical movements of the time sorely needed: a way of coming to terms with failure. Not just personal failure, though punk had a lot to say on the topic, being a culture proudly of and for outcasts, misfits, and losers. Punk was also a riposte to the failure of utopias, the failure of grand ideologies, the failure of hope, the failure of the sixties—the very things that had made it so difficult to be a radical in the 1970s and 1980s, and that had impelled so many activists to invent elaborate strategies of compensation. You didn't have to listen to punk rock to absorb the alternative approach punk offered. Just because you belonged to a generation "born to lose," as the Heartbreakers put it in a 1977 song, didn't mean you had to give up, turn away, accept defeat or pretend that you were winning. If you were angry enough and determined enough, it didn't matter if your movement was small and marginal. You could still exercise the one power that even the tiniest minority retains: the power to harass, disrupt, and annoy.[10]

An in-your-face style defined a whole era of American radicalism, stretching from the mid 1980s well into the 1990s. It marked a shift from the prefigurative politics that held such sway throughout the 1970s and early 1980s, but continued these movements' experiments with decentralized organizational forms. This style was, most notably, the hallmark of ACT UP, the most innovative, influential, and effective radical organization of the late twentieth century. It carried over to the group's many offspring and imitators, among them Queer Nation, the Women's Action Coalition (WAC), and the Lesbian Avengers. More broadly, it linked together many of the otherwise disconnected parts of a scattered political generation, expressing a shared sense of powerlessness and alienation. This style of protest politics was not a creed but a sensibility, common to direct-action movements as disparate as the radical environmental network Earth First!; Roots Against War (a people of color organization created in response to the Gulf War); WHAM! (Women's

Health Action and Mobilization, a reproductive rights group); and ADAPT (American Disabled for Attendant Programs Today, whose organizing helped force the 1990 passage of the Americans with Disabilities Act).

The ranks of all these movements were filled, to a substantial degree, by activists from a generation that had grown up enjoying the fruits of earlier struggles: greater opportunities for women and people of color; more widespread acceptance of lesbians and gays; increased protections for the environment; the right to choose abortion. Since the early 1970s, organized right-wing opposition to these gains had been building, in campaigns like Anita Bryant's successful 1977 bid to repeal a local gay rights ordinance in Dade County, Florida, and in culturally conservative groups like Focus on the Family, founded by right-wing preacher James Dobson that same year. This politics of backlash had entered a new and sharper key in the late eighties. Where the National Right to Life Committee (founded in 1972) favored low-key lobbying and legislative activity, Operation Rescue (founded in 1987) undertook large-scale campaigns of direct action against abortion providers, borrowing blockading tactics from the left to intensify activism on the right. Jerry Falwell's Moral Majority, which since 1979 had promoted a conservative social agenda at the national level with only modest success, gave way in 1989 to Pat Robertson's Christian Coalition, which built an aggressive and sophisticated grassroots political machine capable of winning real local power. On the environmental front, the industry-backed Wise Use movement (launched in 1988) and its extremist cousin, the property rights movement, aggressively and even violently challenged green initiatives of every kind.[11]

The broad dreams of limitless revolution shared by parts of the New Left and the early identity movements were long gone, and instead, the new radicals of the eighties and nineties were continually battling limits. Not just the limits to growth acknowledged in the famous 1972 environmental report of that name, but newer constraints as well: limits born of the enormous budget deficits created by Republican economic policy in the 1980s, which served to stymie any state-funded social reform; limits sets by well-organized opponents from the right's growing social movements, the likes of which radicals in the 1960s and early 1970s had never had to face; and limits, in an era when communism was dead and socialism seemed moribund, to the age-old radical faith that the left had history on its side. The activists of this post-sixties generation were typically radicalized by the sense that their future was being foreclosed: by the threat of nuclear annihilation, ecological catastrophe, or government insolvency; by the erosion of abortion rights or the ravages of AIDS.

The political backdrop for the new wave of direct action was not apathy, although the period of the early and mid eighties was often characterized as quiescent. Dissent was widespread, but its impact was far from evident. Mass mobilizations in that era seemed almost to underscore the scale of progressives' powerlessness: a crowd of at least 250,000 people gathered in Washington in September 1981 for Solidarity Day, the largest labor march in US history, sponsored by the AFL-CIO with support from the NAACP, Greenpeace, and hundreds of other groups. Coming just a month after Reagan had fired the PATCO air-traffic controllers, the demonstration was intended to boost labor's morale, and while it may have done so in the short run, it did little to shore up union membership or influence, both of which were beginning a long period of sharp decline. The immense New York City march and rally for nuclear disarmament in June 1982—far larger than any of the Vietnam antiwar protests, and by some accounts the largest demonstration in US history—was the major exception, a mobilization so large that it successfully conveyed a sense of national moral consensus against the development and use of nuclear weapons. More than a million people joined this protest, held on the occasion of the United Nations Second Special Session on Disarmament, which helped push the Reagan administration toward arms-limitation talks, though there would be no substantive moves towards arms reduction until after the demise of the Soviet Union. The protest was organized in a similar fashion to the large Vietnam protests of the late 1960s, with a central staff and coordinating committee working to spur local mobilizations. Unlike many of those demonstrations, though, this one also included civil disobedience: two days after the big march, more than 1,600 demonstrators were arrested in follow-up direct action at UN missions throughout the city. This type of march-and-civil disobedience hybrid—usually with a sit-down-and-be-arrested character, although sometimes more tactically daring—became a common formula for national actions from this point onward, offering a way to accommodate some of the strategic and tactical differences that had divided the peace movement in 1971.[12]

The eighties also witnessed large grassroots movements against US intervention in Central America, which the Reagan administration viewed as a crucial battleground in its global fight against communism. The CIA under Reagan waged a far-reaching covert war against Nicaragua's revolutionary Sandinista government while supporting El Salvador's ruthless right-wing regime, notorious for eliminating opponents including Catholic archbishop Oscar Romero through death-squad assassinations. Opposition to Reagan's Central American policies loomed large on the progressive agenda in those years, and activism around the issue took many forms, from providing sanctuary to refugees fleeing violence in the region to organizing work brigades to help with the Nicaraguan coffee and cotton harvests. The close relationship between CISPES—the group whose use of monitors at its demonstrations had incensed the organizers of the War Chest Tours in 1984—and the armed guerrillas fighting the Salvadoran regime inspired a whole new wave of FBI harassment and surveillance of activists in the United States, including break-ins, document thefts, and death threats; even with J. Edgar Hoover long in the grave, the bureau remained obsessed with the idea of communist subversion. CISPES had good reasons for wanting to keep the atmosphere calm and controlled at its demonstrations: "We had our own political culture, and we were very attached to the Salvadorans and to the political organizations in El Salvador," recalled Diane Greene Lent, a longtime CISPES staffer who eventually became the group's executive director. "If we had Salvadorans with us, we really didn't want it to get out of hand because they were undocumented." CISPES had explicitly defined itself at its 1985 national gathering as the "North American front of Salvadoran revolution," not the "Central American wing of the US left." They rejected the loose, decentralized structures favored by so

Committee in Solidarity with the People of El Salvador, mid 1980s (designer unknown; courtesy Mike D'Elia)

many movements in the United States in favor of what historian and CISPES organizer Van Gosse called "a time- and goal-specific national program … to which the entire organization held itself accountable through a voluntary discipline." This more centralized and program-driven organizing approach set CISPES apart from most other grassroots groups of the time, even in later years when it embraced more confrontational and vibrant forms of street protest. In Lent's words, "We were supporting a revolution and that's where our analysis and objectives came from."[13]

The Pledge of Resistance, launched in 1984, was the Central American solidarity movement that most carried forward the more anarchist-leaning direct-action tradition of Mayday 1971 and the 1970s anti-nuclear movement. "The Pledge originally started out by saying, we're going to ask you to sign a pledge to resist US intervention in Nicaragua," explained Lisa Fithian, a former Pledge activist who later played a large role in both the Seattle WTO blockade and Occupy Wall Street and served as a direct-action trainer during the black-led uprising against police violence in Ferguson, Missouri. "The idea was that if the US was going to do a military invasion, you'd have thousands of people committed to do civil disobedience." Some 80,000 people signed the Pledge in the movement's first two years, a sizable number. Local Pledge groups formed throughout the United States, organized on an affinity group basis, and undertook both local and nationally coordinated direct actions. Pledge activists in Chicago disrupted holiday shopping at the Neiman-Marcus department store, singing an anti-CIA song to the tune of "Jingle Bells." Most famously, the Pledge organized a 1987 protest at the Concord Naval Weapons Station, in the San Francisco Bay Area, a site that had been an early target of antiwar blockades during the Vietnam War. Several Pledge protesters sat down on the railroad tracks leading from the station in order to block a shipment of munitions to Central America. The train didn't stop. Activist and Vietnam veteran Brian Willson was unable to get off the tracks in time. The train ran over him, and Willson lost both his legs below the knees.[14]

The force of reaction felt overpowering and unstoppable in the 1980s. There were glimmers of hope, like Jesse Jackson's 1984 and 1988 presidential campaigns, which held out the electrifying possibility of a nationwide, multiracial and multi-issue progressive

Pledge of Resistance button, mid 1980s (designer unknown; author's collection)

movement. But no one thought that Jackson could actually *win* a presidential election, and those who wanted to see the Rainbow Coalition take shape as an ongoing grassroots activist organization were sorely disappointed (as many followers of Bernie Sanders would be after his 2016 electoral bid). In the wake of the 1988 campaign, Jackson pushed through by-law changes that expanded and consolidated his power over the organization, undermining local chapters and ensuring that the Rainbow Coalition would never become anything more than a vehicle for his own electoral aspirations.[15]

A feeling of impotence, bordering on futility, permeated many radical efforts of the early and mid eighties. But it didn't stop them. In 1985, for instance, organizers from a wide range of movements collaborated on the "April Actions for Peace, Jobs, and Justice," protesting both domestic budget cuts and US foreign policy. The turnout was more than respectable, with something like 50,000 people attending a large march and rally, and more than 300 arrested in an attempted blockade of the White House. But the effect was unclear. "Is Ronald Reagan going to listen?" asked veteran civil rights activist Anne Braden, as those planning to commit civil disobedience gathered before the action. "Of course not. We're speaking to the people of this country." Yet it often seemed that the people of this country weren't listening either, and protests of this sort were just speaking to the wind. "Sometimes you just have to be out there and say, there is another worldview, and no, we don't like what you're doing … even when you know that demonstration isn't going to dramatically change the political discussion and dynamic of the country," reflected Leslie Cagan, the staff organizer for the 1985 event. "It was not the most important or significant demonstration ever, but it helped keep a community of protest alive."[16]

With the solid gains of the anti-apartheid movement in 1985 and 1986, the mood in some radical circles began to shift. Two springs after the Peace, Jobs, and Justice event, activists from a range of groups working to challenge US foreign policy decided to up the ante, pulling together a weekend-long mobilization that ended up featuring the most striking direct action since Mayday 1971: a non-violent blockade of the Central Intelligence Agency's headquarters in Langley, Virginia. The CIA's role in arming and funding the right-wing contras in Nicaragua and supporting repressive governments throughout Central America, especially the regime in El Salvador, had come under increasing criticism over the course of the 1980s. In late 1986, a group of college students including Amy Carter, the daughter of ex-president Jimmy Carter, made national headlines when they were arrested for a blockade against CIA recruitment on the University of Massachusetts Amherst campus; sixties veteran Abbie Hoffman, visiting the campus to stir up interest in a possible national student organization, was arrested along with them. Their trial the following spring—and acquittal using a necessity defense, a claim that they were compelled to break the law to stop a greater harm from occurring—generated even more publicity and helped build momentum for the planned direct action, with a big crowd of supporters chanting "Langley! Langley!" after the verdict was announced.[17]

The CIA blockade arose out of an improbable organizing context, a larger multi-day mobilization so hampered by caution and cleavages of race that it's surprising it produced an action so bold. The overall event was initiated by David Reed, the head of the faith-based Coalition for a New Foreign Policy, and David Dyson, director of the progressive National Labor Committee in Support of Democracy and Human Rights in Central America. Both wanted to organize a broad, inclusive demonstration against US intervention in Central America that could draw significant religious and labor participation. But the influential role of CISPES in grassroots solidarity activism posed a particular quandary for their planning. CISPES was way too important and well-organized to exclude. Unlike some of the more mainstream labor and religious groups that the conveners sought to involve, however, CISPES wasn't simply seeking a more humane and just approach to US foreign policy: it was rooting for the Salvadoran revolutionaries to win. As Dyson later wrote, "For most religious and labor leaders the FMLN connection was a problem. While clearly 'anti-interventionist' in their own positions ... they were not ready to throw personal or institutional support behind a military victory for the FMLN." So as the coalition for the action began to form, they made a rather unorthodox decision: in their public statements and outreach, they would only list the names of the religious and labor groups on the steering committee, in the hope of downplaying the role of CISPES and other controversial participants. "The majority agreed that ... exposure of the steering committee members would invite red-baiting," explained a post-action evaluation.[18]

The gambit failed rather spectacularly. Withholding the names of the steering committee members made local organizing around the country much more difficult—local Central American solidarity groups, for instance, had no way of knowing which national players were supporting the action. And far from deflecting criticism of the mobilization, the obfuscation seemed to fuel it. Perhaps the mobilization would have been attacked no matter what; there was clearly a coordinated drive to discredit it. AFL-CIO president Lane Kirkland issued the first salvo, writing to state and local chapters of the labor federation to urge them to stay away from the march and rally because they would include supporters of the FMLN and the Sandinistas: "Opposition to Administration policies does not mean," he wrote, "that we are prepared to join with any and all critics of Administration policies." Albert Shanker, the president of the United Federation of Teachers, soon followed with a paid advertorial in the Sunday *New York Times,* urging people to shun the mobilization because it was organized by the "wrong crowd." Jeane Kirkpatrick, the staunch anti-communist who had served as Reagan's ambassador to the United Nations, took to the pages of the *Washington Post* to write that the mobilization had "the smell of hard-left politics." The *Washington Times* went much farther, claiming without a shred of evidence that the demonstration had been bankrolled by Libya's Muammar Qaddafi.[19]

Meanwhile, realizing that the mobilization was shaping up to be overwhelmingly white, the steering committee, after long debate, decided to expand the scope of the event to include the issue of US policy toward South Africa, inviting a number of anti-apartheid groups to join. But if anyone hoped this dilatory addition would inspire significant black participation in the demonstration, the lateness of the invitation and limited staffing for the mobilization all but guaranteed it would not. The anti-apartheid groups did not appreciate the expectation that they should somehow make up for racially skewed organizing by mobilizing black crowds to join an otherwise mostly white event, and tensions around race carried through the entire organizing process. What diversity there was in the crowd that eventually gathered for the big march on April 25 mainly came from the labor contingent, which numbered in the tens of thousands despite the AFL-CIO's condemnation. The steering committee later criticized itself, acknowledging, in the words of the debriefing report, "that the black community was missing from the organizing and should have been included ... from the beginning."[20]

The last thing one might expect out of this embattled and fractured context was a dramatic blockade. From the start, there were strong reservations, especially from labor, about holding any kind of civil disobedience action, even something tame and choreographed. "Labor representatives expressed apprehensions about the inclusion of a civil disobedience action," the post-action report explained, "fearing it would be seen as too much of an escalation given the fragility of the coalition and nervous support from some of the labor signatories." Though the steering committee eventually agreed to hold some kind of action, it was so nervous about this aspect of the weekend that when the official call for the mobilization went out, it referred only in the vaguest terms, seemingly borrowed from A. A. Milne, to "An Event in Which Some Will Engage in Non-violent Civil Disobedience."[21]

But sometimes events take on a life of their own. The initial plan was to hold some form of orchestrated civil disobedience action at the White House. Advocates of direct action objected that the target was a dull and predictable choice, unlikely to excite much media or public interest; the more tactically cautious forces on the steering committee, including labor, countered that the group should simply try to involve more people in the action, as if doing something boring on a bigger scale would somehow make it less boring. Though religious and labor representatives felt that switching the action to CIA headquarters "represented a radical escalation in tactics" and "would threaten the mainstream character of the mobilization," to quote the post-action debrief, the idea prevailed. And once the site was shifted to Langley, the intrinsic drama of the location gave the action new appeal: no one, after all, had ever brought a large protest right up to the gates of CIA headquarters before, much less tried to disrupt the agency's operations by doing so.

The march and rallies that kicked off the weekend were indeed large and broad-based, despite the concerted attacks and inhospitable weather; organizers estimated the turnout at 100,000, while the Capitol Police put the number at 75,000 and the Parks Police offered a lowball estimate of 35,000. Tens of thousands of these were trade unionists, including contingents from the United Auto Workers, the American Federation of State, County, and Municipal Employees, and the Communications Workers of Americas. But the fact of bringing large numbers of people together for a protest held little intrinsic media interest, to organizers' chagrin: coverage was modest, buried, and perfunctory; a page thirty-two account in the *New York Times,* for instance, characterized the day as a "scene reminiscent of [the] 1960s."[22]

On the Sunday between the march and the planned action, some 1,000 people gathered for civil disobedience trainings and last-minute planning on the East Lawn of the Capitol—a small number for a march, but a large turnout for direct action. Early on Monday morning, the protesters swarmed the approaches to CIA headquarters, snarling traffic in and out, using mobile tactics in addition to classic stationary blockades. "We had three marches, three teams," recalled Fithian, whom the steering committee hired to coordinate the action. "The CIA has three entrances, so we had three teams of a lot of people that were going to blockade each entrance. The team that had the Parkway had to traipse through the woods—it was a wild scene." Tom Swan, a longtime progressive activist who was part of one of the affinity groups that went through the woods, remembers the "unnerving" feeling of being followed by police on horseback, but the authorities took a relatively gentle approach to policing the event: there was no riot gear beyond simple helmets, no tear gas, and no attempt to stop protesters from freely roaming through the area in a way that would be hard to imagine today. That helped give a festive quality to the defiance, underscored by sassy banners reading "Criminals in Action," "Covert Illegal Agency," and, in an allusion to the CIA's involvement in the drug trafficking that partially funded the contras, "Cocaine Import Agency." Eight protesters dropped their pants to reveal the message "NO REAGAN" spelled out on their bare bottoms. "It was a weird mix, there was a lot of seriousness about the action and what we were doing, and there was some fear, some nervousness," Swan recalled. "But there was also hopefulness and joyous energy, that we were doing the right thing." By day's end, more than 550 demonstrators were arrested, and the protest was front-page news in the *Washington Post, USA Today,* the *Philadelphia Inquirer,* and other major daily newspapers, drawing far more prominent and extensive coverage than the much larger march two days earlier.[23]

How to evaluate it all? The march had drawn big numbers, while the direct action had attracted big media attention. Both had certainly put some pressure on the Reagan administration, signaling the breadth of opposition to its foreign policy and the likelihood that protests would escalate if Reagan were to consider direct military action against Nicaragua. But surrounding the CIA's headquarters with direct-action blockades didn't seem to affect either the Agency or the Reagan administration to anything like the degree that Mayday 1971 had unsettled Nixon and his staff. Most

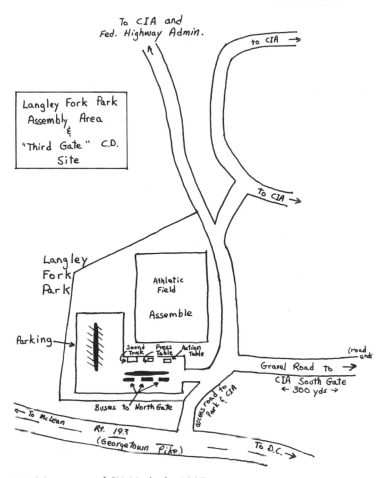

Hand-drawn map of CIA blockade, 1987
(artist: Lisa Fithian; courtesy Lisa Fithian)

CIA employees just arrived extra early that day, and a spokesperson blandly commented, "We respect the demonstrators' rights to express their views in a peaceful, lawful way." A Fairfax county police officer, D.A. Stopper, who was assigned to the demonstration and had also worked at Mayday 1971, observed, "That was different. That one was more frightening. These are just regular ol' people."

Quite frankly, the Reagan administration seemed much less rattled by the feisty blockade than by the prospect of having representatives of revolutionary groups deliver speeches from one of the four rallies that accompanied the march (the steering committee, in this case, having succeeded in scaling up something soporific, adding rally after rally during the planning process to accommodate a plethora of speakers and causes).[24]

From the more circumscribed perspective of movement culture, though, it was clear where the energy and momentum were. The CIA action represented the direction that street protest was going: more confrontational, more ambitious, more participatory, more media savvy. But the idea that the larger mobilization seemed to represent, of uniting disparate movements into some larger single vehicle, had a powerful appeal at the time, too, even if behind the scenes the relationships among the various sectors were rather strained. Some student activists of the time were particularly inspired by the prospect of doing both: uniting disparate movements while moving in a bolder direction tactically. Some months before the CIA action, they began exploring the idea of creating a new "multi-issue, multiracial, and democratically structured" national student organization "to confront the status quo through direct action." This was the project Abbie Hoffman was promoting when he got swept up in the anti-CIA protest at UMass, and he played an important advisory role throughout the process. The organizers called for a national convention to be held at Rutgers University in February 1988, for what they characterized as "the first attempt to form a national student organization since Port Huron." This self-conscious reference to the 1962 Students for a Democratic Society (SDS) founding convention issued from their sense that they were undertaking an historic task: bringing together the disparate parts of a multi-movement, multi-vocal progressive student landscape to create "a united voice of the student left"—an entity that could move youth organizing "beyond the fragments," as sympathetic journalists Vania del Borgo and Maria Margaronis put it in *The Nation*.[25]

The mainly white initiators of this ambitious project were aware of the racial divisions that had characterized campus anti-apartheid organizing just a few years before, and they hoped to build something truly inclusive; their advisory board included not just Abbie Hoffman and noted environmentalist Barry Commoner but also poet Cheryl Clarke and writer and publisher Barbara Smith, both veterans of the Combahee River Collective. In the months before the meeting, conference organizers traveled to campuses around the country to build momentum and recruit participants. But the conference planners had made the same fundamental error as the organizers of the April 25 mobilization: they took a white-defined and white-led project and tried to diversify it through subsequent outreach, an approach that was doomed to fail. In the end, when 700 delegates converged at Rutgers University in February 1988 for what was intended as the founding convention for the new national group, fewer than 5 percent were people of color.[26]

The conference opened with a stirring call from Christine Kelly, a Rutgers student who was one of the principal organizers, to build on what she called the "great upsurge in student activism first marked with the 1985 divestment protests": "We must not be afraid of making real all that lies in our imaginations. We must not allow ourselves to be deterred, derailed, or divided." It was already too late. Before the conference even began, the white students were divided into two broad camps: those who supported the main Rutgers organizers like Kelly and their SDS-inspired vision, and an anarchist-inflected "Independent Caucus" of students from MIT, Berkeley, and other schools who denounced the proposed organizational model as too centralized and bureaucratic (Billy Nessen, from the Coalition for Direct Action at Seabrook and Berkeley's anti-apartheid movement, was part of this grouping). While the Rutgers group worked to organize people in issue-oriented workshops, the Independent Caucus countered that progressive politics should be as much or more about "how we want to live" as about "what issues motivate us." This split seemed certain to bring the conference to a stalemate, but before it could, the twenty-five members of the Students of Color Caucus, working in alliance with gay, lesbian, and bisexual activists at the conference, confronted the body with a more fundamental problem. As Angela Parker, an organizer with DC-SCAR wrote afterward, "We were angry that little or no attempt had been made to involve national or regional students of color groups in the conference planning. And we were angry that a convention with less than 5 percent students of color representation could claim to represent the entire student left." The caucus asked that the establishment of a national organization be postponed until there was greater diversity in the organizing body. Parker explained, "Once again, students of color are being asked to legitimize an organization in which we have not been involved in the decision-making process, or had input in the creation of the agenda. This is a position we are no longer willing to accept."[27]

Shaken and defensive, the white students agreed to support the caucus demands, which effectively ended the project altogether. "It was traumatic because we were at a point where we really had to confront these white activists," DC-SCAR organizer Ray Davis later recalled. "Rutgers was like: Stop this, right now. You didn't do your homework, go get it right or we will boycott this thing and we will tell other people to boycott this thing. It's tiring, it's tough, because we are looked on sometimes to provide not only the 'people of color perspective' but even to actually provide people of color, bring them, get them there." There were deeper political reasons why students of color had been reluctant to throw their weight behind the project—the divisions of race correlated with tactical and political differences as well. Two veteran left organizers and journalists, Michael Albert and Lydia Sargent, reported afterward, "Many of the convention's organizers told us that many [people of color] organizations they solicited did not want to participate … because they did not agree with the direct-action orientation of the Rutgers convention." As *Nation* writers Del Borgo and Margaronis put it in their convention recap, "Most whites' definition of what's radical—direct action, protest politics, global critiques of imperialism—implicitly discredits the choice of many black students to work, for example, against financial aid cuts or in Jesse Jackson's campaign." Though Davis, DC-SCAR, and others continued to work toward cross-racial alliance building in the ensuing years, little progress was made, and many black activists in particular moved in a more nationalist direction.[28]

The new wave of creative direct action that emerged in the late 1980s and early 1990s would play out against this backdrop of racial division and mistrust—more acute than it had been a decade before, in part because there had been more attempts at engagement. Largely led and shaped by whites, as direct action had been since the early 1970s, the new wave of activism would come out of groups with tightly focused issue or identity agendas, not out of efforts to create broad political umbrellas, which might sound promising in theory but were proving dispiriting in practice. Dreams of left unity simply didn't reflect the reality of movements on the ground, which had every reason to protect their hard-won autonomy: the notion of a single "united voice of the left" mainly appealed to those who had never had their voices silenced or marginalized.

"Perhaps it *is* a hopeless quest," wrote Dave Foreman, one of the founders of Earth First!, in 1981, of the newly established group's vow to push a radical environmental agenda. With Ronald Reagan in the White House, and mainstream environmental organizations limiting themselves to an incrementalist program of lobbying and litigation, it seemed rather doubtful that a group "radical in style, positions, philosophy, and organization" could aspire to many concrete accomplishments. Foreman acknowledged these limitations, even as he shrugged them off. "Maybe a species will be saved or a forest will go uncut or a dam will be torn down. Maybe not," Foreman continued. "A monkey wrench thrown into the gears of the machine may not stop it. But it might delay it. Make it cost more. And it feels good to put it there."[29]

He chose his metaphor pointedly. Earth First! had adopted as its motto "No compromise in defense of Mother Earth," and from the outset, the group distinguished itself from more moderate environmental groups by its interest in ecological sabotage, or "violence against machines." Earth First!ers called this practice monkey-wrenching, lifting the term from Edward Abbey's 1975 novel *The Monkey Wrench Gang,* which described the adventures of four ecological idealists as they fought development of the Utah and Arizona wilderness through a combination of "subtle, sophisticated harassment techniques" and "blatant and outrageous industrial sabotage."

The fictional band of vandals pulled up road survey stakes, toppled billboards, poured Karo syrup into the fuel tanks of earth-moving equipment, knocked down power lines, and even derailed a coal train.[30]

Abbey's account, in turn, was based on real events. In the years of the ecology movement's infancy, from roughly 1969 to 1974, there had been a nationwide outbreak of grassroots sabotage directed at environmentally destructive businesses. First came "The Fox," a northern Illinois man who gained national fame for a series of daring actions against polluters. These included scaling an enormous industrial smokestack and sealing it with a homemade plug, blocking a sewage pipe from discharging foul wastes into a local stream, and dumping US Steel's own toxic sludge on the carpeted floor of the company's executive suites. Meanwhile, small teams of "billboard bandits" chopped down hundreds of advertisements along Michigan roadways, prompting local farmers (who derived income from the billboards) to form armed posses in the vain hope of catching them. In Arizona, a group called the Eco-Raiders quickly graduated from cutting down the signs that advertised new housing developments in the desert outside Tucson to trashing the construction sites themselves. They broke windows, snipped electrical wires, damaged plumbing pipes, and poured both sand and sugar into the tanks of bulldozers, always leaving behind a spray-painted exhortation to "Stop Sprawl." These were merely the most organized and publicized capers of this sort: anyone who "gets stoned and feels like wrecking," explained one sympathizer in 1973, could become an Eco-Raider.[31]

Environmental Action, the fairly moderate group behind the first Earth Day, openly and actively encouraged "ecotage," with little concern that the tactics would be viewed as extremist. The group even held a contest for the best sabotage tips, compiling the most intriguing entries in a paperback guide published by Simon & Schuster—the contest winners were Miami's Eco-Commandos, who cemented the discharge pipes of two industrial polluters and dumped dye into the city's sewage treatment plant to show the spread of raw waste to the area's waterways. "Ecotage is merely an attempt of some members of a generation which has had its future stolen [to combat despair]," explained Sam Love, the organizer of the contest. "Our senses are dulled to traditional ways of bringing pressure. Harassment is one of the few catalysts left to make people respond to problems."[32]

In one sense, then, the founding of Earth First! was a return to a bygone tactical militancy after a decade of increasingly tepid and professionalized mainstream environmental advocacy. In the movement's first decade of existence, when self-styled "rednecks for wilderness" like Foreman held sway, monkeywrenching was central to Earth First!'s mystique. Judi Bari, one of Earth First!'s best-known organizers, once called it "an aggressively prankster organization," and many of the group's actions were delightfully impish: forcing the closure of a Colorado golf course by inscribing ecological graffiti in the greens; burying salt under a dirt airstrip in Idaho so that moose and deer would rip up the runway; putting cow pies over the intake vents of a Forest Service supervisor's office air conditioner. Other Earth First! tactics were more controversial, notably "tree-spiking," or driving metal spikes into trees slated for logging in order to damage sawmill blades and discourage further cutting. Though lauded by proponents as "an extremely effective method of deterring timber sales," the practice was denounced by Bari and many others in the movement after a mill worker in Northern California was seriously injured in 1987 while cutting a spiked tree. In another blow to the monkey wrenching approach, four Earth First! activists were arrested in 1989—and later convicted and jailed—for attempting to sabotage a federal power plant; Dave Foreman was arrested as a conspirator, a charge he plead guilty to in exchange for a reduced sentence.[33]

Earth First!'s broader interest in what a dedicated, disruptive minority can accomplish was very much of its time, a reflection of the post-sixties shift from countercultural aspirations toward majoritarian revolution to the subcultural resignation that radicals were necessarily permanent outsiders. Greenpeace's famous campaigns to save whales and baby seals from commercial slaughter, which began in the mid seventies, were a key precedent. They relied on the bold actions of a handful of activists who traveled to remote hunting grounds and placed their bodies between the killers and their prey. Images of these risky interventions (relayed not only via the press, but also through the first-ever issue-oriented direct mail campaign) sparked public outrage, ultimately leading to new restrictions on whaling and sealing operations. Similarly, beginning in 1980, small groups of religiously inspired radical pacifists led by Daniel and Phillip Berrigan—militant Catholic brothers who had famously burned draft records with homemade napalm at the height of the Vietnam antiwar movement—undertook a series of "Plowshares" actions, in which they used hammers to damage actual nuclear weapons, generating huge amounts of publicity for their cause. These protests also entailed great personal risks: in the most famous case, eight activists who hammered on the nose cones of two warheads inside a General Electric plant in September 1980 were sentenced to five- to ten-year prison terms for their acts.[34]

Earth First! and the other new direct-action movements of the 1980s and early 1990s differed from these earlier efforts partly in temperament: they were pushier and more cynical. A North Carolina environmental activist, Buck Young, wryly observed about Earth First!, "It isn't an environmental group that makes you think of hippies and Bambi and wildflowers," conjuring up instead "the right of a wolf to rip the lungs out of Bambi." But what most distinguished this crop of activists was how they viewed themselves in relationship to mainstream America. Where both Greenpeace and Plowshares opted for a prophetic role, undertaking actions that they hoped would appeal to the consciences of millions, the new wave of radicals had little expectation of gaining widespread sympathy for their positions, at least not in the foreseeable future. They were movements comprised of people who were willful outsiders, unwilling outcasts or both. Their basic strategy toward their opponents, in the words of the late New York AIDS activist Aldyn McKean, was straightforward: "Make it more costly for those in power to resist than to give in." These movements certainly raised broad critiques of existing structures of power, but above all they were determined to win concrete battles—to protect some of the country's very last remaining parcels of old-growth forest from logging, for instance, or to speed the government approval process for medications that might treat HIV. They used direct action so extensively for a simple reason: it worked. As the old IWW slogan revived by Earth First! succinctly put it, "Direct action gets the goods."[35]

This character was most typical of ACT UP, the movement that made the most effective use of the new punk-inflected style of outrageous and mediagenic direct action, pushing through an array of AIDS-related policy changes that saved vast numbers of lives—millions of lives, by most accounts. Among many other accomplishments, ACT UP's activism transformed the testing and approval process for experimental medications in the United States, spurring life-saving treatment breakthroughs; forced pharmaceutical companies to lower the price of key AIDS drugs; and persuaded the government to broaden its definition of AIDS in a way that brought needed treatment to women, poor people, and others previously excluded. Moreover, ACT UP achieved all of this in a remarkably short time, despite being largely comprised of what one contemporary zine sardonically called "diseased pariahs," often viciously rejected by the culture at large.[36]

The year preceding ACT UP's 1987 founding was an especially dire time for gays and lesbians in the United States, and not only because of the huge numbers of gay men who were dying of a then virtually untreatable disease. HIV was spreading rapidly in the mid 1980s—almost 150,000 Americans were becoming infected each year at that point, with the infections almost always proving fatal—and by the end of 1986, nearly 25,000 people in the United States had already died. AIDS hysteria was fueling new attacks on gay and lesbian civil rights, which had been far from secure to begin with. In June 1986, the United States Supreme Court upheld Georgia's anti-sodomy law in the infamous *Bowers* v. *Hardwick* case, ruling that it was constitutional for the state to prosecute homosexuals for consensual sexual acts in the privacy of their own home. More setbacks followed: the Chicago City Council defeated a gay rights bill, California's Governor George Deukmejian vetoed a bill protecting people with AIDS from discrimination, and the Vatican banned the gay Catholic group Dignity from meeting on Church grounds. Columnist William F. Buckley suggested that everyone who was HIV positive be tattooed on the forearm and buttocks, while followers of neo-Nazi wingnut Lyndon LaRouche succeeded in placing an initiative on the California ballot that, had it passed, would have mandated quarantines for people with AIDS. Meanwhile, the *New York Times* (which at this point still would not allow its writers to use the word "gay") insultingly editorialized that it was "not time, yet, to panic over AIDS" because there was little evidence so far of heterosexual transmission.[37]

The first stirrings of an organized, militant response to these developments came from a group called Citizens for Medical Justice in San Francisco, which blockaded the entrance to Governor Deukmejian's office in retaliation for his veto, and from a New York outfit named the Lavender Hill Mob, founded by former activists from the early-1970s Gay Activists Alliance. Drawing on the GAA's experience with zaps, the Mob organized a series of small but bold actions in late 1986: disrupting a public address by New York's Catholic archbishop John Cardinal O'Connor; occupying the office of Republican senator Alphonse D'Amato; heckling right-wing radio talk show host Bob Grant during a public speech. In February 1987, members of the Mob traveled to Atlanta, where they disrupted a conference on antibody testing sponsored by the Centers for Disease Control and denounced mainstream gay leaders for their moderation. "We should be yelling, we should be screaming, about this issue!" exclaimed Lavender Hill activist Bill Bahlman at one point in the proceedings. "We shouldn't be sitting, talking rationally about this!"[38]

Less than three weeks later, at a meeting convened by playwright and gadfly Larry Kramer, ACT UP's flagship New York chapter was born. The group described itself, in a statement read at the start of each meeting, as "a diverse, non-partisan group of individuals united in anger and committed to direct action to end the AIDS crisis," and from the beginning, ACT UP's radicalism was principally defined by temper and tactics: by collective rage, born of overwhelming grief, channeled into very aggressive and targeted action. Illness and death were constant presences in ACT UP, powerful radicalizing forces that made its experience unlike that of any previous social movement. (Death, and grief, would later profoundly shape the Black Lives Matter movement.) "Living with AIDS in this country is like living through a war that's happening only for those people in the trenches," observed gay film historian and ACT UP/NY activist Vito Russo in a 1988 speech. "Every time a shell explodes you look around to discover that you've lost more of your friends. But nobody else notices—it isn't happening to them." To join ACT UP, whatever your HIV status, was to be part of a movement of people literally fighting for their lives, a movement whose members were continually dying. The fury—and fear—were potent inspirations, driving people to undertake daring actions and drawing them together in tight camaraderie. "Part of what bonded us and what made ACT UP such an incredible, amazing family," remembered New York activist Zoe Leonard, "was that we literally cleaned up each other's shit and went to each other's funerals."[39]

From the start, ACT UP acted with aggressiveness, audacity, and a panache that had been mostly missing from radical activism for decades. They blockaded Wall Street to decry the exorbitant price of existing AIDS medications. They shut down the Maryland headquarters of the Food and Drug Administration in 1988 to demand that it expedite the release of dozens of promising new drugs. They disrupted a broadcast of *CBS Evening News* during the Gulf War, shouting "Fight AIDS, not Arabs" on air in front of a startled Dan Rather. In their most controversial action of all, ACT UP, along with the reproductive rights group WHAM!, disrupted mass at New York's St. Patrick's Cathedral to protest the Catholic Church's opposition to safer-sex education, condom use, and abortion rights. ACT UP favored the grand and arresting gesture, whether it was throwing the ashes of dead loved ones on the White House lawn or shutting down the Golden Gate Bridge. They used dramatic props, ranging from mock coffins and headstones to jugs full of used hypodermic needles and brightly colored smoke bombs. Their posters and other protest graphics were bold and eye-catching, far slicker than anything to be found in activist circles at the time, and emblazoned with stark and unforgettable slogans: SILENCE=DEATH, STOP THE CHURCH, MEN: USE CONDOMS OR BEAT IT. At the group's height in 1991, ACT UP boasted eighty-seven chapters throughout the United States, not just in heavily gay cities like San Francisco and Atlanta or progressive college towns like Madison and Austin, but in an unpredictable array of locales: Boise, Wichita,

ACT UP button, 1987
(designer: Silence=Death
Project; author's collection)

Cleveland, Pittsburgh, Shreveport, Tallahassee.[40]

Direct action was fundamental to ACT UP's identity, and the group generated it at an astounding rate. In part this was because so many members left their jobs to subsist on disability or personal savings during what they knew might be the final months of their lives. "At that point, if you found out you were HIV positive, or you had an opportunistic infection, the odds were truly against you," recalled ACT UP/NY activist David Crane, "and there was no reason to do *anything* other than ACT UP. Nothing." The New York chapter developed a particularly effective system for swift and emphatic actions. As ACT UP/NY activist Mike Spiegel explained, "If somebody wanted to start a fax campaign to a pharmaceutical company, they would basically go over to one corner and hold their hand up, and the facilitator would say, 'OK, everybody who wants to work on that, go over there.' And whatever they did, they got to call themselves ACT UP doing it." The overall membership—"the floor," as ACT UP/NYers called it—"could generally approve or disapprove of an idea, but people were pretty loose about how it got carried out," Spiegel continued. Hardly a week went by in the peak years of the crisis without some kind of direct action on AIDS. In Milwaukee, ACT UP activists distributed condoms outside an Ash Wednesday mass at Marquette University; in Des Moines, they held a die-in at the state capitol to protest the governor's plan to veto AIDS appropriations. In Kansas City, Missouri, ACT UP compelled Payless Shoe Stores to adopt a policy against employment discrimination based on HIV status; in New Orleans, a civil disobedience action at City Hall brought improvements in AIDS services at the municipal hospital.[41]

ACT UP's distinctive character was also shaped by the unprecedented and volatile combination of forces that made up the movement. Before the advent of AIDS, gay men and lesbians had mostly been arm's-length allies. They shared the status of sexual minorities, but throughout much of the seventies and eighties, they had a tendency to view each other with suspicion and even disdain. Certainly there was little common ground between the lesbian-feminist desire to separate from patriarchal culture and the sexual liberationist agenda of many gay men. There were even fewer political contexts in which gays and lesbians came together across lines of race or class. But as AIDS decimated the gay community, significant numbers of lesbians rallied to the side of gay men, importantly shaping the activist response to the disease. And as the character of the epidemic evolved, spreading disproportionately among communities of color, ACT UP's overwhelmingly white initial membership was increasingly joined by a significant (though never large) number of black and Latino activists, who worked to transform the movement's agenda.

The small group of veteran white lesbian organizers who helped shape ACT UP/NY, and their counterparts in the dozens of other ACT UP chapters that sprung up by 1990, formed a bridge between the new AIDS activism and the direct-action radicalism of the 1970s and 1980s. These women brought extensive experience with large-scale civil disobedience campaigns based on their earlier work in the anti-nuclear and anti-intervention movements and their participation in events like the two Women's Pentagon Actions; through their work in the anti-apartheid movement, they'd experienced firsthand how careful targeting could yield success. They taught their fellow AIDS activists concrete skills: how to set up effective legal support before a protest, how to train marshals for a march. They also introduced the group to some of the by then established organizational conventions of direct-action protest, including the use of affinity groups. Moreover, lesbians in ACT UP drew on the work of the women's health and reproductive rights movements, applying feminist—often socialist-feminist—critiques of the medical establishment and principles of medical self-determination to the fight against AIDS.[42]

While ACT UP was deeply influenced by prior direct-action traditions, the group had scant connection to the traditional left. Isolated individuals within ACT UP had long left pedigrees: for instance, Mike Spiegel, active in the New York chapter, had been national secretary of SDS in 1967 and 1968; Avram Finkelstein, part of the collective that designed the famous SILENCE=DEATH logo, was a red-diaper baby who grew up with leftist politics. There were also a few unpleasant early run-ins with the sort of socialist sects who are always looking to attach themselves to movements with real appeal and momentum, having so very little of their own. But otherwise, ACT UP developed its brand of radical activism at a distance from many of the organizations and institutions that made up the left at that time. This separation was in most respects beneficial, for it helped ACT UP to innovate in areas where much of the left had grown stale: in tactics, message, and tone. If that meant activists sometimes found themselves lacking a sense of political history and thereby reinventing the wheel—"People in ACT UP thought that tabling was a new idea," remembered Maxine Wolfe, one of the seasoned lesbian activists in ACT UP/NY, with bemusement—it also freed the movement from acting by simple force of habit. As an example, Wolfe cited rallies, a tedious yet unquestioned staple of left-wing organizing: "In ACT UP, people *hate* rallies instinctively. Nobody can stand to be there listening to people preach to the converted—they don't understand why you don't get everybody and go *do* something." The many movements that took inspiration from ACT UP carried this character forward. As Sarah Schulman explained in a 1994 interview about her organizing with the Lesbian Avengers, "We don't use rallies with speakers, we don't do marches or demonstrations with signs. We don't have agreement on analysis. We don't have theoretical discussions. We don't do anything [older lefts] did." In the *Lesbian Avenger Handbook*, she advised activists who might start their own Avenger group, "Avoid old stale tactics at all costs. Chanting, picketing and the like no longer make an impression; standing passively and listening to speakers is boring and disempowering. Look for daring, new participatory tactics depending on the nature of your action."[43]

The political grounding that lesbians gave to ACT UP was complemented by the sensibility and skills of the movement's most notable neophytes: affluent white gay professionals with considerable cultural and financial capital at their disposal. "I think a lot of men initially came to ACT UP because it was the first time in their life that their white male privilege wasn't working for them," recalled Amy Bauer, a seasoned lesbian activist who anchored many of ACT UP/NY's direct-action trainings, who now goes by the name Jamie Bauer. "They were outraged that the government wasn't taking it seriously, that they couldn't get the drugs, that this wasn't put at the forefront of the whole medical establishment." The ranks of those radicalized by the AIDS crisis included numerous advertising, public relations, and media professionals—people who, were it not for the accident of epidemiology, would never have found themselves protesting and raising hell. For example, ACT UP/NY activist Bob Rafsky, who helped the group craft its media strategy, was the executive vice president of a public relations firm until he began devoting himself full-time to AIDS activism; Michelangelo Signorile had been a publicist, pushing juicy celebrity tidbits to gossip columnists. ACT UP borrowed freely and without compunction from corporate culture to communicate its message and demands. "ACT UP has always talked about corporate greed," noted David Norton, an activist with the group's Seattle chapter, in 1992, "but people within ACT UP have also worked within these same corporations and used that access to help ACT UP."[44]

This quality was one reason why ACT UP looked and felt different from the movements that came before it. It mostly rejected the homespun aesthetic of groups like the Clamshell Alliance and the Women's Pentagon Action in favor of bold, professional design. For a grassroots group, ACT UP had striking access to resources. As feminist writer Alexandra Juhasz put it in an interview with the ACT UP Oral History Project, "If you did something through ACT UP, it had infrastructure, it had support. If you did it anywhere else, it didn't." For women like Juhasz, there was a discomfort in being "a feminist who knows that no women's organization we'll ever belong to will have the clout of ACT UP; that no lesbian organization will ever have the clout of ACT UP." ACT UP also had a level of sophistication in dealing with the mainstream media that few recent movements could match; its press packets were professional in quality, its contact lists enviable. Before each significant ACT UP/NY action, former *CBS Morning News* producer Ann Northrop, a key figure in the movement, would work with the group to refine its message into broadcast-quality soundbites. At the main press conference for the 1988 FDA protest, one of the most important of the group's early actions, organizers cleverly had participants from all around the country line up with signs identifying them by hometown, and sure enough, local reporters flocked to them for quotes "like dogs thrown a steak bone," in Signorile's words.[45]

ACT UP's structure and process varied from chapter to chapter, but on the whole, the group emphatically embraced the democratic and decentralized organizational values of the direct-action tradition. In New York, the group used Robert's Rules of Order; in San Francisco, until procedural disagreements fueled a 1990 split, ACT UP operated by consensus decision-making. There was no national ACT UP office or central coordinating body tying chapters to one another, only a loose network. In what by now had become standard movement practice, ACT UP organized into affinity groups for its actions. Some were formed for one occasion only, while others continued from action to action over a period of years. Their ingenuity and nerve could be impressive. At the dramatic 1988 FDA action, the WAVE 3 affinity group finagled a way into the agency building and sent out memos on FDA letterhead to agency officials, detailing the policy changes they wanted to see. In April 1989, four men calling themselves the Power Tools not only occupied an executive office at the headquarters of pharmaceutical giant Burroughs Wellcome, but barricaded themselves inside by attaching steel plates to the doors. ACT UP was committed to internal democracy, but its affinity groups were more practical than prefigurative in character, facilitating actions that relied upon surprise, or giving manageable structure to mass protests. The group never adopted the spokescouncil structure pioneered by the anti-nuclear movement, in which each affinity group participates in overall decision-making through a spokesperson. Affinity groups in ACT UP had a further dimension unlike any other movement's: they provided support for those who were grieving. David Crane recalled that the Candelabras affinity group of ACT UP/NY wrote to the parents of one member after he died. "We had become a major component of his social life throughout his illness, and he had become part of our emotional life," he remembered. "We wrote the letter as a consolation to his parents, but also to let them know what he had been accomplishing, that maybe they didn't know about."[46]

ACT UP's agenda seemed simple and straightforward at first. "What do we want?" activists shouted at the group's first action, "A cure!" In the group's earliest days, the solution to the crisis seemed to be getting experimental medications out of the testing pipeline: "There's one issue—and that's getting drugs into the bodies of sick people as soon as possible," Vito Russo explained in 1988. "There's no agenda other than that. It's outside the political framework, left versus right, or top versus bottom." When ACT UP blockaded the FDA headquarters, activists chanted, in a reference to the one AIDS medication available at the time, "AZT is not enough, give us all the other stuff!" "Drugs-into-bodies" became a powerful ACT UP mantra, and captured the urgent necessity not just of accelerating the drug approval process but of transforming how potential treatments were developed, tested, and made available.[47]

But everything quickly became more complicated. The medications that were then in development did not turn out to be cures; yelling for their expedited release was not saving lives. ACT UP had defined itself as a direct-action group, but direct action alone wasn't proving effective. Activists in ACT UP/NY's Treatment and Data Committee began learning everything they could about both the science behind HIV infection and treatment and the governmental procedures that regulated the testing and release of medications. Out of this intensive study, they developed their own detailed AIDS treatment plan, and some activists began meeting with both government and pharmaceutical company officials. This shift came at the same time that others in ACT UP were raising a different set of questions, about equity and access to health care—in the words of activist Elias Guerrero, the "root causes of why people couldn't get drugs into bodies."[48]

These questions were being posed most powerfully by the small but growing number of people of color in ACT UP. In its earliest days, ACT UP was almost completely monochromatic: "It was 400 white people in the room, and I would see one black man and one Mexican man over there," recalled Robert Vasquez-Pacheco of the

New York chapter's first meetings. "We stood out, as my grand-mother would say, like a fly in a glass of milk."[49] Nor had much of the group's membership previously given much thought to questions of race, class, or equity: as activist Kendall Thomas put it, "The overwhelming majority of the people who were coming to those meetings had no analysis at all of what racism was, how they were implicated in the structures of racialization and racism—had no sense of themselves as being raced." Some members of ACT UP/NY soon formed first the Majority Action Committee and later a Latino Caucus and an Asian Pacific Islander Caucus to recruit more people of color for the group, support those who joined, and serve as vehicles for education and action.[50]

The caucuses, and their counterparts in other ACT UP chapters around the country, took on a wide variety of projects: distributing condoms and safer sex information in black, Latino, and Asian nightclubs and other venues where people of color gathered; pressuring Kings County Hospital, a Brooklyn hospital with mainly low-income patients of color, to improve its treatment of patients with HIV; organizing a national People of Color AIDS Activist conference. Ron Medley of ACT UP/NY described the Majority Action Committee as "one of the last organizations I remember where blacks and whites cooperated with each other on a very high plane. It was basically gay black men and straight white women—some of whom were social workers—basically designing direct actions and doing a lot of outreach in the minority communities, and just hanging in there through thick and through thin—with all the ups and downs that were going on in ACT UP." The caucus structure allowed for autonomy, making it possible for groups within ACT UP to pursue their own agendas whether or not they were fully embraced by the organization as a whole. "It's important for those groups who are affected the most to be at the forefront, leading the fight, or our issues are going to be on the back burner," remarked Cathy Chang of ACT UP/NY's Latino Caucus in 1992, when this work was in full swing. "When it boils down to it, people are going to fight for themselves first."[51] But by 1990, tensions around race, gender, class, and political strategy had already begun to pull some ACT UP chapters apart. In New York, Kendall Thomas recalled:

Just really acrimonious floor fights about whether or not the floor should support a demand coming from the Women's Caucus that the CDC recognize infections and illnesses that seem to be specific to women with HIV, as part of the "official" definition of Acquired Immuno-Deficiency Syndrome. Whether or not the floor should situate its demands for greater and more vigilant research into drug therapies within a larger critique of the US healthcare system and the racialized character of access to it and treatment within it. Whether the floor ought to authorize and support aggressive out-reach to communities of people who were being affected by HIV/AIDS, who didn't come from the East Village, the West Village or the Upper West Side.[52]

The San Francisco chapter was the first to split: the trigger was a proposal, supported largely by white men, to replace the chapter's consensus decision-making process with "super-majority rule," in which a motion would carry with an 80 percent vote. After the Sixth International Conference on AIDS was held in San Francisco in June 1990, and greeted with huge and deftly organized protests, the chapter's membership tripled. For the most part, these newcomers were white men, many of them HIV positive. Members of the Women's and People of Color Caucuses felt that their issues were being pushed aside by these recent arrivals, and countered their sense of marginalization by using their power under consensus process to block proposals, including the proposal to scuttle the consensus process. These maneuvers in turn angered a large number of white gay men, who walked out of ACT UP/San Francisco and formed a separate chapter, which they called ACT UP/Golden Gate.[53]

The real divisions, however, went far deeper than process. "There is a split in this organization—if I may be so bold—among those of us who want to focus on the top quarter with AIDS and those who want to focus on the bottom third," declared ACT UP/San Francisco Women's Caucus member Kate Raphael. "If you do the latter it leads you to look at AIDS in the broader context," which, for Raphael and others, meant addressing race, class, and gender issues both within the organization and in society at large.

"You have a group in ACT UP of white men who had a great deal of privilege until they got sick, and a lot of them still have a lot of class and white skin privilege," said Deeg Gold. What they failed to acknowledge, she added, was that solely "finding a cure for AIDS will not stop the epidemic," because in a vastly unequal healthcare system, only the privileged would have access to a cure.[54]

Those who left the San Francisco chapter viewed the matter quite differently. Explained one such activist, Bill Struzenberg, "Put very succinctly," he said, "we have to find a cure before we fight for access. The other people are coming from the other side; they want us to find access before a cure." For many who formed ACT UP/ Golden Gate, personal mortality loomed—quite understandably —far larger than any broader political considerations. "If we have to deal with racism and sexism and homophobia, we will not start moving forward until I am dead," said Jesse Dobson. "I am not proud of [downplaying those questions], but I will not let my growth in those areas stop me fighting AIDS. I will not build a coalition on the dead bodies of my community!"[55]

Meanwhile, in New York, parallel tensions led members of the Treatment and Data Committee to separate from the chapter and form their own organization, the Treatment Action Group (TAG), in January 1992. Mark Harrington, one of the most prominent treatment activists to leave ACT UP, recounted how the experience of a first major meeting with government officials transformed some activists' perspectives. "There was a lot of euphoria, but there was also a wistfulness about crossing over. From then on we were sort of inside/outside, and not just outside; and [we] sort of lost innocence," he recalled. "I knew that we would never be so pure and fervent in our belief that we were right, because we were actually going to be engaged and, therefore be more responsible for some of the things that actually happened." But this hard-won access proved controversial among other AIDS activists; supporters and opponents of the inside/outside approach viewed it in exactly opposite ways. "ACT UP has never just been an outside angry street group," explained Jon Winkleman. "A lot of our big successes have come from being out on the streets and then sitting down at the table when we got access." But as ACT UP's identity and political vision had been so strongly shaped by its embrace of direct action, sitting down to negotiate with pharmaceutical executives or government officials inevitably felt like a betrayal to some. "When we became both the inside and the outside ... the people who got on the inside became so entranced by their role that they forgot there was an outside," declared Maxine Wolfe in 1992. "The government doesn't listen to us because we're smart," she said. "They listen to us because we're smart and we can threaten them."[56]

Many ACT UP chapters began to wane or closed up shop beginning in 1993, two years before the scientific advance that would save millions of lives. The 1995 advent of protease inhibitors, thanks in substantial part to the years of intense ACT UP pressure, provided the long-sought breakthrough in AIDS treatment, helping turn HIV infection into a manageable long-term health condition for many patients rather than a nearly certain death sentence. Many movements crumble altogether before they reach their aims; in ACT UP's case, the bitter splits that marked the years when hope had faltered were mostly overcome by subsequent AIDS activists, who made questions of equity and access to medical care central in their work over subsequent decades, building on the early organizing of the Majority Action Committee and others.[57]

Along the way, ACT UP's example had profoundly changed the nature of activism in the United States. "ACT UP just created—I don't know what the word is—a restlessness or momentum," explained René Francisco Poitevin, one of the founders of Roots Against War, a San Francisco Bay Area people of color group that played an important role in the movement against the 1991 Persian Gulf War. "We were like: we know that shit works. It can make a lot of trouble. So here we go." Recalled WHAM! activist Tracy Morgan, whose group used intense direct-action counter-blockades to keep abortion clinics targeted by Operation Rescue open to clients, "You couldn't not be inspired by ACT UP at that point. ACT UP really taught us how to organize: how to prepare a fact sheet, how to deal with the media, what a pre-action meeting is." None of ACT UP's many imitators would have quite the same alchemy that it did, nor would they have nearly the same effect. It was one thing to imitate ACT UP's fierce style and tactics, and quite another to develop

Queer Nation stickers, circa 1990 (designer unknown; author's collection)

a focused direct-action strategy with objectives that were at once concrete and far-reaching. As catalysts of cultural change, though, some of the groups directly inspired by ACT UP had important and enduring influence. Queer Nation, for instance, founded in 1990 by ACT UP activists with a broad agenda of fighting homophobia and promoting LGBT visibility, did much to popularize the notion of queer identity with its brash propaganda and showy protests. "We're here, we're queer, get used to it!" wasn't the sort of intervention that could readily translate into policy prescriptions; it was, however, exactly the kind that could, and did, change lives.[58]

At about the same time that ACT UP chapters were dividing in the early 1990s, the Earth First! movement was splitting over strikingly similar matters: how much to integrate social issues into their activism. While one of Earth First!'s founders, Mike Roselle, had taken part in the Vietnam antiwar movement and cited the Yippies as a major influence on his activism, he was atypical of the first generation. Earth First! co-founder Dave Foreman, a registered Republican who had supported the Barry Goldwater campaign back in 1964, was more conservative than most. But he set the initial tone for the movement, with his disdain for any activism besides wilderness preservation and disinterest in any tactics besides monkeywrenching, media stunts, speech-making, and small-scale backwoods heroics in the Greenpeace vein. The philosophy of "deep ecology" that the old guard espoused began from a critique of the anthropocentrism that has been at the core of Western thought since at least the time of the Greeks. Instead of using humans as the yardstick by which to measure progress, they argued for the intrinsic worth of nature. Wilderness should be protected not for any benefit that might accrue to humanity in the process (as, say, when pollutants are filtered from the air), but for its own sake, because it exists.

Foreman and his cohort went farther, making grotesque calls for large-scale human depopulation in the name of restoring the wild. "The worst thing we could do in Ethiopia is to give aid," said Foreman in one representative 1986 interview, "the best thing would be to just let nature seek its own balance, to let the people there just starve." Meanwhile, an anonymous eco-radical calling himself Miss Ann Thropy (later identified as Christopher Manes) wrote a notorious 1987 essay in the *Earth First! Journal* lauding the potential of the AIDS epidemic to decimate human populations. "[As] radical environmentalists," he asserted, "we can see AIDS not as a problem, but a necessary solution."[59]

"They didn't like people," explained Mac Scott, who was an early-1990s Earth First! activist in the Pacific Northwest, "which is a really bad base to organize from. You know, I'm against speciesism and all that, but the fact is that we don't know how to organize wolves and bears and foxes. We can organize people, that's our species." The fact was, the old guard didn't want to organize. But a new wave of eco-radicals who joined Earth First! in the late eighties and early nineties did. The new guard of environmental radicals was comprised of activists whose politics had been importantly shaped by one or more other recent social movements, from feminism and gay rights to anti-nuclear activism and the Central American and South African solidarity movements. This newer generation of activists was more interested in crafting effective direct-action campaigns than they were in the doctrinal debates and lone-wolf gestures of the Foreman generation ("big man goes into big wilderness to save big trees," Earth First!er Judi Bari described it). And while they fully embraced the goal of wilderness preservation, they didn't separate it from questions of social and economic justice and found the old guard's misanthropy not just distasteful but baffling. "For me, wilderness has no meaning without civilization," said Earth First! activist Ramin Karimpour in 1992. "I don't want to live in a world where I can't go see a really great movie and have a really great pizza."[60]

No one exemplified and shaped the new guard more than Judi Bari, who became nationally famous in 1990 when a bomb exploded in a car carrying her and fellow activist Darryl Cherney, on the eve of their ambitious Redwood Summer campaign. (Though Bari was nearly killed by the explosion, she and Cherney were arrested almost immediately afterwards and charged with having placed the bomb. The authorities never provided proof, the charges were never pursued, and both Bari and Cherney believed the FBI was in fact behind the explosion.) Bari, a carpenter and lifelong radical who said she "majored in anti–Vietnam War rioting" at college, helped build a high-profile forest-preservation campaign in Northern California through old-fashioned outreach, organizing, and non-violent direct action. Though Bari herself didn't attend the Women's Pentagon Actions, she was deeply influenced by the ecofeminist tradition they represented, and she was heavily involved in the Pledge of Resistance campaign in the 1980s, serving as a regional coordinator. "Little did I know," she wrote in 1992, "that by combining the more feminine elements of collectivism and non-violence with the spunk and outrageousness of Earth First!, we would spark a mass movement."[61]

Redwood Summer took place on a scale that dwarfed previous Earth First! actions. Thousands of mostly young activists from throughout the country converged on Humboldt and Mendocino Counties in a bid to stop or at least slow the logging of ancient trees there, using "equal measures of guerrilla theater and guerrilla war," as one newspaper account put it. After taking part in everything from a "Redwoodstock" music festival to backwoods forest blockades, a

Poster for Redwood Summer, 1990 (designer: Tom Yeates; courtesy David Solnit)

number of these activists—the majority of them women—went on to start or reinvigorate Earth First! groups in the places they came from; following Bari's lead, feminism would shape both the politics and practices of this second wave of Earth First! The decision to name the mobilization after the civil rights movement's storied Freedom Summer and the accompanying call for "Freedom Riders for the Forest" were rather presumptuous for an event so deeply rooted in white activist culture. (Cherney elaborated: "We believe that the Earth deserves civil rights the same as people do.") But the analogy held insofar as the violence that they faced over the course of the summer was very real, albeit on a much smaller scale than Mississippi in 1964: Bari received repeated death threats, and a logging truck rammed her car from behind, sending her and her children to the hospital.[62]

And while the movement took few steps toward reckoning with race, a sincere and important effort at bridge-building across class lines was at its core. In a move that would pave the way for the labor–environmental alliance at the Seattle WTO protests nearly a decade later, Bari pushed the movement to drop its longstanding disdain for loggers, focusing its ire on the timber bosses instead, and seeing timber workers as potential political allies. As a radical union organizer in the late seventies, Bari challenged not only her employers—first Grand Union supermarkets, and later the US Postal Service—but also complacent trade unions that did little to improve their members' plight. "The interests [of environmentalists and timber workers] coincide because both the forests and the workers are exploited by out-of-town corporations, whose policy is to liquidate the forests and then leave," she declared in a 1993 interview. "Cut-and-run is equally damaging to the ecology and the economy. The area that they leave behind is devastated, and to log in a manner that you are cutting yourself out of work is certainly not in the interest of the loggers."[63]

For the old guard, Redwood Summer was the last straw. "I'm tired of being sidetracked by eco-feminism, sanctuary, anarchy, woo-woo, coalition building, bleeding heart humanists against misanthropy, sexist animal lovers for gay rights, and all of the other egotistical fodder for human chauvinistic cause-lovers," wrote

Earth First! co-founder Howie Wolke shortly afterwards. Wolke, Foreman, deep ecology theorist Bill Devall, and others left Earth First!, saying the movement had become "sidetracked by anthropocentric concerns." The break-up was briefly in the public eye, but the movement was already heading so far away from the direction the old guard had charted that the split was soon nearly forgotten. By the late 1990s, many active Earth First!ers didn't even know about the prankster "rednecks for wilderness" phase, or the history of noxious musings about AIDS and famine. The departure of the old guard opened up political space for new relationships, and in particular for tentative steps toward cross-racial alliance building, mainly with Native American activists, work that helped lay the political groundwork for a major wave of direct-action-oriented climate activism in the new millennium. Representatives of the American Indian Movement attended a post–Redwood Summer conference to evaluate new directions for Earth First! organizing, and spoke of the common ground between the movements; Earth First!ers and native organizers would go on to collaborate on a variety of local campaigns, including a late-1990s effort to stop construction of a highway through Indian burial grounds in Minnesota.[64]

The Lesbian Avengers were one of the last groups to take direct inspiration from ACT UP, forming in 1992, when the AIDS activist group was entering its most dispiriting phase. The founding of the Avengers grew out of a desire to direct lesbian organizing energies—which had been key but largely invisible in so many movements—to issues directly facing lesbians *as* lesbians. As had become the pattern with many successful direct-action groups, activists in other cities who felt an affinity with the Avengers quickly formed their own chapters, with more than fifty chapters in total. This process was greatly facilitated by a comprehensive handbook ("a handy guide to homemade revolution") produced by the New York group, which included everything from sample logos and graphics to a detailed action checklist ("Do you have a clear message, dramatic visuals? ... Have you leaked info to the media? ... Do you have bail money in case of arrest?").[65]

Lesbian Avengers logo, 1992
(designer: Carrie Moyer;
courtesy Sarah Dougher)

"Lesbians have been in the forefront of every movement for social change," declared an Avenger broadsheet, "from abolition to revolution, from AIDS activism to peace and anti-nuclear efforts, civil rights, feminism, the lesbian and gay rights movement, the labor movement, housing and environmentalism. Yet our participation is ignored. OFTEN WITH OUR COMPLICITY." Distributed at the first Dyke March, held in Washington, DC on the eve of the large and very mainstream 1993 National March on Washington for Gay, Lesbian, and Bi Equal Rights, the broadsheet offered witty summaries of the Avenger approach:

LESBIAN AVENGERS BELIEVE IN CREATIVE ACTIVISM: LOUD, BOLD, SEXY, SILLY, FIERCE, TASTY AND DRAMATIC. ARREST OPTIONAL. THINK DEMONSTRATIONS ARE A GOOD TIME AND A GREAT PLACE TO CRUISE WOMEN.
LESBIAN AVENGERS BELIEVE CONFRONTATION FOSTERS GROWTH AND STRONG BONES. BELIEVE IN RECRUITMENT. NOT BY THE ARMY; NOT OF STRAIGHT WOMEN. DON'T MIND HANDCUFFS AT ALL.[66]

The Avengers logo featured an image of a bomb, intended to be mischievous—a choice that would have evoked hardcore militancy two decades earlier, when the Weather Underground was still blowing up corporate and military targets, and come across as foolhardy a decade later, after the 9/11 attacks closed down the political space for dissent. At the early Dyke Marches, and at numerous other events, groups of Avengers would do fire-eating performances, to symbolize their collective fearlessness and to memorialize a man and woman in Oregon who had been killed in a homophobic fire-bombing. The marches were the antithesis of the inward-looking

First New York City Dyke March, 1993 (photo: © Carolina Kroon)

"women's space" created by lesbian feminists in the 1970s. They weren't safe havens from the wider world but loud and very public interventions, made possible by the years of community building and consciousness-raising that had come before. "The streets belong to the dykes," marchers chanted at the first Dyke March as everywhere lesbians were kissing, shouting, dancing, taking off their shirts, while gay men lined the march route and cheered the women on. Some Avengers set off stink bombs inside the Capitol Building, an action they had earlier taken at the Times Square Army Recruitment Center and St. Patrick's Cathedral (any of which would likely have brought terrorism charges had they tried it in 2002 instead of 1992). Their communiques ended with a call to rage: "GET MAD! GET EVEN! JOIN THE LESBIAN AVENGERS AND JOIN THE RIOT."[67]

But for all of this bravado, the Lesbian Avengers' most successful move was a shift away from the tone of anger and confrontation that had colored so much radical direct action over the previous several years. By 1993, especially in LGBTQ circles, the culture of fury and defiance was playing itself out. "I just can't live with all that anger anymore, personally," explained queer activist Rachel

Pepper on the eve of the 1993 March on Washington of Lesbian, Gay, and Bi Equal Rights, echoing the sentiments of many. "I'd rather take my anger and translate it into something more positive than screaming at people all the time." As the Lesbian Avengers shifted from planting stink bombs and eating fire to working on concrete campaigns, they began to explore the subversive potential of being sweet.[68]

One of the earliest actions by the New York group was an early-morning meet-and-greet outside a Queens elementary school in response to right-wing backlash against schools chancellor Joseph A. Fernandez's proposed multicultural, gay-positive Rainbow Curriculum. Accompanied by a spirited marching band (playing "We Are Family" and "When the Dykes Come Marching In"), the Lesbian Avengers handed out balloons to the arriving first graders. The balloons were lavender, with the simple message, "Ask About Lesbian Lives." It was a cleverly disarming approach: what was a homophobic parent going to do, tell his or her child that the nice women handing out pretty balloons were in fact deviants and perverts? In New Orleans, a group of Lesbian Avengers took over a streetcar and handed out lollipops with the message "Lick Homophobia." In West Springfield, Massachusetts, Avengers distributed candy and handwritten valentines to grade-school kids on Valentine's Day, telling them that "girls who love girls and women who love women are OK!!!"[69]

The most ambitious of the group's undertakings was the Lesbian Avengers Civil Rights Organizing Project, a response both to right-wing anti-gay ballot initiatives and the strategies used by mainstream gay and lesbian organizations to fight them. Beginning in Colorado in 1992 and continuing throughout the early 1990s, religious conservatives used popular referendums in an array of states and localities to prohibit legal protections for gays and lesbians on the grounds that they constituted "special rights." The hate-filled campaigns to promote the ballot initiatives were not just loathsome in themselves; they were invariably accompanied by a steep rise in anti-gay violence.

The measures came at a time when mainstream groups like the National Gay and Lesbian Task Force (NGLTF) and the Human

Rights Campaign Fund (HRCF) were gaining in size and influence, and promoting what would ultimately be very successful apple-pie issues: marriage equality and access to the military. To more radical LGBTQ activists, who viewed marriage and the military as oppressive institutions that ought to be abolished, this approach undercut the liberationist foundations of the movement. After years of fiery AIDS and queer activism had greatly increased lesbian and gay visibility on the national stage, it seemed, in the 1993 words of radical San Francisco activist Annette Gaudino, "like the gays have jumped on all the gains the queers have made in the culture."[70]

These political divisions shaped the 1990s campaigns to defeat anti-gay ballot initiatives. Most followed a mainstream model, backed by NGLTF and HRCF, which relied on extensive polling, professional staff, and "message control." That control meant, in most cases, a decision *not* to use the words "gay," "lesbian," or "homosexual," for fear of alienating straight voters. "What they did in their campaigns," recalled Lesbian Avenger Elizabeth Meister, "was put out literature with extremely vague slogans. They were basically closeted about the whole thing." For the 1994 effort to defeat an anti-gay initiative in Idaho, for example, the mainstream campaign's primary slogans were "Proposition One: It's Expensive," and "No Government Intervention in Private Lives." Volunteers were told, when phone banking or canvassing, not to make any explicit references to gays and lesbians in their descriptions of the ballot measure. In some cases, volunteers actually had to sign an agreement that they would not speak to the media or write letters to the editor about the initiative without approval from the central campaign committee.[71]

The New York chapter of the Lesbian Avengers put out a call to gay and lesbian organizations in Idaho, offering to help run a very different kind of campaign with any group that requested it. "We wanted to demonstrate that you could run an 'out' campaign and not lose votes for being out," Meister explains. A group of lesbians from Moscow, Idaho invited the Avengers to come, and together more than a dozen activists, half of them working full-time, spent several weeks organizing in three northern Idaho counties. One centerpiece of this Civil Rights Organizing Project was an old-fashioned door-to-door canvass, albeit with a twist: the tactics might be conventional, but the sensibility was drawn from the direct-action world. "Each team would be two people: one of the Lesbian Avengers from the New York area, and one of the local people," remembered Avenger activist Eileen Clancy. "We'd knock on the door and we'd say, 'Hi, do you know about Proposition One?' ... Then one of us would come out on their doorstep, saying something like, 'Well, the reason this is important to me is because I'm a lesbian, and this is what it could mean to me: I could lose my job, I could be thrown out of my apartment, I could be thrown out of a restaurant.' The idea was to get people to engage and have a real conversation and see a real human being there."[72]

It was, in Clancy's words, an "extremely bold" approach—and it worked. Statewide, Proposition One was defeated by a tiny margin: 50.4 percent, or just 3,098 votes out of a total state population of 1 million. In the three counties where the Avengers focused their efforts, with a combined population of 85,000, the measure was defeated by 4,785 votes. In one rural town where the Lesbian Avengers Civil Rights Organizing Project did extensive canvassing, the "No" votes prevailed by a stunning 75 percent margin. "I don't know that I had ever been involved in a campaign like that on any issue that had ever won in a way that you could clearly demarcate," said Clancy. "I'd had the sense of working on things and building things before, and some successes here and there in the skirmishes of the Reagan-Bush years, but never the sense of actually winning a political battle in that clear-cut way—and it was *great*." What was radical about it? Nothing, and everything: an anti-discrimination ballot campaign might seem like a classic example of mainstream political involvement, the antithesis of direct action, but in that time and place, nobody else but a group of radicals would have conducted it.[73]

Radicalism along one dimension of identity, though, didn't necessarily correlate to radicalism in all others. Ten months before launching the Idaho initiative, a group of New York Avengers had organized a caravan to support activists in Lewiston, Maine who were fighting against a local anti-gay initiative there. They called this project a Freedom Ride. No one had objected in 1990 when

Earth First! invited "Freedom Riders for the Forest" to join its "Mississippi Summer in the Redwoods," or for that matter in 1988 when ACT UP/NY traveled to towns throughout the South and called the trip a "Freedom Ride." These movements used the name in part to evoke the sense of menace and danger they faced: in one town in Florida, where an arsonist had burned down the home of three HIV-positive hemophiliac children a year before, the AIDS activists were greeted by a huge crowd shouting, "Go home, faggots!" But in 1993, with activists of color increasingly calling on white-majority movements to deal with race and racism, a controversy broke out over the use of the term.[75]

Combahee co-founder Barbara Smith and a Kitchen Table Press colleague in Albany, New York, one of the stops on the Avengers' ride, wrote to the group and asked them to drop the name. The rationale, Smith explained at the time, was straightforward: "Appropriation of the term is offensive because the organization has no demonstrated involvement in anti-racist organizing." The group was not all white, but at that point, it hadn't foregrounded race in its work (some Avengers later worked to change that), and to Smith, that was crucial. In a 2016 interview, Smith elaborated, "How dare you say that you're going to have a Freedom Ride when you have no identifiable anti-racist practice?" She continued, "Lesbian Avenger politics were not multi-issue and radical as I remember. When I say radical, I don't mean in your face, lobbing verbal grenades—radical means having a deep understanding of structural oppression and being willing to eradicate that." Being criticized so publicly by one of the country's most prominent black lesbians stung, but after debating the question, the Avengers rebuffed the request: They made some changes to their press release but kept the Freedom Ride name. Elizabeth Meister, who joined the group at the tail end of this dispute, later agreed with Smith's objection. "Looking back on it, I think the reference to the Freedom Ride was disrespectful. It was a cheeky use of it—everything we did was cheeky," she recalled in a 2016 interview, "and I did not get how offensive that was." She continued, "It's the biggest regret of my activism in the 1990s that I didn't fully appreciate race, and I was so taken by the sexiness of being a Lesbian Avenger that I wasn't as thoughtful as I could have been." Autonomy had been the guiding principle for identity-based movements for decades, and had taken them far; but increasingly, as movements mixed and interacted and sometimes clashed, they would find themselves needing to contend with another crucial standard, that of accountability.[75]

All of the groups that embraced confrontational direct action in the late eighties and early nineties ultimately came up against another problem, this one intractable: how quickly their most outrageous actions became old hat, especially to the novelty-obsessed corporate media. In 1990, Earth First!ers in southern Illinois made front-page news in their area when they planted a 1962 Chevy Biscayne at the entrance of a timber sale they were fighting. ("It's big, it takes more than two people to move and it can't be arrested," quipped the *Southern Illinoisan*.) But you can't pull a stunt like that twice. "At the time when we did it, it was pretty bold," said Shawnee Earth First!'s Ramin Karimpour two years later. "Now you can bury an RV and four or five Pintos and nobody even looks the other way." Just three years after the first ACT UP direct action, members were already seeing a declining rate of return from their dramatic tactics. "Civil disobedience and arrests have degenerated into a type of macabre performance art," declared ACT UP/DC activist Eric Pollard in 1990. "It has worked for a long time, but we are getting to the point now where the media are not titillated by these types of actions."[76]

Waves of activism always recede, for one reason or another: because they succeed; because they fail; because movements sabotage themselves, or are sabotaged from the outside; because the organizers who create them burn out, or sell out, or become discouraged, or win something real and move on to another fight. The activist style that was so novel and edgy in the late eighties ran its course by the mid nineties, but the movements that created it transformed the practice of radical organizing in the United States in lasting ways. Their bold imagery, sophistication, daring, and political flair found their way into everything from the hip-hop criminal justice activism of California's Third Eye Movement to the blockades that famously stopped the WTO meetings in Seattle.

Most importantly, their concreteness and radical pragmatism showed that even relatively powerless outsiders could win meaningful victories when their actions were strategic rather than simply symbolic or expressive. And when movements with this orientation began to collaborate and combine, their political ambitions grew.

4

Turned Up

At evening rush hour on April 25, 1995, the day before New York City's Republican mayor Rudolph Giuliani was to release a harsh new city budget, a racially diverse group of activists representing an array of causes simultaneously shut down four major arteries into Manhattan—the Brooklyn Bridge, the Manhattan Bridge, the Brooklyn Battery Tunnel, and the Queens Midtown Tunnel—in a surprise coordinated action. One group featured AIDS and disability activists, including ACT UP/NY, concerned with impending cuts to public hospitals and other health-care services. Another, with representation from the Committee Against Anti-Asian Violence (CAAAV) and the National Congress for Puerto Rican Rights, was focused on questions of police brutality and racial and homophobic violence. The third featured a group of homeless activists and their allies protesting planned cuts to affordable housing and public assistance programs. And the fourth was comprised of radical students from the City University of New York (CUNY), fresh from a massive student walkout and disruptive street protest a month before in response to a major impending tuition hike.

The blockades brought traffic to a standstill and left the police furious (an NYPD commander called the protests "childish" and "criminal"). It would be a stretch to say the protests had any concrete impact on the ensuing budget process, other than emphatically signaling disagreement, but they accomplished something else: they modeled a new kind of direct-action-based, cross-racial political collaboration. Eric Tang of CAAAV described the action as the product of "a coalition with progressive organizations in New York, which advocate on behalf of and organize the disenfranchised—homeless, people with AIDS, black, Latinos, Asian Americans, gays and lesbians." But the term "coalition" didn't quite capture how different this model of collaboration was from the classic structures used for so many political initiatives over the years, including many of the march-and-civil-disobedience protests from the 1980s onward.

Most participants in the April 25 action had come of age in an era of movement multiplicity; rather than seeing it as an obstacle to be overcome, as left critics of identity politics typically did, they cherished it as a source of political validation and strength. As Andrew Hsiao and Karen Houppert wrote in a contemporary account of the protest, "They have cut their teeth on identity politics, and for them there is little point in abandoning the movements that allowed them to gain a political voice in the first place." The organizers, many of them people of color and all experienced with multiracial organizing, were also cognizant of the divisions in movement circles, particularly the strains around race and representation. So they planned an action, as they described it in one of their planning memos, that "does not require us to work as one, to resolve our contradictions and suspicions, in order to pull it off." Though there was close coordination around everything from logistics to messaging to media work, each of the four actions was planned independently, reflecting the priorities and sensibilities of each cluster of groups. It was an action, in the words of organizer Esther Kaplan, "that allowed maximum autonomy for each organization involved." For the activists knew, Kaplan explained, "that part of what limited the effectiveness of coalitions … was that none of us could really imagine a single organization that everyone could trust." As a set of actions that relied on the element of surprise to succeed, the April

Activists blockade the Queens Midtown Tunnel, 1995
(photo: © Carolina Kroon)

25 blockades were organized with great discretion; information about logistics was closely held by only a few people, in a manner reminiscent of the 1985 Columbia anti-apartheid blockade. This kind of security culture would often characterize direct actions with strong people of color involvement in the years to come, as a way of offsetting some of the concern about the safety of participants. By overcoming longstanding distrust to pull off such a daring set of actions, the organizers of April 25 pointed toward a vision of how movements might coalesce without subsuming difference, which would be a precondition for any radical undertaking with broad scope from this point forward.[1]

Across the decade of the 1990s, an unmistakable if partial set of realignments took place across many parts of the complex activist landscape, signaling a greater political ambition, a growing willingness to collaborate, and a new understanding that the political expressions of these alliances could be as rich and multi-vocal as the panoply of movements that created them. A major milestone was the creation early in the decade of the environmental justice movement out of the many local and grassroots efforts, overwhelmingly led by people of color, to address environmental racism, from the siting of toxic facilities in low-income communities of color to the whiteness of the major environmental groups of the time. The Indigenous Environmental Network (founded in 1990) brought hundreds of Native American activists together into an enduring coordinating structure to work on issues ranging from native sovereignty to fracking and natural-gas pipelines. More than 600 people gathered in the fall of 1991 for the National People of Color Leadership Summit, which organizers described in their call to action as raising "the life and death struggles of indigenous and grassroots communities of color to an unprecedented multinational integrated level." The event brought together movements that, in the words of summit participant Paul Ruffins, "see ecology through the lens of social justice," with the goal of transforming environmentalism in the United States away from a white-led movement focused on wildlife and wilderness. Their central precept was self-determination, captured in the title of an important early movement document: "We speak for ourselves."[2]

Meanwhile, across the hemisphere, many had taken inspiration and heart from the 1994 Zapatista uprising in Mexico, at once an armed rebellion against the Mexican government and an innovative social movement shaped by a novel mix of Mayan, anarchist, socialist, and other political influences. The Zapatistas offered a sweeping critique of neoliberalism and stood out for their irreverent spirit, firm grounding in the culture of indigenous resistance, and rejection of vanguardism in favor of a radically democratic vision of networked resistance. What one supporter, Manuel Callahan, called the Zapatistas' "commitment to difference rather than identity, dialogue over command, and autonomy in opposition to state or market control" resonated powerfully with movements in the United States that were looking for new ways to broaden their critiques and amplify their impact. ACT UP chapters in Philadelphia, New York, and elsewhere were taking on both the federal government and the pharmaceutical industry to expand access to life-saving AIDS drugs for people in South Africa. College activists around the country joined together in the spring of 1998 to form United Students Against Sweatshops and were addressing global labor abuses in a concrete way by pressuring their campuses to stop selling collegiate apparel produced in sweatshops. The Ruckus Society, created amid the intense backwoods forest fights of the mid 1990s, was taking the high-profile tactics of Greenpeace and Earth First! and spreading them to new movements through trainings and workshops. Anarchists were organizing on a new scale, with 700 convening to share skills and strategies at a counter-countercon-vention outside the 1996 Democratic convention in Chicago called Active Resistance, designed "to address and transform how we live, how we connect, how we grow," as the organizers put it in an event overview. Creative new undertakings, from Critical Mass bike rides to Reclaim the Streets protest parties, were bringing mirth and wit to street activism while contesting the privatization and polic-ing of public space. And these varied streams were combining in interesting and powerful new ways, as in the successful late-1990s direct-action fight to save hundreds of New York City community gardens that brought together veterans of ACT UP, Lesbian Aveng-ers, Earth First!, and other movements to block bulldozers and disrupt real-estate auctions.[3]

Meanwhile, a wave of mid-1990s forest defense actions showed how tactical innovation could go hand-in-hand with a rising rad-icalism. In 1995, President Bill Clinton signed the Emergency Salvage Timber rider into law, which permitted a logging free-for-all on public lands. This sell-out galvanized a new set of militant and savvy Earth First! protest campaigns throughout the West, especially in Oregon and Idaho—campaigns that were at once prag-matic fights to preserve very specific parcels of old-growth forest and exercises in utopian dreaming. The most important and influ-ential of these was the effort to preserve a forest in Oregon's Warner Creek watershed that had been torched by an arsonist, rendering it eligible for logging under the salvage rider. When the cutting was about to begin, a group of protesters blocked the main logging road and maintained the blockade for an impressive 343 days. "There were these two signs on the gate, white and red striped signs like candy canes with reflectors on them so that automobiles would see the gate," remembered a young man named Cloud, who took part in the encampment. "So we wrote 'Cascadia Free State'—Cascadia on one, and Free State on the other, both in duct tape, and claimed it as our own." The eleven-month Cascadia Free State was a prefigurative experiment in principles of self-management, a "temporary autonomous zone" where activists lived out their dreams of the good society. The ideal of creating an anarchist free state, however ephemeral, was an old one; the Coalition for Direct Action at Seabrook had, for instance, dreamed of building one through their thwarted early-1980s occupation attempt. But the Warner Creek activists weren't just building a backwoods commune; they were quite literally holding logging equipment at bay with their bodies, in one of those rare but exhilarating instances when direct action functioned not at all symbolically but as an actual monkey wrench in the gears of power.[4]

A major reason why the Cascadia Free State lasted as long as it did was because the blockade employed lockdown devices, which make it more difficult and expensive for the authorities to remove protesters from a site. Any barricade or fortification that activists create is ultimately symbolic; the police will always have more force at their disposal and the equipment to knock it town or tear it apart. But if a person is attached to the blockade, and would be injured if the obstacle were simply demolished, it's a whole different game. Lockdown devices were first developed by radical environmentalists in Australia in the 1980s and soon spread, first to the anti-roads movement in Great Britain and then to backwoods campaigns in North America. The simplest of them are called lockboxes, and are made of steel or PVC pipes with a crossbar welded at the midway point inside them. The activists who are going to lock down place a chain bracelet around each of their wrists with a clip or carabiner hanging from it. Then they insert their arms into the pipe and clip onto the crossbar inside. In this way, they can lock themselves to, say, the axle of a logging truck, or link together with others in a circle. To remove them, the authorities have to cut the pipes off without cutting the demonstrators, which can take hours.

At Warner Creek, the blockading devices were inventive, numerous, and very difficult to dislodge. Activists installed what they called "sleeping dragons"—lockboxes embedded in concrete and buried underground—in the road leading to the site, and covered them with fire doors with arm-sized holes in the middle. To stop logging equipment from coming up the road, a forest defender had only to lie down on one of the doors—perhaps the one nicknamed "Morrison"—reach down through the hole in the door, and attach to the underground lockbox: the resulting obstacle was devilishly hard to remove. For the Cove-Mallard campaign in Idaho, another longstanding backwoods blockade, activists built similar barricades with buried barrels; they also dangled from huge road-blocking tripods made of logs. These kinds of techniques became so integral to the movement's approach to protest that when Earth First! put out a direct-action manual in 1997, it included only perfunctory information on longstanding organizing practices like forming affinity groups or making decision by consensus and instead mainly focused on detailed instructions for creating lockboxes, tripods, sleeping dragons, and other devices of this sort.[5]

Earth First! direct-action manual, 1997 (designer: DAM Collective; author's collection)

Effective as they could be for saving old-growth forest—the Warner Creek sale was eventually canceled and the land protected—these techniques were designed for the intrepid few, not for mass actions. And authorities quickly raised the stakes even higher by using pain-compliance techniques to dismantle blockades. In the most widely publicized incident, in 1997, four North California Earth First! activists who were blockading the office of an anti-environmental congressperson in Eureka had pepper spray applied directly to their eyes with cotton swabs. The incident was video-taped, and on it you can hear the blood-curdling screams of the young Earth First!ers as the caustic chemical—which according to manufacturers' guidelines should not be used within two feet of a person's body—burns their eyes. The police violence used against this and other lockdown blockades pushed a number of activists in a more militant direction, leading a small but influential number of organizers to reject nonviolence as passivity and turn to property-destroying Black Bloc actions in subsequent years. "When you lock yourself to something, you're subjecting yourself to a reaction—a reaction to your action," explained John Bowling, an Earth First!er who had trained activists in lockdown techniques, in late 1999, a few days before the Seattle WTO protests. "And we've seen an overwhelming, unconscionable expression of police brutality, just sheer torture, used on people who are peaceful in their intent, who are not a flight risk. I think what that has done is radicalized people, and actions are gaining in intensity as a result of that."[6]

One of the most momentous developments for activism in the United States during this period took place elsewhere, in the global *encuentros,* or gatherings, that grew out of the Zapatista movement and into the People's Global Action (PGA), a decentralized struc-ture for coordinating grassroots resistance movements around the world. PGA was dedicated to the project of working "to weave a variety of struggles into one struggle that never loses its multiplicity," and it began calling for world-wide days of action against capitalist globalization, using major summit meetings as the occasion to raise a radical critique. The first coincided with the May 1998 World Trade Organization ministerial in Geneva, and involved coordi-nated protests in some sixty cities. For the second, on what was dubbed "J18"—the June 18, 1999 G8 summit in Germany—PGA called for dramatic "carnivals against capital" around the globe. More than one hundred cities on five continents responded with festive defiance, including Boston, San Francisco, Washington, DC, and New York.[7]

A larger mood shift was underway from a politics of anger to one of hope. Some members of a radical street-theater group called Art and Revolution, co-founded by David Solnit at the 1996 Active Resistance anarchist gathering, began to dream about what might happen for the third PGA global day of action, scheduled to coincide with the November 30, 1999 meeting of the World Trade Organization in Seattle. They began reaching out to others with extensive direct-action experience, including Ruckus and the Rainforest Action Network, with a bold vision of "people on the street breaking down corporate globalization and showing glimpses of the world as it could be—global liberation," to quote from one of the invitations they circulated. Over the ensuing months, this informal planning network developed into the Direct Action Network (DAN) and put out as its goal the complete shutdown of the WTO ministerial meeting. As the circle of people working to mobilize for Seattle expanded and grew, they called on fellow activists to join them in creating a protest "reflecting some of the diversity of the groups and communities affected by the WTO and corporate globalization" and organized with "mutual respect for a wide variety of nonviolent action styles reflecting our different groups and communities."[8]

Nothing quite prepared even the most optimistic planners and observers for what would unfold on the streets of Seattle. Rarely has a large-scale protest come off as splendidly as the extraordinary WTO blockade of November 30, 1999, or "N30," as it was called in the activist shorthand of the time. An organizing collective handled the advance planning, the budgeting, and overall logistics. For a week beforehand, organizers held trainings on everything from basic principles of nonviolent protest to Earth First! lockdown techniques in a sprawling warehouse just east of downtown Seattle, dubbed the convergence center. People built protest props

in abundance: colorful puppets and flags and banners and costumes, many with focused messages about the WTO and the perils
of corporate-driven trade agreements, and others with open-ended
calls to "RESIST" and "IMAGINE." Thousands of people formed
themselves into affinity groups and committed to blockading particular areas around the convention center. Organizers had divided
the surrounding cityscape into thirteen sections, like pieces of
pie, and "clusters" of affinity groups took responsibility for each
wedge, deciding among themselves how they would position themselves in the streets to prevent WTO delegates from reaching the
summit meeting. Large action spokescouncils used consensus decision-making to coordinate how the cluster actions would unfold,
while robustly organized legal, medical, media, and other working
groups worked autonomously to provide key forms of support.

Mobilizing postcard for
Seattle WTO actions,
1999 (designer: Hugh
D'Andrade; author's
collection)

Seattle was the moment when the mass direct-action model that activists had been developing and refining since Mayday 1971 worked most smoothly and brilliantly. On the morning of N30, as protesters assembled throughout the city, the atmosphere was a true carnival of resistance and hope. Something on the order of 50,000 people had converged on the city to protest the WTO Ministerial meeting; the portion of those demonstrators who came to participate in disruptive direct action was smaller but still numbered in the thousands, and their energy and exuberance set the tone in the streets. There were marching bands and Radical Cheerleaders and dancing and celebration as activists moved into place to block key intersections. In some places, they simply locked arms; in others, they locked themselves to concrete blocks or to each other with reinforced PVC pipes. Though the action had been openly and publicly planned in the standard approach of predominantly white direct-action movements of the time, the authorities were caught off guard by its scale and efficacy, and cheers rose up all over downtown Seattle as delegates were repeatedly turned away from the planned opening ceremony by the simple stubborn force of people's defiance. "This is what democracy looks like!" the crowd chanted when the ceremony was canceled, energized by the thrilling realization that their direct action had, however briefly, actually brought the WTO meeting to a halt. It was the most ambitious direct-action undertaking in thirty years, profoundly collaborative and participatory in character, and astoundingly it had worked, disrupting not just the meetings but also the negotiating process and helping to derail the planned agreement. Longtime direct-action organizer Brad Will, who had been centrally involved in both the forest campaigns of the West Coast and the squatter and community garden campaigns of the East Coast, described the sense of exhilaration and empowerment: "*This is it*, everyone's here—this is it. Just my heart swelling. Pride. *This* is what I had in mind, and never thought was going to happen."[9]

That was when the police attacks began: Seattle was the culmination of years of rising radicalism, and the beginning of years of rising repression. The mayor declared a state of emergency, the governor called in the National Guard, and the streets soon were under an ominous militarized occupation. Police used pepper spray, tear gas, and rubber bullets to try to subdue the crowd, in one of the most aggressive and violent responses to nonviolent protest since Mayday 1971. In most media accounts of the day, the police assault with tear gas and rubber bullets was presented as though it had been a response to the window-smashing and other vandalism committed by several dozen roving Black Bloc anarchists, many of whom had participated in, and been radicalized by, the backwoods "free state" at Warner Creek and subsequent Earth First! encampments. But in fact the property destruction took place well away from the blockades and with almost no intervention or direct response by the police. The authorities saved their biggest firepower for the lockdown blockades, where activists were bombarded with chemical weapons in the hope of dislodging them. Yarrow Rain King, a young woman from Humboldt County who had locked down in an intersection with about twenty other activists, described how the police came and went around the circle pepper spraying everyone directly in the face, not once but a brutal four times. Despite the burning pain, no one unclipped from the lockboxes: "We just sat through it, and we all were just calming each other down and crying and just pushing through it, because that's what we felt like we had to do." Few of the direct-action protesters were discouraged by the attacks; if anything, the repression inspired some of the thousands of other WTO opponents on the streets, such as the huge crowd assembled for an official labor march that day, to join in solidarity with the blockaders. Certainly the police violence left blockaders with the sense that what they were doing was important and right: "It was more than a protest," wrote activist, author, and direct-action trainer Starhawk afterwards. "It was an uprising of a vision of true abundance, a celebration of life and creativity and connection, that remained joyful in the face of brutality and brought alive the creative forces that can truly counter those of injustice and control."[10]

Many different streams of direct-action work had come together in Seattle, and there was a powerful and unmistakable alchemy as they combined. Lisa Fithian, whose own organizing background included the 1987 Pledge of Resistance CIA blockade, ACT UP's daring FDA 1988 occupation, and years of work with the more militant pockets within organized labor, enumerated some of the forces at play: "You had anti-nuke people. You had the other more radical environmentalists, the Earth First!ers, the Greenpeace types. You had people who came out of the Central American solidarity movement. You had people who came out of the women's movement and anti-militarism. And then you had a certain number of cultural workers in resistance." There wasn't a significant organized LGBTQ presence, but the legacy of ACT UP's sophisticated approach to street activism was evident everywhere, and there was an explicitly queer dimension to the carnival in the streets. Movements had certainly joined together before at national convention protests, among many other contexts, but the synergy in Seattle was on a different scale. "I had never seen that kind of convergence of influences in one place at one time without a lot of tension or struggle," Fithian explained. "That was very empowering, and very instructive for a lot of people that it can be done, that we don't all have to be on one program, we don't all have to have one message, we don't all have to have one tactic." Crucially, the direct action was focused upon a very concrete objective: disrupt the WTO's negotiations by interfering with the meeting. But both the action and the extraordinary gathering of forces that made it possible were sustained by a vision of systemic change more ambitious than anything seen outside of the far fringes for many years. The language of revolution had largely dropped out of the discourse of the left for decades; in Seattle, it made something of a comeback, with all the defiant impracticality it implied. As David Solnit optimistically phrased it two months after the WTO meeting, "Most of the [recent] past mass movements in this country have been around single issues like disarmament or Central America or forests. This is a movement that at the core is challenging an entire system—bringing people from all the different fights and very clearly saying that the economic system of this country and this world is wrong, and we're going to overthrow it and build a new one in the wake of it."[11]

That call for system change came most strongly from the most misunderstood of the many converging streams of activism: the anarchists. Openly anarchist currents had been a small part of the mix in US radical circles since the early twentieth century, and experienced a modest revival during and after the sixties—quite a few activists in the more militant wings of the late-1970s anti-nuclear movement, including the Coalition for Direct Action at Seabrook, identified as anarchists, as did many of the punk protesters behind the 1984 Democratic convention protests in San Francisco, to take just two examples. And anti-authoritarian impulses had strongly shaped the character of direct-action organizing from the early 1970s onward; the directly democratic organizational forms of prefigurative activism were efforts to model the sort of society anarchists hoped to create. Beginning in the late 1980s, though, this diffuse anarchist presence within broader grassroots movements was increasingly complemented by an expanding world of explicitly anarchist endeavors, from groups like Food Not Bombs to anarchist publishing houses, bookstores, "infoshops," and gatherings like the 1996 Active Resistance conference. There was a strongly white and subcultural quality to many of these projects, though the scene grew more diverse over time. Within this larger anarchist world, the Black Bloc in Seattle represented just one small militant strain; while it predictably sparked movement debates about the political merits of property destruction wherever it appeared, it was never as influential as either the visionary and prefigurative strain or the nut-and-bolts, movement-building aspects of anarchist activism.[12]

The Seattle mobilization was as successful as it was in significant part because it built on years of this low-visibility, infrastructure-building work. As anarchist journalist and organizer Chris Crass wrote afterwards, "While the media obsesses over anarchists who destroyed property, the real story was that anarchists were simply everywhere doing a hundred different things. Anarchists were doing jail support, media work, making meals for thousands, doing dishes, facilitating strategy meetings, leading workshops, and discussion groups. Anarchists were doing medical support work, security at the warehouse space, communications between affinity groups and clusters, organizing marches and blockades and lockdowns and tripod sits and forming human chains. Anarchists were making puppets, banners, signs, leaflets, press releases, stickers, and costumes." And with so much of the preparatory work on display in the convergence center or visible in the public workings of the action spokescouncils, Seattle served as a large-scale training ground in the mechanics of mobilization.[13]

Not everything went flawlessly in Seattle, to be sure. Though the event became famous for showcasing a "Teamsters and turtles" alliance between labor and environmentalists, in fact the relations between organized labor and the direct-action camp were strained, for both had scheduled their marquee events on the same day. Some labor leaders were unhappy that the blockades interfered with the big march they had organized for November 30, though large numbers of rank-and-file members simply abandoned the planned route and joined the direct action, especially after the tear-gassing

Confetti thrown by the Black Bloc in Seattle, 1999 (designer unknown; author's collection)

began. The Black Bloc, meanwhile, decided to be nihilistic in their practices as well as their messages, scheduling their property-destroying spree for not just the same day but the very same time as the direct-action blockade, despite repeated appeals from DAN organizers that they not undertake actions that would endanger the blockaders and justify police violence against them. If there was an upside to these conflicts, it was that they spurred a new movement practice that carried forward into future mobilizations, including the fall 2014 Ferguson October mobilization: the adoption of what organizers called solidarity principles, carefully negotiated agreements among groups about tactics, timing, and mutual respect.

Of the many important streams of recent activism, though, one was only represented in Seattle on the tiniest scale. During the same late-1990s period when direct-action forest defense, anti-sweatshop, and public space activism were on the rise, there was a steady growth of people-of-color-led movement work focused on policing, prisons, and race. The mass incarceration that had begun in the late 1970s and 1980s had accelerated enormously during the presidency of Bill Clinton; his "tough on crime" policies, combined with the ongoing War on Drugs, led to skyrocketing rates of imprisonment for young blacks and Latinos. As scholar Keeanga-Yamahtta Taylor succinctly put it, "By the end of Clinton's term, Black incarceration rates had tripled and the United States was locking up a larger proportion of its population than any other country on earth." Those imprisoned were mainly men; as grassroots organizing against this crisis began to build, women, particularly queer-identified women, played a central role shaping the activist response, grounding their work in the women of color feminism of the eighties onward, now increasingly referred to as intersectional politics. Activists involved in the CUNY fights of 1995 in New York formed the Student Liberation Action Movement (SLAM!), a multiracial organization that tackled issues ranging from immigrant rights to police brutality to economic inequality. On the West Coast, the Ella Baker Center for Human Rights (founded in 1996) launched campaigns against racist abuses in the criminal justice system. The Black Radical Congress (founded in 1998) brought 2,000 organizers and scholars of African descent together into a new national network. The landmark 1998 Critical Resistance conference in Berkeley brought 3,500 activists and scholars together to analyze the growth of the prison-industrial complex and refine grassroots strategies for resisting it; the gathering developed into an enduring national organization. The founding of *ColorLines* magazine that same year provided an important and influential new platform for writing on race and activism.[14]

Direct action was not at the center of any of this work for an array of reasons, including the heightened risks activists of color faced when engaging with the very same system of criminal injustice they were critiquing. But amid the growing activist sense of an acute crisis around policing and prisons, that was beginning to change. When four New York police officers killed unarmed Guinean immigrant Amadou Diallo with a barrage of forty-one bullets in early 1999, a number of organizers—including Richie Perez of the National Congress for Puerto Rican Rights, who had been a key planner of the April 1995 bridge-and-tunnel blockades—launched a civil disobedience campaign modeled on the Free South Africa Movement apartheid protests of the 1980s. For a whole month that spring, demonstrators gathered day after day to block the entrance of One Police Plaza, the headquarters of the New York City Police Department; nearly 1,200 people were arrested. They were negotiated arrests, much like those outside the South African Embassy fifteen years before had been, but the huge increase in mass incarceration over those intervening years meant it was no small matter to participate, especially for the young people of color joining the protest. "Folks were scared, and this was an easy one," Perez recalled afterwards. "Young blacks and Latinos are not eager to do civil disobedience, because many of them have been through the system or have been touched by the system in one way or another, or have loved ones that have. There's been a tremendous increase of police interference in people's lives, and people want to get away from it, they don't want more of it."[15]

Perhaps if this rising stream of people-of-color-led organizing had been completely unrepresented in Seattle, the mostly white character of the mobilization would have been little noticed or discussed. But something much more interesting happened: among the crowd of 50,000 protesters in Seattle, there was a small delegation of about forty young people of color, organized by a group called Just Act (Youth ACTion for Global JUSTice). They showed up at the convergence space, the bustling headquarters for the direct-action preparations, not quite sure what to expect. "When we walked in," one attendee recalled, "the room was filled with young whites calling themselves anarchists. There was a pungent smell, many had not showered. We just couldn't relate to the scene so our whole group left right away." But while these young people of color found the culture of the white anarchist scene to be hugely off-putting, they were both intrigued and impressed by the organizing methods and skills that had gone into the mobilization. Said another attendee afterwards, "We should have stayed. We didn't see that we had a lot to learn from them." Rashidi Omari of the hip-hop group Company of Prophets recalled, "Later I went back and talked to people, and they were discussing tactics, very smart. Those folks were really ready for action. It was limiting for people of color to let that one experience affect their whole picture of white activists."

These comments, and others much like them, were showcased in a *ColorLines* article by veteran racial-justice activist Elizabeth "Betita" Martinez, entitled "Where Was the Color in Seattle? Looking for Reasons Why the Great Battle Was So White." The piece was published a few months after the mobilization, when excitement about the showdown in Seattle and the promise of the burgeoning movement against corporate globalization was high. It opened with a quote from organizer Jinee Kim, an activist with a Bay Area group called the Third Eye Movement, recalling a moment outside the jail where N30 arrestees had been taken. "A big crowd of people was chanting 'This Is What Democracy Looks Like!' At first it sounded kind of nice," Kim recalled. "But then I thought: is this really what democracy looks like? Nobody here looks like me." The essay was widely reprinted and discussed, making it one of the most influential pieces of writing on direct action in thirty years.[16]

The piece sparked not one but several conversations. It prompted many white organizers to reckon with race in a more focused and serious way than they had done before. "It was amazing the impact that one article had," observed Jia Ching Chen, who played a key role in bringing the delegation of activists of color to Seattle. "People talked about how few people of color were up in Seattle, but the JustAct contingent, that small number of people were instrumental in promoting this dialogue around these issues and this analysis around globalization in the US. The amount that that small group of people and that article has been able to influence the broader movement dialogue and agenda has been phenomenal." Questions of race had never been wholly absent from the direct-action campaigns of the previous decades. But when the white-led direct-action tradition was becoming formalized in the 1970s, race had come up only tangentially, as when white activists in the anti-nuclear movement lamented the absence of people of color from among their ranks but seemed flummoxed by how to deal with it. In the 1980s, divisions of race had often seemed intractable, as in the anti-apartheid movement at UC Berkeley or the Rutgers student conference of 1988, and when white activists interacted with movements of color, there was often conflict, much of it born of white obliviousness. In direct-action movements of the 1990s like ACT UP that had solid people of color caucuses, though the engagement was largely more productive and constructive than in earlier movements, the process was often bumpy. The post-Seattle wake-up call to white activists on race was certainly long overdue, but it did seem that at last they were ready to listen—or enough of them were to be able to make a change. "White people, especially white progressives confronted by racism, get really scared and often really guilty and immobilized," remarked Direct Action Network organizer Mac Scott in April 2000, on the eve of the next big global justice mobilization, a protest outside the International Monetary Fund and World Bank meetings in Washington, DC. "But there's been a lot of debate and a lot of good news. People are starting to debate the issue, starting to wrap our heads around the right way to go about building these bridges, supporting movements of color rather than expecting them to support our movements. And doing that respectfully, and accepting [their] leadership."[17]

The discussion among activists of color also now had a different character. Yes, white activists were being called out about the mono-chromatic character of their movement culture, but the situation was different from, say, Berkeley in 1985, when anti-apartheid activists of color viewed the white direct-action movement's methods and approach as not just exclusionary but also counter-productive and politically unappealing. The shutdown in Seattle was so electri-fying, and the direct-action model was employed so smoothly and powerfully, that many key racial-justice activists were also inspired. "Being there was an incredible awakening," one activist of color told Martinez. "I saw the future," said another. "I was blown away, impressed, and reinvigorated by Seattle," echoed SLAM! organizer Sandra Barros. But that sense of inspiration was accompanied by a powerful sense of the obstacles that would stand in the way of a similarly ambitious mobilization by movements of color—and a critique of what journalist Andrew Hsiao called "an insider's culture of privileged militancy." "I thought it was great. Absolutely wonder-ful, on multiple levels," commented SLAM! and Critical Resistance organizer Kai Lumumba Barrow in a 2000 interview. "I also felt disconnected, and I felt envious—player hate. They had the equip-ment, they had the contacts—why don't we have this stuff to do this work?"[18]

An intense flurry of organizing took place in the ensuing twenty-two months, as a wide range of movements worked in different ways to build on the momentum of Seattle, and a smaller but significant subset worked, as part of that project, to redress the direct-action movement's shortcomings on race. While few people had come to Seattle viewing themselves as part of a single broad movement for global justice, many left feeling that one had been forged there in the streets. But the strategic clarity that had given power to the WTO fight proved elusive as the newly consolidating movement against corporate globalization began to plot its next steps. The Direct Action Network grew into a decentralized but coordinated association of a dozen local groups around the country with big hopes and a broad transformative vision. As the New York City affiliate, NYC-DAN, put it in an outreach brochure, "We support and struggle for direct democracy; local autonomy; a globalism based on relations between people not between assets; and a society in which everyone has the freedom and security to realize his or her full potential."[19]

In practice, though, protesting corporate globalization in the period after Seattle largely came to mean surrounding other big summit meetings, like the April 16, 2000 meeting of the World Bank and International Monetary Fund (known in movement shorthand as A16), or holding protests in solidarity with summit protests in other places. It was enormously exciting to feel that activists were taking on big targets with energy and vision, intervening at a high level in the debate over the course of global trade negotiations. Some 20,000 protesters gathered in DC for A16, and the protests made front-page news nationwide. But there was something of a sense that A16 was a less-perfectly-executed replay of N30. Organizers used the same slices-of-pie approach to blockading the meetings, but this time, in an odd departure from the generally open organizing process, one section was claimed in advance for a secret affinity group action that did not successfully materialize. Daily life in DC was certainly disrupted, but with a big gap in the planned blockade, the IMF/World Bank meeting proceeded more or less as planned. That couldn't help but be a disappointment when the stated goal was again to stop delegates from reaching the event. The focus on protesting outside big summit meetings seemed to impose a narrow action teleology: the immediate goal always became shutting the meeting down. That in turn required channeling a large share of the movement's energies into the minutiae of street maneuvers. Organizers spent endless hours before the actions planning how to use radio communications, bike runners, and bullhorns to deploy protesters as needed, with the hope of once again creating a blockade as seamless as the one in Seattle. These logistical discussions became almost paramilitary in character, with activists discussing "scouts" and "recon" and referring to themselves as "tac" (tactical teams) or "comms."

There was a mounting sense that, for some participants anyway, the point of the direct action had become pulling off an impressive direct action, with direct action becoming not just a method of protest but a political identity in itself, separate from any pragmatic

or strategic considerations. For those with more prefigurative leanings, it wasn't necessarily whether the blockade succeeded but how
the process unfolded that had the greatest significance: some participants gauged success by the extent to which activists employed
the direct-action movement's version of direct democracy through
affinity groups, consensus process, spokescouncils and the like. A16
was also something of a replay of Seattle on race—indeed, some
observers thought there was an even lower percentage of people of
color within the crowd of protesters than in Seattle, a particularly
dismal showing in the majority-black city of DC. "A16 was indeed a
sea of white," activist Eric Tang of New York's Third World Within
told a reporter for *ColorLines*. Though the groups spearheading the
mobilization had put effort into outreach to organizations and communities of color, the effort was no more productive than similar
attempts in the past had been. As activist and political analyst Van
Jones wryly noted, "The point isn't to make the movement look like
a Benetton ad. The question is: how will this convergence change
the movement?"[20]

The 2000 Democratic and Republican convention protests
provided some answers to this question, as the direct-action
movement, still predominantly white, tried something different:
partnering with grassroots movements of color to help move their
priorities and agendas forward. That type of solidarity work had
been a key part of Art and Revolution's orientation even before it
catalyzed the Seattle shutdown: the group had collaborated with
organizations such as the United Farm Workers, Jobs with Justice,
Critical Resistance, and the Coalition on Homelessness, making
specific, circumscribed contributions like creating mediagenic
protest props and signs while supporting (rather than seeking to
shape) the partner movement's tactical choices, message framing,
and overall strategy. For white activists looking to improve their
movements' track record on race, this approach stood out as a viable
and constructive alternative to the dead-end strategy of trying to
use outreach to diversify their existing groups and movements.

In the meantime, some movements of color focused on questions
of criminal injustice were embracing bolder tactics, beginning to
take greater risks in response to a sense of rising crisis. When the

four police officers who killed Amadou Diallo were acquitted in early 2000, thousands took over the streets in New York for large, passionate, and unpermitted protests, while a hundred were arrested in civil disobedience actions at the United Nations. In the Bay Area, a group called Third Force, which arose as a project of the Ella Baker Center, spearheaded an inventive campaign against a draconian juvenile justice ballot measure, Proposition 21. The proposition consolidated and expanded what activists were beginning to term the "school-to-prison pipeline," allowing fourteen-year-olds to be prosecuted as adults, and it provided harsh punishment for minor crimes like graffiti and activities defined as "gang-related." Third Eye and allied groups catalyzed large middle-school and high-school walkouts with thousands of participants, and organized a series of public concerts and hip-hop rallies. Hip-hop shaped the style and tone of these young black and brown activists' organizing in much the same way that punk had done for white activists a generation before, providing not just a soundtrack but a sensibility: "a carving out of more social space, more identity space," in the words of activist–scholar Tricia Rose. "Hip-hop is the movement," explained organizer Pecolia Manigo. "It's how we do our outreach, raise funds and educate people."[21]

The movement's boldest action came at its most disappointing hour, after Proposition 21 passed statewide by a wide margin. The following day, hundreds of young people converged outside San Francisco's Hilton Hotel, whose chief executive had provided financial backing for the measure, and then occupied its lobby with a raucous sit-in at which 150 young people were arrested. Jia Ching Chen, who was arrested at the action, explained to a reporter for the *San Francisco Examiner,* "It's about the criminalization and incarceration of an entire generation of young people of color. And we're not going to take it." Disrupting the Hilton was a display of defiance rather than a strictly strategic intervention, and it showcased the vibrant culture of resistance that had built up around the campaign. Instead of relying on timeworn and predictable chants of the "Hey hey! Ho ho!" variety, the protesters reworked the Sugar Hill Gang's classic "Rapper's Delight," filling the hotel lobby with rhythmic chants of "Hotel, Motel, and the Hilton—If you start a war on youth, you ain't gonna win!" Explained organizer Edget Betru afterwards, "The goal was to say, we're not defeated or demoralized; we're energized and we're moving on, building upon this ... It was much more celebratory than you'd imagine for an action the day after the thing passes."[22]

The fight had energized and radicalized a whole new cohort of activists, whose tactical boldness and stylistic experimentation set them apart both from their counterparts in the anti-apartheid movement a generation earlier and from the mostly white direct-action movement of Seattle and A16. As Chen, whose organizing work spanned both worlds, observed in late 2000, "Even though they might have common inspiration, like Gandhi and King, the kind of tradition that's come through the anti-nuclear movement and Greenpeace to Ruckus is really different than the tradition that comes through the civil rights movement and the direct action of groups like the Young Lords to the Third Eye Movement." The new upsurge of activism around the prison industrial complex was shaped by a broad array of historical influences, including the civil rights movement, the Black Panther Party, and the women of color feminism pioneered by the Combahee River Collective, all of which gave it a very different political flavor than white-majority direct-action protest. But that tradition had an impact, as well. "Our grounding comes out of radical feminism and Third World communism," explained Sandra Barros of SLAM!, "but there's definitely the influence of anarchist tactics and organizing models as well."[23]

SLAM! and the Direct Action Network, particularly its New York and Philadelphia affiliates, decided to join as partners for protests against the 2000 Republican National Convention, along with ACT UP/Philadelphia, the Prison Moratorium Project, CAAAV, and a diverse array of other groups. Kai Lumumba Barrow recalled the lengthy political debates it took to persuade white direct-action activists to pivot from their focus on trade agreements and corporate globalization and throw their energies into a mobilization focused on policing and prisons. "There was a lot of energy and excitement about raising questions around neoliberalism and globalization. And then there were some of us who felt like, yes, that's true, however, we felt like we needed to link these issues of global capital to conditions of people of color in the US." Barrow continued, "So, we had to be like, 'Look, we are bringing what this movement does not have, which is people of color, predominantly young people of color, predominantly female-bodied and queer and poor people of color, who are coming to this action from our own particular experiences, our own analysis, which is completely different from the analysis that is currently existing. And that has value.'" Added Chen, "There was still a lot of contention, there were still a lot of people saying, this isn't a broad enough message, thinking globalization represented an anti-democratic process but not seeing that it historically hasn't existed without race oppression."[24]

The groups ultimately agreed to collaborate on an August 1 day of direct action against the prison industrial complex. The mobilizing materials for R2K, as activists nicknamed the mobilization, featured stylized images of people of color engaged in protest, conveying the hope that the demographics of this event would be very

Mobilizing broadsheet for the 2000 convention protests
(designers: Eulan Atkinson and Jed Brandt; author's collection)

different from Seattle and A16. The tactical plan was very different, too. Instead of trying to coordinate a single seamless blockade, and doing so in a public spokescouncil meeting, the activists decided to deploy affinity groups in surprise disruptions all around downtown Philadelphia. "If you plan on doing direct action during the convention," a handbook created by the Philadelphia Direct Action Group cautioned, "make the cops' job harder by NOT TALKING ABOUT IT! Try to limit details to yourself, members of your affinity group, and those members of legal and strategic support that NEED to know them." Organizers had one big surprise they worked extra hard to keep secret, a clever merging of two now classic elements of direct-action street protest: some of the giant puppets that activists used as protest props to dramatize the issues at hand would on this occasion double as lockdown devices, enabling activists to create mediagenic and difficult-to-remove street blockades at key sites throughout the city.[25]

Or rather, they would have done so, if the puppets hadn't been confiscated first. The authorities had a surprise of their own: four state police officers posing as union carpenters had infiltrated the activists' warehouse space, playfully dubbed the Ministry of Puppetganda, and learned of the plan. Hours before the blockade puppets were to be deployed, police surrounded and raided the warehouse, telling the media it was a "nerve center of criminal activity." Seventy activists, including a number of key organizers, were arrested and charged with multiple misdemeanors, while authorities destroyed all of the protest props—not just the ones designed for blockading, but all of the beautiful hand-painted signs, banners, and flags. The police had not only successfully disrupted the disruption, they had very effectively deprived the protesters of their main means for conveying their messages to the public. The August 1 direct action went forward anyway and did block intersections and snarl traffic around the city. But without the props that communicated the activists' critique of policing and prisons, the action came off as chaos for its own sake, and the reporting focused almost exclusively on cat-and-mouse skirmishes between protesters and police. "Demonstrators Nearly Steal the Spotlight at Convention," declared a *New York Times* headline the next day, but the article made only the most oblique mention of why the protesters were out in the streets, foregrounding instead an exasperated bystander's assessment: "They're just rebels without a cause."[26]

The raid on the Ministry of Puppetganda was just one facet of a well-designed police plan for what scholars B. Edwards Gillham and J.A. Noakes have termed "strategic incapacitation," designed to thwart the August 1 protests and hobble the movements that had converged to make them happen. Police in Philadelphia avoided using the tear gas and rubber bullets that had proved so controversial in Seattle, but they used brute force to disperse the street gatherings, and swept up hundreds of people, charging many with multiple misdemeanors. Relying on extensive surveillance, they followed and detained key organizers. Three such activists, including Kate Sorensen from ACT UP/Philadelphia and John Sellers from the Ruckus Society, were arrested while talking on their cellphones and charged with felony possession of an instrument of crime; bail for Sorensen and Sellers was set at a jaw-dropping $1 million each. Organizers of color had long talked about how much more vulnerable they and their movements were when engaging in direct action, and the concerted repression in Philadelphia seemed both to prove their point and to underscore the post-Seattle shifts in the policing of protest: as movements had grown more ambitious and better organized, so had governmental efforts to neutralize them. RNC protest organizers and arrestees spent years fighting the charges, most of which were ultimately dropped. It was a bitter irony that participants in a mobilization focused on criminal injustice would see so much of their energy diverted into dealing with police and the courts afterwards.[27]

Even so, many organizers felt that August 1 had been an important step forward. Barros reflected, "Historically, the people of color left and what might traditionally be seen as a white anarchist scene were seen as separate and disparate. What we learned from R2K is that we actually have so much to learn from one another. I found the Direct Action Network in particular to be very highly organized and sophisticated. There were really amazing structures of organization that were not only strategically and tactically important [for] actually shutting the city down, but that were amazing experiments in democracy." Barrow described the experience of cross-racial collaboration as a real advance, "We cried together, we fought together, we called out racism when it came up, we called out entitlement when we thought we should call it out, we cussed at each other, and then we leaned on each other." Another SLAM! activist, Kazembe Balagun, concluded, "Direct action, done correctly, can foster solidarity across racial and gender lines, and that's something we definitely learned."[28]

The process had been a struggle for everyone involved; for the mostly white direct-action movement, the progress it represented, though real, was small. Lesley Wood, a white organizer with DAN-NYC, recalled, "We did an anti-racism training in DAN, and it was incredibly frustrating, because people constantly found ways to talk about something else. We were saying, 'This is an anti-racism training,' and it was like, 'Let's talk about gender, or sexuality'—or anything other than racism." She added, "There's a real frustration in organizing since Philadelphia, in that people felt that other people are pushing their issues on them. Seeing race as an 'issue' as opposed to a way of organizing, an intrinsic part of the way we organize." As the next big mobilization approached—a huge convergence around the IMF/World Bank meetings planned for late September 2001—there was cautious optimism that this set of protests could challenge corporate globalization in a more inclusive way, building on the relationships forged through the convention protests and other work. Intriguing behind-the-scenes negotiations between representatives of organized labor, the direct-action movement, and the Black Bloc were addressing how to coexist in the streets despite differing tactical approaches. There were reasons to hope that the mobilization would showcase an expanding, multi-vocal, and ever-more-confident radicalism to counter the forward march of corporate globalization.[29]

But the September 2001 global justice mobilization never happened, because 9/11 did. The attacks on the World Trade Center and the Pentagon utterly transformed the climate for activism, along with so much else, overnight. It's difficult to overstate how grief and fear changed the character of public life in the period after 9/11. To the very limited extent that people gathered in public at all in the period after the attacks, given the wide unease, it was for candlelight peace vigils, not impassioned protests, and certainly not carnivalesque ones. The theatricality and exuberance that had given the global justice protests such charisma and impact now seemed grotesquely inappropriate to a country in mourning. Militancy in any form seemed completely out of the question, and for a time, even the tamest forms of street protest, like simple marches or rallies, seemed too confrontational for the country's solemn mood.

Calling for peace after 9/11 (designer: American Friends Service Committee; author's collection)

When the United States went to war against Afghanistan, not quite a month after 9/11, modest and somber gatherings of committed peace activists were nearly the only sizable public expressions of dissent; though protest actions did take place on more than a hundred campuses, they were small and subdued. Several months later, what remained of the global justice movement in New York tried to mount a series of protests against meetings of the World Economic Forum, but the actions were largely thwarted by a massive police operation that the *New York Times* termed a "security lockdown."[30]

As it became clear over the ensuing year that the Bush administration was going to use 9/11 as the pretext to wage war against Iraq as well, a nationwide antiwar movement began to coalesce. Of course there were some important continuities between this work and the global justice organizing that had been underway since Seattle, and the movement gained its most important focal point when the European Social Forum set February 15, 2003 as a coordinated international day of action against the war, extending the practice initiated by People's Global Action. But the antiwar movement's character, style, and approach were very different from those of the direct-action global justice movement. Where the global justice movement's roots stretched back to Mayday 1971, with its decentralized organizing practices and its no-business-as-usual style of public disruption, the Iraq antiwar movement was closer in spirit and structure to the National Peace Action Coalition (NPAC) of the Vietnam era, the formation that advocated mobilizing the broadest possible opposition to the war and used lowest-common-denominator demands and strictly legal tactics to do so. United for Peace and Justice (UFPJ), the huge coalition that initiated the February 15 protests in the United States and served as the major vehicle for antiwar organizing in the ensuing years, was certainly not controlled by a single behind-the-scenes organization the way NPAC was steered by the Socialist Workers Party. But UFPJ's strategic choices were more strongly shaped by longstanding pacifist groups and various strains of the tactically cautious socialist-leaning left than they were by the anarchist-inflected direct-action tradition, which played more of a supporting than a driving role in the coalition's work.

The mobilizing materials for February 15 in New York conveyed something of this character, featuring just one simple and inclusive slogan—The World Says No to War—alongside an impressively diverse list of cities around the world where coordinated protests were to take place, a nod to the now-eclipsed global justice movement. February 15 was the single largest day of protest ever in world history, with estimates of the global turnout ranging anywhere from 6 million to as high as 30 million. It was a grassroots mobilization on a massive scale, pulled together with extraordinary speed. There were protests in hundreds of sites around the United States, and nearly 800 cities and towns worldwide, on every continent. With perhaps close to a million people in attendance, the New York rally was by far the largest demonstration in the United States since the enormous 1982 anti-nuclear protest in Central Park, and was organized in a fraction of the time; scores of organizations large and small threw their weight behind the effort. In the days leading up to the event, hundreds of volunteers fanned out around the city, distributing more than a million leaflets at every major subway stop in the five boroughs.[31]

Right from the outset, UFPJ faced a major choice about how confrontational an approach to protest it would take. The 9/11

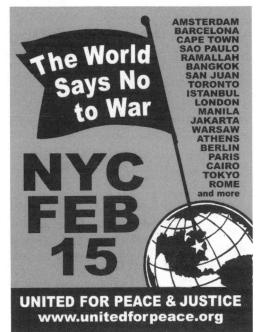

Mobilizing sticker for February 15, 2003 antiwar protest (designer: L.A. Kauffman; author's collection)

attacks—and the anti-terrorist Patriot Act passed soon thereafter —had given authorities at every level of government an easy and politically safe pretext for limiting demonstrations, and the NYPD, collaborating closely with the federal government, emphatically refused to issue a march permit for February 15, allowing only a stationary rally to take place. Some within the nascent antiwar coalition, including those with direct-action leanings, wanted the group to march anyway, hoping that an intense show of defiance would both reopen the public space for dissent and deter the Bush administration from its rush to war. But the coalition's steering committee chose, both on this occasion and at other times when the authorities moved to constrain its events, including at the 2004 Republican National Convention in New York, to accept the restrictions in order to have a legally permitted event, which the largest number of people could potentially attend. And one decisive reason it did so was because of race: UFPJ pledged to be a truly multiracial coalition early on, dedicating three-quarters of the speaking slots at the New York rally and half of its steering committee positions to people of color. If the movement was to represent the breadth of opposition to the war, many felt, and not be overwhelmingly white like the global justice movement, it couldn't opt for the kind of confrontation that would make significant numbers of people, especially people of color, feel unsafe participating.

This approach clearly helped UFPJ amass huge numbers of people in the streets. President Bush, however, simply brushed off the massive and unprecedented outpouring of antiwar sentiment. When asked what he thought about the largest-ever demonstrations in world history, Bush replied, "Size of protest—it's like deciding, well, I'm going to decide policy based upon a focus group." Would Bush have held off on attacking Iraq if, instead of millions assembling peacefully in the streets, there had been a smaller number—say, tens of thousands—marching in defiance of the protest restrictions? Almost certainly not. But might the Bush administration have felt that it had less of a free hand to conduct a war based on brazen lies if the protests had been more confrontational? The question is as unanswerable as it is intriguing. The political temper of the time was too subdued for there to have been anything like a replay of Mayday 1971; there simply wasn't broad support for a disruption of that character and scale. But the experience of February 15 inevitably threw into question the premise behind the mass-mobilizing model: that the best way to have a large political impact was to mobilize the largest number of people. Numbers alone didn't necessarily mean anything.[32]

The day after the US government launched its invasion of Iraq, hundreds of thousands of people marched in anger and sadness through the streets of New York City in a permitted UPFJ event. Preventing the war had perhaps been a quixotic undertaking all along, but there was something uniquely dispiriting about having organized the largest display of popular dissent in world history only to have it ignored. Alongside UFPJ's mass-mobilizing work, there were a few attempts at more disruptive action, which the coalition supported but didn't throw its full weight behind: in San Francisco, the group Direct Action to Stop the War blockaded streets throughout the financial district; in New York, hundreds shut down Fifth Avenue with a die-in. The climate for this style of disruptive protest was decidedly uncongenial, however. When demonstrators tried to hold an April 2003 direct action against the Carlyle Group, a war profiteer, the NYPD simply swept everyone off the sidewalk in preemptive mass arrests, in a sign of the ever-more-repressive policing tactics being used to shut down unruly dissent.[33]

Between the post-9/11 mood shift and the clampdown on public protest, a chill descended over grassroots activism. UFPJ teamed up with what remained of the grassroots global justice movement to protest against the Free Trade Area of the Americas summit in Miami in late 2003. The authorities responded to the modest mobilization with a vast and ominous show of force, banning most public gatherings and using everything from surveillance to pre-emptive arrests to stymie the organizing. As the ACLU described it afterwards, "Police officers from more than three dozen law enforcement agencies converged on downtown Miami to create an almost surreal backdrop that included armored vehicles on the ground and helicopters dotting the skyline above. The police marched in lines wearing full riot gear and wielding batons, tear gas, pepper spray and beanbag rifles to control the crowds of demonstrators."[34]

Huge protests, the largest of which were coordinated by UFPJ, greeted President Bush and the Republicans when they held their 2004 party convention in New York City the following summer. But after a time in the 1990s when grassroots activists could feel that some momentum was on their side, and that direct action was serving as a powerful mechanism to win concrete victories, it was back to that dismal 1980s feeling again, the sense that sometimes you protest just to register a public objection to policies you have no hope of changing.

Hope was, of course, what Barack Obama promised the nation when he ran for president in 2008. His charisma, his upbeat message, and the prospect of electing the country's first black president energized and activated huge numbers of people—especially young people, and especially young people of color. Obama's campaign operation mobilized volunteers on a previously unseen scale, providing thousands of Millennials with their first experience of direct political engagement. Even before his election, though, the global economy was beginning to tumble into what would become the worst recession since the Great Depression, triggered by the collapse of the subprime mortgage industry after years of reckless lending. In this 2007–09 period of crisis, millions of people lost their homes to foreclosure, and millions more lost their jobs in the economic downturn, while banks received billions in taxpayer-funded bailouts. When the heightened expectations of a generation inspired by the notion of "change we can believe in" collided with the bitter realities of an economy grossly skewed to favor the very wealthiest, the disillusionment and sense of outrage sparked a broad new movement with the most sweeping critique of the existing economic order since the sixties.

Declaring themselves the representatives of the 99 percent— that is, of the vast majority of the country's population, arrayed against the power of the wealthiest 1 percent—a small and intrepid group of activists converged on Wall Street in September 2011 and, finding the immediate vicinity of the New York Stock Exchange blocked off by police, proceeded to create a protest encampment in nearby Zuccotti Park. A declaration issued by the occupiers' governing body, an open-to-all general assembly that made its decisions by consensus, explained the rationale for the encampment, "No true democracy is attainable when the process is determined by economic power. We come to you at a time when corporations, which place profit over people, self-interest over justice, and oppression over equality, run our governments." Activists had tried to take on Wall Street through direct action without much success many times before, but somehow this bold and improbable intervention captured the imagination of thousands. Large crowds converged at Zuccotti and transformed it into a bustling hub for political debate and action they called Occupy Wall Street (OWS), while people in dozens of locations across the United States were inspired to establish Occupy encampments of their own over the ensuing weeks.[35]

While all of the encampments foregrounded issues of debt, economic inequality, and corporate rule, the Occupy movement as a whole famously declined to spell out concrete demands or goals. Its signature political move was what two participants, Amy Schrager Lang and Daniel Lang/Levitsky, called "dreaming in public": sparking sustained debate about what a radically transformed, egalitarian society might look like. As activist Marina Sitrin, one of the many veterans of the global justice movement who became deeply involved in Occupy, put it, "Most of us believe that what is most important is to open space for conversations—for democracy —real, direct, and participatory democracy." Although roving protest actions launched from the encampments might target specific banks and financial institutions, Occupy was less interested in trying to wrest concrete concessions from powerful opponents than in reimagining the larger economic and political order.[36]

The operation of the encampments provided one important laboratory for this undertaking, for in classic prefigurative fashion, they were organized with the hope that they might serve as models for self-managed societies run through directly democratic means. Managing a sustained encampment this way, however, proved to be a more challenging endeavor than, say, organizing a one-day summit blockade using consensus process and representative spokescouncils, as direct-action movements of the past had done. OWS made the task harder still by opting for a general assembly structure in which any person could walk up and fully participate in the encampment's decisions, and by having that assembly make decisions about budgetary and logistical matters which other direct-action movements, like the one that targeted the WTO in Seattle, had delegated to a planning collective. With amplified sound prohibited without a permit in New York City, the Occupiers used what they called the "People's Mic" to broadcast their messages—those standing closest to the speaker in a crowd would repeat his or her words one line at a time, in an effective but time-consuming mechanism—and relied heavily on hand signals to communicate everything from agreement to objections to how the consensus process was unfolding. On the occasions when it all worked smoothly, it was exhilarating: "I felt close to tears a few times," wrote activist Adrienne Maree Brown, "seeing unexpected diversity in the crowd, seeing the self-organized systems emerging for creation of art, sharing of information, health and wellness."[37]

Over time, though, major problems plagued the encampments, as indeed had often been the case at similar activist encampments in the past, such as the troubled anti-apartheid occupation at UC Berkeley in 1985. There were numerous reports of sexual harassment and even assault; a noisy drum circle made neighbors edgy and sleeping difficult. The police did their part to make the encampment unmanageable by steering large numbers of homeless people there; the Occupiers welcomed them, but some had serious mental health or substance abuse problems that couldn't be readily addressed. Meanwhile, the consensus process was proving spectacularly unworkable in such a wide-open setting. It had always been a weakness of the prefigurative model that it rested on a vision of the world in which people were obliged to spend a great deal of time and energy in meetings. The proceedings of the general assembly stretched on for hours, often without resolving the issues at hand; increasingly, unaccountable informal leaders made pressing decisions behind the scenes and outside of the formal process. The large sums of money that had flowed into Occupy's coffers early in the

AGREE   UNSURE   DISAGREE   BLOCK

POINT OF PROCESS   POINT OF INFORMATION   I HAVE A QUESTION   WRAP IT UP

Reaching consensus at Occupy Wall Street (design: Adam Koford; Creative Commons license)

movement—OWS had nearly $400,000 in the bank as of its one-month anniversary—only made the process more fraught.[38]

And encampments weren't just hard to sustain, they were easy to evict, with sanitation, public health, and safety providing ready rationales. After mayors from nearly forty cities conferred by conference call, a nationwide wave of police actions shut down encampments all across the country. The New York encampment was raided and destroyed in mid-November, not quite two months after its inception; all told, some 7,000 Occupiers from 122 different encampments were arrested that fall. Creating a sustained physical space for dreaming in public was, it transpired, both beyond the movement's capacity for self-governance and well beyond anything local and federal authorities would tolerate.[39]

But in opening up something less tangible—that is, political space—Occupy was extraordinarily successful. Occupy created a new sense of political possibility after the long dismal years of retrenchment post-9/11, and veterans of the encampments fanned out across the country to launch or support an extraordinarily diverse range of activist initiatives, most of which had the kind of concrete-ness and pragmatism that Occupy itself pointedly spurned. In cities throughout the country, Occupy Our Homes took over abandoned and foreclosed properties, both to provide housing for needy families and to shed a spotlight on abusive lending practices. Through its Rolling Jubilee project, an Occupy offshoot called Strike Debt bought up medical debt for pennies on the dollar and abolished it, powerfully highlighting the arbitrariness of financial obligations; it also organized a debtors' strike of students defrauded by for-profit colleges. When Hurricane Sandy ravaged the New York metropolitan region and emergency personnel were slow to respond, Occupy Sandy drew on the experiences of Zuccotti to organize a highly efficient and multifaceted relief and cleanup effort.

In many ways, Occupy was reminiscent of the Women's Pentagon Actions that took place thirty years before: the same unbounded visionary quality that arguably circumscribed its immediate real-world impact proved remarkably generative and influential for subsequent activist projects. Dreaming in public, it seemed, could be an inspiring prelude to later work for concrete change. Many of these post-Occupy undertakings were solidly multiracial collaborations, with veterans of Occupy providing a direct-action edge to the organizing. And nationwide, Occupy also reinvigorated key aspects of the direct-action movement's infrastructure that had atrophied since the heyday of global justice organizing, such as street medic collectives and legal support.

Occupy had benefited, too, from the real if modest improvements in cross-racial political organizing that had taken place after Seattle, including within the antiwar movement, and this character shaped its subsequent influence. Veterans of the 1999 WTO showdown played important roles in Occupy, but so too did veterans of SLAM!, the 2000 Philly RNC mobilization, and other multiracial direct-action projects. Of course there were conflicts around race in the encampments, but there was much wider participation by people of color than in any of the global justice mobilizations. That meant, among other things, that race-based concerns were addressed sooner than they had been an activist generation before. The original draft of OWS's founding document, for instance, had a sentence invoking the ostensible unity of the 99 percent, that referred to the Occupiers as "one people, formerly divided by the color of our skin, gender, sexual orientation, religion, or lack thereof." Several activists of color objected to this post-racial language, arguing that the deep realities of race couldn't be wished away by rhetorical fiat, and used the blocking mechanism provided for by the consensus process to force further discussion. "And so, there in that circle, on that street corner, we did a crash course on white privilege, structural racism, and oppression," recalled activist Manissa Maharawal. The group agreed to remove the line, "and when we walked away," Maharawal wrote, "I felt like something important had just happened, that we had just pushed the movement a little bit closer to the movement I would like to see, one that takes into account historical and current inequalities, oppressions, racisms, [and] relations of power."[40]

Among the many organizing endeavors partly influenced by the example and experience of Occupy was one catalyzed by the cold-blooded murder in February 2012 of black Florida teenager

Trayvon Martin. Martin was walking back to a family friend's house from a convenience store, carrying a bag of candy and wearing a hooded sweatshirt, when George Zimmerman—a self-appointed neighborhood watch captain—confronted him and shot him dead, claiming self-defense under the state's "stand your ground" law. Martin was only seventeen years old, a high school junior who had done nothing more dramatic than run an ordinary errand, and he was killed simply because Zimmerman saw his blackness as a threat. Martin's murder underscored that the election of a black president four years earlier had done little to protect black Americans from racially motivated violence, whether at the hands of vigilantes like Zimmerman or, more typically, the police, and coverage of the case at one point eclipsed that of the presidential election campaigns then underway. Some sizable protests followed the murder, including a defiant Million Hoodies March in New York City that attracted an estimated 5,000 participants.[41]

But it was when a Florida jury acquitted Zimmerman on all charges in July 2013 that the level of outrage became politically transformative, sparking an intensive new wave of black-led activism. Most notably, the verdict spurred the creation of the social media hashtag #BlackLivesMatter, which would first provide the focal point for an urgent online conversation about the state of black America and ultimately grow into a grassroots national movement. Alicia Garza, one of the creators of the phrase and the Black Lives Matter organization, recalled, "When [Zimmerman] was acquitted, it felt like a gut punch. And I remember sitting with friends and talking and there was nothing to say, but we just wanted to be around each other." She continued, "I was basically sending love notes to black people and saying, we're enough. We are enough, and we don't deserve to die, and we don't deserve to be shot down in the streets like dogs because somebody else is fucking scared of us. And our presence is important and we matter. Our lives matter, black lives matter." Garza's friend and collaborator Patrisse Cullors immediately saw the political potential of the three-word phrase and famously put a hashtag in front of it. Even then, at its inception, Black Lives Matter was more than a solely online intervention. Garza, Cullors, and their colleague Opal Tometi were all organizers by disposition and experience. As Garza tells it, Tometi quickly saw ways to build on the hashtag: "We should create space for our folks to be able to tell our stories, share grief, share rage, collaborate together," she recalls Tometi saying. "People are in motion right now, and we have a real contribution to offer." Tometi created a Facebook page, a Tumblr, and other online infrastructure for the project, and the team behind #BlackLivesMatter soon began organizing a series of conference calls to extend the project's impact beyond education and consciousness-raising, developing strategies, in Garza's words for "how we also catalyze that work onto the streets."[42]

In Florida, a group of activists who called themselves the Dream Defenders were already in motion; two months after Martin's murder, they had organized a three-day march to the Florida municipality where he was killed, culminating in a sit-in at the local police station to demand accountability. Then, four days after Zimmerman was acquitted, the Dream Defenders converged on the Florida Capitol to launch an occupation. "We thought of the tactic before we even thought of what we were going to demand," remembered organizer Umi Selah, then known as Phillip Agnew. "We were going on the fly a lot during that time. But we knew we had to go to a seat of power and confront a person or body of people that could give us what we needed." The demonstrators remained for a full month, drawing on the experience of Occupy to manage the logistics of their statehouse encampment. Though they ended their occupation without achieving the goal they had settled upon—passage of a legislative package that would repeal "Stand Your Ground" and implement related reforms—their choice of direct-action tactics reflected a growing impatience and determination in black activist circles.[43]

It was not activists, however, but ordinary people pushed beyond all endurance who elevated the intensifying fight for black lives to a level not seen in a generation. When white police officer Darren Wilson shot and killed unarmed black teenager Michael Brown in the town of Ferguson, Missouri on August 9, 2014, and local police then left his body lying in the neighborhood's main thoroughfare for more than four hours, it was simply too much for local residents to bear. The Ferguson police department had a long history of blatant anti-black bias, which the federal Department of Justice would later detail in a scathing report. The 2015 DOJ report determined that police routinely violated the constitutional rights of the community's black residents, with black people in Ferguson stopped, arrested, convicted, imprisoned, and fined at hugely disproportionate rates, and had a longstanding history of using excessive force in encounters with black residents.[44]

On that August afternoon in 2014, people poured out into the streets of the Canfield Green apartment complex in shock and outrage, joined by Mike Brown's grieving mother, Lezley McSpadden, and his stepfather, Louis Head, who carried a sign reading, "Ferguson Police Just Executed My Unarmed Son." As word of the killing spread on social media, and especially on Twitter, many more joined the stunned crowd on the street, which was stained with the eighteen-year-old's blood. "They stole this baby's future away," tweeted Johnetta Elzie, one of the first observers on the scene, who went on to play a key role in amplifying the protest response on social media and shaping the national conversation about Ferguson over the ensuing months. The *St. Louis Post-Dispatch* immediately termed the crowd's anguished response a "mob reaction," though at that point all people had done was to gather publicly in grief and anger. The police responded by bringing in SWAT teams, armored personnel vehicles, dogs, and tear gas, opting for the kind of militarized response to dissent that had become a hallmark of American policing since the era of the global justice movement—and employing an ominous arsenal of military-grade equipment supplied to local police through a post-9/11 Department of Defense program.[45]

Kayla Reed, then a twenty-four-year-old pharmacy technician who had gone to the same school district as Brown and grew up close to where he was killed, recalled the scene on the streets of Ferguson that first night. "I went to pick up my friend, and we went out there, and [Mike Brown's body] wasn't on the street anymore, but there were still a lot of people. I remember the cops responding so intensely, with dogs and mace. I was in complete disbelief." She continued, "The next day, I wanted to see what was going on, and I came out, and it just became this thing where I felt like I had to be there. I wanted to help in any way I could, whether it was giving out water or face masks or just protesting. I had no skills around how to do any of this, just a desire to want to help, and a feeling of obligation to my people."[46]

Many felt a similar calling; crowds continued to gather in the streets of Ferguson each day, spilling out from the neighborhood where Brown lived onto the major nearby thoroughfare West Florissant Avenue. Maurice Moe Mitchell, a longtime black organizer who came to Ferguson from New York a few days after the killing to lend a hand, recalled, "When I got there, all of West Florissant, all of the adjoining sections were packed with people, with black people: young to old, everyone, all spectrums, transgender, gay, straight, church people, Nation of Islam—everybody was there. It was like the hugest political block party and it was totally decentralized and anarchistic—there was nobody organizing it." The scene on the streets was unlike anything he had encountered in his lifetime. "It was just everywhere, and I was like, I can't believe I'm witnessing this, this is what I dreamed of, this idea that black people could spontaneously organize ourselves across difference and respond to state violence in this type of way with this type of resistance." Kayla Reed recalled the ways that the people out on the streets, many of whom she knew from high school and college, took care of one another. "I remember you would see people stopping by who had to go to work, but they would drop off cases of water, or drop off food," she said. "People brought out their barbecue pits and made sure everybody was eating. It was this real, organic family reunion, it looked like. But when you looked on the opposite side of the street, it was this police line, this militarized police force. So there was this spirit of community, but there was a righteous anger that was brewing in the midst of it."[47]

A pattern quickly developed to the days. Derek Laney, a staff organizer with Missourians Organized for Reform and Empowerment (MORE), a progressive community group with a history of economic and social justice work, remembered, "Every afternoon, evening, and night, people would be in the street, and every night, police would arrest people. They would demand that folks disperse, and people would obviously refuse. They were like, we're angry, we're hurt, we're grieving, you've not only killed one of our children but you treat us with disrespect, because of our sense of outrage about that murder, and we're not going anywhere. So they would stay until they were teargassed, they would stay until riot-gear-clad police officers would chase them down and arrest them." The aggression and violence of the police response only solidified people's commitment to hold the streets as long as they possibly could. Rev. Osagyefo Sekou, a radical theologian and longtime activist who grew up in St. Louis, described the protesters in the streets as "everyday people—queer and woman-led, and poor. They won't bow down. They don't give a fuck, which is their greatest asset and their biggest liability." It was, in Mitchell's words, "an organic, grass-roots uprising of working-class and poor black people, young black people, and a lot of young people who we as a society have completely written off." Though the protesters were overwhelmingly nonviolent, in stark contrast to the police, on occasion the rage spilled over into property destruction, most notably the burning and looting of a QuikTrip gas station that had served as a gathering spot in the first days after Brown's killing.[48]

From the outset, there were some people on the streets and some leaders from the local black community who tried to calm the angriest protesters. Their efforts were mostly rebuffed. "Many African-American civic leaders in St. Louis said they were frustrated by their inability to guide the protesters," reported Julie Bosman in the *New York Times* a week after Brown's killing, in an article head-lined, "Lack of Leadership and a Generational Split Hinder Protests in Ferguson." But the young people in the streets weren't inter-ested in being led or guided, especially by elders of the civil-rights generation—they were taking action and exercising leadership on their own terms. Cherrell Brown, another longtime activist who came to Ferguson shortly after the protests began, recalled, "There were so many young people who weren't waiting on organizations, they were taking to the streets and self-organizing, and it was really beautiful to see." When national figures like Al Sharpton and Jesse Jackson came to Ferguson to show solidarity, many of the protesters were leery of having them play a prominent role. Brown continued, "Young people were saying, we're tired of people coming in and telling us what to do, dictating how this should go, it's our turn." Mitchell recalled witnessing some older people trying to encourage the young protesters to go home. "And they're like, 'Get off the streets, you're going to get hurt,' and the [protesters were] like, 'We're going to get hurt anyhow.' 'You're going to go to jail,' and they're like 'We're going to jail anyhow, so at least we can go to jail on our terms, at least we can go to jail doing something right.' And I was just blown away by that, that level of clarity of political analysis and clarity of purpose," said Mitchell. "I don't think people really give young working-class and poor black kids, especially kids in gangs, or kids who look a certain way and have tattoos on them or who dress a certain way, talk a certain way, that type of credit in terms of the sophistication of their political analysis."[49]

Because the initial uprising in Ferguson didn't have a single leader or organization at the helm, and because social media played such an important role in publicizing the protests and framing their significance for the wider world, few perceived the organizing structures that were quickly—and quietly—put in place to support the protesters in the street and, over time, to help make Ferguson the spark for a nationwide upsurge of organizing for black lives. Riots often burn out in a matter of days, as soon as law enforcement gets the upper hand and enough participants are behind bars. There were many reasons why the uprising in Ferguson was different, evolving into a sustained, ongoing movement in a way that other similar eruptions did not, such as the much larger 1992 riots that broke out in Los Angeles after a mostly white jury acquitted four police officers who had been filmed viciously beating black motorist Rodney King. The single most important factor was the tenacity and persistence of Ferguson's street protesters, who stood up to the militarized police over and over again, despite being teargassed, shot with rubber bullets, chased, beaten, and arrested. But their courage and commitment might not have had the enduring national and international impact that it did without another key factor that was almost unknown outside the movement: the behind-the-scenes support work of seasoned organizers, who decided from the start to do whatever they could to help build this eruption of grief and anger into something with broad political significance.

As Reed put it, "There was this amazing thing that most people on West Florissant didn't know, that these organizations that existed were coming together to create infrastructure to protect the people." The progressive activist community in the St. Louis area in August 2014 was not large, but it began to mobilize a response almost as soon as word began to spread of Mike Brown's killing. Two organizations in particular anchored the effort. The first, and politically most influential, was the Organization for Black Struggle (OBS), an all-black group whose work in the region stretched back to 1980. OBS was formed during the era of activist entrenchment and institution-building, a time when, in the words of the organization's official history, "there was a vacuum of Black radical leadership that could boldly speak and act." Over its thirty-five-year history, OBS had played a role in everything from the 1980s anti-apartheid movement to the work of the Black Radical Congress in the late 1990s to longstanding community efforts to reform policing in the region. Like many black organizations, however, it had limited funding and had no paid staff at the time of Mike Brown's killing (an influx of funding allowed it to hire several people, including Kayla Reed, over the course of the fall of 2014). The second organization, MORE, defined itself as a "direct-action organization challenging corporate power," in the words of its longtime director, Jeff Ordower. Rooted in the Saul Alinsky tradition of community organizing, MORE had played a supportive role in St. Louis's version of Occupy and had recently been active in the Show Me $15 campaign, part of the feisty national drive to raise the minimum wage for fast food and other low-income workers. MORE had a multiracial base and staff but white leadership, which contributed to some tensions that later arose over its involvement.[50]

OBS and MORE were savvy enough not to try to lead, direct, or speak for the protesters. Instead, they looked for ways to support them, and in particular to create the conditions that would allow the uprising to be sustained over time. A core group of organizers began meeting daily almost immediately after Brown's killing, swiftly setting up infrastructure such as a text messaging loop to facilitate rapid communication on the streets and a jail-support operation to provide both bail money and legal representation to those arrested in the protests. Michael McPhearson, the St. Louis–based director of Veterans for Peace who was part of the initial core group and helped build a citywide coordinating body known as the Don't Shoot Coalition, explained how this support work helped bolster and prolong the nightly protests, especially after the governor declared a state of emergency and imposed a curfew. "MORE and OBS decided that they were going to support people trying to hold the street and not make them go home if that's what they wanted to do," he recalled. "The young people were the ones that led the actual street presence in Ferguson—not OBS, not MORE. But they wouldn't have been able to maintain it, because a lot of them would have been in jail." The numbers in the street in Ferguson, after all, weren't huge—keeping a few dozen key players behind bars might have been all that the authorities needed to break the momentum.[51]

Over those first days and weeks, with protesters out in the streets night after night, support flowed into Ferguson from many different sources, often coordinated by the core organizing group. As McPhearson explained, "We were able to gather resources that people in the street didn't have access to, or time to gather." A collective of activist street medics from Chicago came to help protesters deal with the tear gas, rubber bullets, and trauma. Experienced activist lawyers helped set up an operation to provide legal services to those arrested in the protests. A church within walking distance volunteered to serve as a safe space and organizing hub. Ordinary people and local service organizations provided free food and water for the folks in the street. People from all around the country donated large sums to the bail fund. One small stream within this larger river of support came from the historically white direct-action world, from the organizing tradition that stretched back through Occupy to the global justice movement, all the way back to Mayday 1971. The white direct-action activist contribution was modest and circumscribed, never part of the strategic core of organizing in Ferguson—the key organizers were very clear that this was a movement for black self-determination, not a wide-open political space to be flooded and overwhelmed by well-meaning white people. But the moment was strikingly reminiscent of another instance of cross-racial solidarity that had taken place nearly thirty-five years before at Mayday 1971, when veterans of the black civil rights movement organized their caravan to bring food and other supplies to the thousands of mostly white protesters who had been arrested after trying to shut down the federal government in protest of the Vietnam War. Then, as in Ferguson, the gestures of support had a political resonance beyond the concrete assistance being offered, highlighting the longer, deeper influences that carried over from one movement to the next. It was a moment of connection that seemed also to mark a pivot point, a time when the energy behind direct-action organizing was propelling American radicalism in a new direction.

For, after the initial eruption in Ferguson began, direct-action organizing would be embraced in black activist circles with a boldness and innovation not seen since the heyday of the civil rights movement, spurring a nationwide outbreak of disruptive protest that focused the country's attention on the issues of state violence and anti-black racism. The forms that direct action took within the burgeoning movement for black lives were varied and drew heavily not just on longstanding traditions of black organizing and struggle, going back to the civil rights days, but also on what now were two decades of sustained experience with direct-action organizing around police, prison, and other issues in communities of color. By 2014, practices like affinity groups, decentralized coordinating structures, and lockdown blockades had long been employed and recontextualized by black and brown organizers in a variety of movements. "Things have come full circle," remarked Terry Marshall—an activist with SLAM! in the 1990s, a participant in the people of color delegation that attended the WTO protests in Seattle in 1999, and an organizer with Occupy Wall Street in 2011—after spending time in Ferguson. "There's a whole new generation of young black people who are upholding direct action." Most recently, Occupy had played a modest role in helping catalyze the wave of new black activism, and some of its specific organizing practices, such as mic checks and hand signals, carried over. But the new movement departed from Occupy in striking ways. As Mitchell explained it, "We had two big differences from Occupy: We're not a leaderless movement. We're not leaderless, we're leaderful. And we have demands—lots of demands, very specific demands, 400 years of demands." (Indeed, two years after Mike Brown's killing, the Movement for Black Lives, a coalition of more than 50 groups including Black Lives Matter, released "A Vision for Black Lives," an ambitious and comprehensive platform filled with both broad visions for change and highly detailed policy proposals.)[52]

A host of new local black-led groups quickly formed out of the Ferguson protests, including Millennial Activists United, Lost Voices, Tribe X, and the Black Souljaz. As Rev. Sekou explained, "All these new formations just popped up, because there was no infrastructure as a container for young rage that had a radical edge." These groups carried forward the composition and political character of predecessors like SLAM! and Third Eye: they tended to be women- and queer-led, with intersectional feminist politics. These groups not only held down the street protests but greatly amplified their message through skillful use of social media, both as mobilizing tool and a way to frame public discussion. As had been the case in so many movements of different kinds over the previous four decades, the central place of women, especially queer women, in this work profoundly shaped its character. "From the beginning, women have been the ones leading the work and really holding down every piece of the movement—the people on the streets, the people who were getting arrested, the people behind the scenes providing support, organizing locally and nationally," recalled Julia Ho, a young organizer who joined the staff of MORE two months before Michael Brown's killing. "Women were carrying the work of all of that, every single aspect of that. And a significant number of queer women, and queer people and trans people, were always there from the beginning." She continued, "I think that absolutely changed the narrative about what the movement was about, that it wasn't just about police and police brutality but it was about state violence across many different identities and many different experiences."[53]

At the same time that organizers in the St. Louis area were working to sustain the energy of the initial uprising, there were large numbers of organizers, activists, and ordinary people from all over the country who wanted to come to Ferguson, to bear witness to the events unfolding there and show support. This dynamic created its own set of challenges. Initially, the word from some key local organizers was that outsiders shouldn't come. But the Black Lives Matter network put out a call for people to converge in Ferguson on Labor Day weekend and more than 500 responded. Lead organizers Darnell Moore and Patrisse Cullors called the initiative a Freedom Ride, invoking "the spirit of the early 1960s interstate Freedom Rides in the racially segregated south," even as they gave it a twenty-first-century spin, both by framing it as a black-focused rather than an interracial mobilization and by giving it an explicitly intersectional character. As Moore explained to *ColorLines* journalist Akiba Solomon, "It has historically been the case that racial justice has been only thought to be the work of black men … Our history has conveniently invisibilized black women and queer and trans people. But if the mantra of this trip is 'black life matters,' it's important to us to emphasize that *all* black lives matter. This is an opportunity to expand a racial justice framework in an equitable way that includes all of us." This framing placed the growing movement squarely in the tradition that stretched back to the work of the Combahee River Collective in the 1970s. As Combahee co-founder Barbara Smith observed in 2016, "It's exactly what we said in Combahee, that if black women were free, everyone else would have to be." She continued, "I believe this is the first time that there has ever been a movement in the United States that wasn't specifically about sexuality and gender oppression but said, by the way, the people we see as key in doing this organizing are women and queer and trans. It's such a vindication for what we were asserting back in the Seventies and thereafter."[54]

The organizing process, it must be said, was bumpy. As Alicia Garza recalled, "When we got there, there was a real tension because people had been flooding to Ferguson for a couple of weeks by then. Jamala Rogers from the Organization for Black Struggle said it's like disaster tourism in the movement. People want to come see and get tear-gassed and be a part of the action, and it's like, 'This shit is happening in your community, and you don't need to come here to see it, you can fight right where you are and really

help grow this,' right?" But there's no substitute for firsthand experience, and for all the ways that the influx of people from around
the country put strains on an already overburdened community
of local organizers, going to Ferguson proved transformative for
many participants. As journalist Kristin Braswell wrote afterwards,
"Speaking to the residents of Ferguson, I know now what kind of
pain seeps through its streets. The evening news cannot frame this
type of visceral experience; only the people on the ground, living
these tales firsthand can. The people of Ferguson are hurt, enraged,
and true seekers of justice." After a weekend filled with everything
from protests and meetings to a community barbeque and church
service, the Freedom Riders each committed to take at least three
actions in their hometowns to build the movement for black lives.[55]

The overall success of the Black Lives Matter Freedom Ride,
in Mitchell's words, "opened people to the idea that people from
the outside could come if they're grounded in good values and do
good work, and so folks were like, okay, let's have a mobilization."
Organizers began planning for a direct-action-focused four-day
convening, to be called Ferguson October, designed less to rally supporters to Ferguson, though it obviously did that, than to boost and
strengthen the movement nationally by providing inspiration, training, and action experience. "We are in a movement moment," read
the call to action on the mobilization website, inviting people from
around the country to join in a "weekend of resistance ... to build
momentum for a nationwide movement against police violence."
Thousands responded to the call and converged on St. Louis, many
mobilized through the organizational networks that racial justice
and policing activists had been building for years, others reached
through the potent means of social media. In historian Donna
Murch's powerful description, "In the name of Michael Brown, a
beautiful black storm against state violence is brewing so dense it
has created a gravity of its own, drawing in people from all over
the US."[56]

As Mitchell described it, "The whole point of Ferguson
October was as an organizing opportunity, period, end of story."
The structure of the weekend was predicated on an acknowledge-
ment that the growing movement was, and would continue to be,

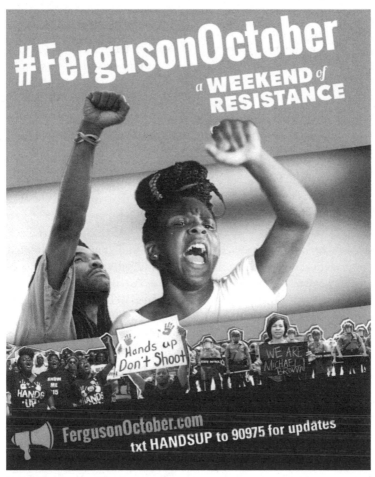

Mobilizing postcard for Ferguson October
(designer: Angus Maguire; author's collection)

emphatically decentralized. Though many people, both then and afterwards, would call it the Black Lives Matter movement because of the wide resonance of the phrase and the hashtag, in fact the BLM network—and the chapter-based organization it soon evolved into—were only one part of a complex and sprawling ecosystem, with plenty of tensions and political disagreements behind the scenes. Ferguson October was designed not as a single unitary mobilization but a container that could hold and support the full array of groups and tendencies; dozens of events and actions took place over the weekend. Most of the direct actions were organized in secrecy to preserve an element of surprise and only announced through text-messaging once they began. Groups of protesters blockaded streets, disrupted shopping at an upscale mall, interrupted a Rams football game with a big banner drop, engaged in civil disobedience outside the Ferguson police headquarters, flooded City Hall, and walked out from classes at St. Louis Community College. Mitchell recalled, "A very, very broad spectrum of entities participated during that moment. Organizations that would never ever work with each other ... used Ferguson October as a vehicle to extend their organizing." He continued, "It was decentralized enough for everybody to make use of it and it was coordinated enough for there to be coherence to it." Indeed, it was so decentralized that some key actions that weekend, like an occupation of St. Louis University that lasted for several days, were organized autonomously by activists critical of the larger convening. A number of the protesters who had sustained the street actions in Ferguson felt that the national movement was being built on their local work and sacrifice, while they were being left behind. "There's a reason why you don't see a Black Lives Matter chapter in St. Louis," commented organizer Julia Ho. "There was a general attitude of distrust around the money, the fame, people's perception of who is profiting off of movements, a feeling of folks being exploited by a national movement."[57]

Ferguson October did not attract anywhere near the level of media attention that the original uprising in August did, but that wasn't its central goal; movement-building was. One outgrowth of the weekend's work was the creation of a new direct-action training collective BlackOUT by a circle of black activists whose firsthand organizing experiences included everything from SLAM! to the Seattle WTO mobilization to work with Greenpeace and Occupy. As collective member Celeste Faison, a Bay Area organizer whose background included a stint as outreach director of the Ruckus Society, recalled, "When we got to Ferguson most of the training team were white allies. We noticed that there was a shortage of black direct-action trainers. We looked at each other and said we need to develop some more folks to train our people and coordinate actions." Meanwhile, the organizers of Ferguson October used the contacts and infrastructure from the weekend convening to build a new coordinating structure, Ferguson Action.[58]

When a grand jury decided in late November 2014 not to indict Darren Wilson, the police officer who had killed Michael Brown, Ferguson Action, Black Lives Matter, the Dream Defenders, and other national networks had already been coordinating plans for weeks via regular conference calls. In Ferguson itself, heartbroken residents took to the streets and some in the crowd burned down a dozen businesses. But everywhere else, the protests were marked by disruption, not destruction. In St. Louis, protesters blocked Interstate 44. In Chicago, they shut down Lake Shore Drive. In Los Angeles, they blockaded Interstate 10. In New York City, they shut down the Manhattan, Brooklyn, and Triboro Bridges. In just the first forty-eight hours after the verdict, protests took place in at least 170 cities all across the country. Their character—and the character of the broad and ever-more-organized movement that was growing and taking shape around them—reflected a powerful melding of many strains of radical activism from the previous forty years. The new movement was black-led, with broad multiracial support; decentralized in its structure, and importantly spearheaded by women and queer organizers; shaped by intersectionality, driven by disruptive protest, and at once visionary and pragmatic. Inside the protests, it was far too soon to tell whether they were just a venting of anger that would have no lasting effect or the first step toward achieving real change. The electricity, though, was palpable: as organizers had hoped, direct action had indeed sparked a major new chapter in the history of American radicalism. And the distinctive approaches to organizing and resistance that radical activists had created over four challenging decades of political reinvention would shape their responses to the crises ahead.

Acknowledgments

I've worked on this project for so very long that I'll never be able to thank all the people who helped me along the way. Quite a few have passed away, for it's been 25 years since I first began formulating my answer to the question that opens this book. The vagaries of memory guarantee there will be others whose names and assistance I don't now recall. And this book was importantly shaped by the periods when I wasn't working on it—by the years in which my focus was on organizing, rather than writing about organizing, and by an extended hiatus when my attention and energies were elsewhere altogether—and thus by collaborations and conversations that are difficult to credit.

I experienced a good deal of the history recounted here first-hand; I've been an activist, and immersed in multiple worlds of American radicalism, since 1980. I was in the crowd at the big anti-apartheid rally at Columbia University in 1986, and I attended the 1988 National Student Convention. I participated in some of ACT UP/NY's earliest protests, went to the first Dyke Marches, spent time at some of Earth First!'s backwoods encampments. In many cases, my role went well beyond observing or reporting. My first protest arrest was in 1992, and I've planned or taken part in more direct actions than I can count. I was in the thick of a number of events described in the book—for instance, I was a tactical coordinator and street tactics trainer at the April 16, 2000 direct action against the World Bank and International Monetary Fund. And I was centrally involved in the antiwar protests of 2003 and 2004 as the staff mobilizing coordinator for United for Peace and Justice. I learned from many brilliant, dedicated organizers through the course of these experiences, and those lessons profoundly influenced this book.

Research for this project was not only conducted in the streets, of course. I'm grateful to the staffs of numerous archives and research institutions for assistance, including the Lesbian Herstory Archives, the New York Public Library, the San Francisco Public Library, the State Historical Society of Wisconsin, and the Swarthmore College Peace Collection. Many activists opened their personal archives to me as well; I'm especially grateful to Lisa Fithian and David Solnit for allowing me full access to their extensive files, as well as for taking time on many occasions to help fill gaps in my knowledge. Over the decades, I interviewed hundreds of activists for this project; the earliest interview quoted here dates from 1990. I learned from every conversation, including the many interviews that I didn't end up quoting, and I'm very grateful to everyone who made time to speak with me.

A special tip of the hat to Mike Davis, one of the first champions of this project; I will always regret that I turned down Verso's offer to acquire the book in 1991. Steve Duncombe merits particular mention and huge thanks for having supported this endeavor from the initial idea all the way through to final manuscript edits. My perspective on social movements and the left was deeply influenced by my colleagues at *Socialist Review*, who cheered on the earliest version of the book, and especially by Marcy Darnovsky, Barbara Epstein, Jeffrey Escoffier, Michael Rosenthal, Pam Rosenthal, Francine Winddance Twine, and Ara Wilson.

Many other people encouraged and assisted me when I returned to the project in the late 1990s, including Andrew Boyd, Leslie Cagan, Eileen Clancy, David Crane, Ron Hayduk, Erin Kelly, Mark Leger, Elizabeth Meister, Kelly Moore, and Benjamin Heim Shepard. Big thanks to Ron Kuby for legal assistance when it mattered most. I wrote significant sections of that version of the manuscript at Blue Mountain Center, whose support I gratefully acknowledge; it was also there where I later made the difficult decision in fall 2002 to set the book aside to organize against the Iraq War. Harriet Barlow responded in the best possible way, by offering BMC's facilities and support to that work.

Twelve years later, I dug my dusty manuscript out of the closet and decided to rework it and bring it up to date. Many of the book's longtime supporters provided crucial help, and several important circles of friends and associates encouraged and assisted me along the way. Huge thanks to Josh Glenn, of course, with special gratitude to Melissa Gira Grant, Richard Nash, Lynn Peril, Astra Taylor, Deborah Wassertzug, Jessamyn West, and Judith Zissman. Others whose support and assistance helped me reach the finish line include Terry Dame, Lisa Guido, Elissa Jiji, Brooke Lehman, Laurie McIntosh, Gerry Gomez Pearlberg, Lex Pelger, Joanne Rendell, Marina Sitrin, Lenora Todaro, and Lesley Wood.

Thanks to Andrew Hsiao for bringing the book back to Verso, shepherding it through the editorial process, and improving it with his comments and feedback. I'm grateful to the whole team at Verso for their work on the book, especially Anne Rumberger, Wes House, and Duncan Ranslem. Thanks to Adrienne Crew and the Author's Guild for contract advice, Keith Dodds for the cover design, Kenya (Robinson) and Jacob Covey for preparing the illustrations for reproduction, Angelica Sgouros for copyedits, Michael Goldstein and Judy Rosen for proofreading, and Mandy Keifitz for the index.

My biggest thanks are to my mom, Jean Kauffman, who does not share my politics or approve of my methods, but who has supported me every single step of the way. And big love and gratitude to N. and D., sources of endless delight and inspiration.

Notes

I   MAYDAY

1. Haldeman is quoted in Tom Wells, *The War Within: America's Battle Over Vietnam* (New York: Henry Holt and Company, 1994), p. 484; *Mayday Tactical Manual*, 1971, author's collection, p. 3. This chapter draws extensively from a previously published essay: L.A. Kauffman, "Ending a War, Inventing a Movement: Mayday 1971," *Radical Society* (December 2002).
2. Mark Goff, "Washington, DC—Spring 1971," *The Bugle-American* (May 13–19, 1971).
3. Richard Halloran, "The Mayday Tribe vs. the US Government," *New York Times* (May 9, 1971); Mary McGrory is quoted in Noam Chomsky, "Mayday: The Case for Civil Disobedience," *New York Review of Books* (June 17, 1971); Carl Bernstein, "Rennie Davis: Make Clear ... We Failed," *Washington Post* (May 4, 1971).
4. Rehnquist is quoted in an American Civil Liberties Union report, *Mayday 1971: Order Without Law* (July 1972), p. 14; Von Hoffman is quoted in Chomksy, "Mayday: The Case for Civil Disobedience." The Nixon quotation comes from "The Biggest Bust: Washington Prevails over the Protesters—At a Price," *Newsweek* (May 17, 1971). Magruder and Helms are quoted in Tom Wells, *The War Within: America's Battle Over Vietnam* (New York: Henry Holt and Company, 1994), p. 512. See George W. Hopkins, "'May Day' 1971: Civil Disobedience and the Vietnam Antiwar Movement," in Melvin Small and William D. Hoover, eds., *Give Peace a*

   Chance: Exploring the Vietnam Antiwar Movement (Syracuse, NY: Syracuse University Press, 1992), pp. 71–88.

5. Clark Kerr, quoted in Kirkpatrick Sale, *SDS* (New York: Vintage Books, 1973), p. 636.

6. Undated Mayday Tribe publication, *May Flowers*, author's collection; David Dellinger, "Why Go to Washington?" *Spring Movement* (April 8, 1971). This broadsheet is from the private collection of Ed Hedemann, who graciously shared this and other Mayday materials with me.

7. Fred Halstead, *Out Now!: A Participant's Account of the American Movement Against the Vietnam War* (New York: Monad Press, 1978). For a retrospective look at NPAC's approach by a political sympathizer, see Carole Seligman, "Lessons of a Winning Antiwar Movement," *Socialist Action* (June 1999).

8. Doug Jenness, "The May Day Tribe: Where It Goes Wrong," *The Militant* (May 14, 1971).

9. This undated broadsheet is also from the Hedemann collection. For PCPJ's perspective on the dispute, see David McReynolds, "Guerrilla War in the Movement," *WIN* (March 15, 1971).

10. Interview with Jerry Coffin, Troy, NY, February 8, 2000.

11. Brian Purnell, *Fighting Jim Crow in the County of Queens: The Congress of Racial Equality in Brooklyn* (Lexington: The University Press of Kentucky, 2013), pp. 249–78; Johnson is quoted in Joseph Tirella, "'A Gun to the Heart of the City,'" *Slate* (April 22, 2014), slate.com; Robert Alden, "CORE Maps Tie-Up on Roads to Fair," *New York Times* (April 10, 1964); Joseph Lelyveld, "CORE Suspends Chapter for Urging Tie-Up at Fair," *New York Times* (April 11, 1964); Joseph Lelyveld, "CORE Split Grows over Plan to Jam Traffic at Fair," *New York Times* (April 12, 1964); Fred Powledge, "CORE Groups Split on Protest Plans," *New York Times* (April 18, 1964); and Homer Bigart, "Fair Opens, Rights Stall-in Fails; Protesters Drown Out Johnson; 300 Arrested in Demonstrations," *New York Times* (April 23, 1964).

12. Hal Straus, "The War of Numbers vs. the War in the Streets," *Berkeley Barb* (May 7–13, 1971); Mayday Tribe, "Getting it Together," undated leaflet, Hedemann collection; "April 24th Anti-War Rally: 250,000 People Come to DC So What?" *Quicksilver Times* (April 30–May 13, 1971). The question of movement marshals was particularly contentious at that time, because of what had happened during the national demonstration that was hastily organized in May 1970 to respond to the Cambodia invasion. The planning was marred by bitter fighting between the factions that would eventually become NPAC and PCPJ—the Trotskyists and the pacifists—over whether there would be civil disobedience at this protest. Perhaps as many as 20,000 of the protesters were willing to risk arrest, including some members of Congress. But the Socialist Workers Party had supplied most

of the marshals, who infuriated the direct-action camp by maneuvering on the ground to prevent civil disobedience from happening.

13. *Mayday Tactical Manual*, p. 3; Gandhi is quoted in Harris Wofford, Jr., "Non-Violence and the Law: The Law Needs Help," in Hugo Adam Bedau, ed., *Civil Disobedience: Theory and Practice* (New York: Pegasus, 1969).

14. Coffin interview; telephone interview with S.J. Avery, November 5, 2000.

15. Maris Cakars, "Meaning of Mayday," *WIN* (June 1971); *Mayday Tactical Manual*, p. 4; "Mayday! Washington," undated leaflet, Hedemann collection; also see Robin Reisig, "Gandhi with a Raised Fist," *The Village Voice* (May 13, 1971).

16. *Mayday Tactical Manual*, p. 3.

17. "In this Issue," *Liberation* (February 1972); interview with Ed Hedemann, New York, NY, November 10, 1999. On the larger debates over organizational structures and decision-making methods in the civil rights movement, the New Left, and the women's liberation movement, see Francesca Polletta's essential study *Freedom Is An Endless Meeting: Democracy in American Social Movements* (Chicago and London: University of Chicago Press, 2002).

18. *Anti-Mass: Methods of Organization for Collectives* (Columbus OH: Amok & Peace Press, n.d.). As one example of its dissemination in this period, see the lengthy excerpts in the July 30–August 13, 1971 issue of *Quicksilver Times*, a DC-based underground newspaper that wholeheartedly supported the Mayday actions.

19. Stokely Carmichael and Charles V. Hamilton, *Black Power: The Politics of Liberation in America* (New York: Random House, 1967), p. 37. As samples of the rhetoric and activism of the other "power" and "liberation" movements, see the following: On the Puerto Rican Power movement: Frank Browning, "From Rumble to Revolution: The Young Lords," *Ramparts* (October 1970), and The Young Lords Party and Michael Abramson, *Palante: Young Lords Party* (New York: McGraw-Hill Book Company, 1971). On the Chicano Power movement: Carlos Muñoz, *Youth, Identity, Power: The Chicano Movement* (London and New York: Verso, 1989). On the Yellow Power movement: Amy Uyematsu, "The Emergence of Yellow Power in America," *Gidra* (October 1969), and William Wei, *The Asian American Movement* (Philedlphia: Temple University Press, 1993). On the Red Power movement: Alvin M. Josephy, Jr., *Red Power: The American Indians' Fight for Freedom* (Lincoln and London: University of Nebraska Press, 1971), and Adam Fortunate Eagle, *Alcatraz! Alcatraz!: The Indian Occupation of 1969–1971* (Berkeley: Heyday Books, 1992). On the Women's Liberation movement: Robin Morgan, ed., *Sisterhood Is Powerful: An Anthology of Writings from the Women's Liberation Movement* (New York: Vintage Books, 1970). On the Gay Liberation movement: Karla Jay and

Allen Young, *Out of the Closets: Voices of Gay Liberation* (New York: Douglas Book Corporation, 1972).

20. "Sources of private troubles" is a quote from SDS's founding document, the Port Huron Statement, which is reprinted in numerous sixties anthologies and in James Miller, *"Democracy Is in the Streets": From Port Huron to the Siege of Chicago* (New York: Simon and Schuster, 1987), pp. 329–74. The description of small feminist groups is from Jo Freeman, *The Politics of Women's Liberation* (New York: David McKay Company, 1975), p. 103. On the continuity between the New Left and women's liberation, see Alice Echols, "We Gotta Get Out of This Place: Notes Toward a Remapping of the Sixties," *Socialist Review* 92/2 (April–June 1992). On feminist influences upon Mayday, see "Women Build for Mayday," *Quicksilver Times* (April 30–May 13, 1971); Mariette, "Here We Are We've Been Detained, Not a One of Us Has Been Arraigned," *off our backs* (May 27, 1971); and "Sexism in Peace City," *The Fifth Estate* (May 20–26, 1971).

21. Telephone interview with Murray Bookchin, November 6, 2000; on the Iberian Anarchist Federation and its *grupos de afinidad,* see George Woodcock, *Anarchism: A History of Libertarian Ideas and Movements* (Cleveland: World Publishing, 1962), pp. 381–93.

22. See Sale, *SDS*, pp. 375–9; Todd Gitlin, *The Sixties: Years of Hope, Days of Rage* (New York: Bantam Books, 1987), pp. 247–60; Wells, *The War Within*, pp. 172–203, 212–19; and Terry H. Anderson, *The Movement and the Sixties: Protest in America from Greensboro to Wounded Knee* (New York and Oxford: Oxford University Press, 1995), pp. 177–82. The phrase "disruptive confrontation" is from a November 1967 article by Marty Jezer, reprinted in Mitchell Goodman, ed., *The Movement Toward a New America: The Beginnings of Long Revolution* (Philadelphia and New York: Pilgrim Press and Alfred A. Knopf, 1970), p. 470.

23. Ron Hahne, *Black Mask and Up Against the Wall Motherfucker: The Incomplete Works of Ron Hahne, Ben Morea, and the Black Mask Group* (London: Unpopular Books & Sabotage Editions, 1993), p. 119; telephone interview with Ben Morea, July 4, 2000; Bookchin interview. On the Motherfucker actions, see Osha Neumann, "Motherfuckers Then and Now: My Sixties Problem," in Marcy Darnovsky, Barbara Epstein, and Richard Flacks, eds., *Cultural Politics and Social Movements* (Philadelphia: Temple University Press, 1995), pp. 55–73.

24. Quoted in Hahne, *Black Mask and Up Against the Wall Motherfucker,* pp. 121 and 112.

25. Telephone interview with Jeff Jones, June 20, 2000. On the Days of Rage and Weatherman more generally, see Ron Jacobs, *The Way the Wind Blew: A History of the Weather Underground* (London and New York: Verso, 1997), especiallly pp. 54–60, and Dan Berger, *Outlaws of America: The Weather*

Underground and the Politics of Solidarity (Oakland CA: AK Press, 2006), especially pp. 103–16.

26. Interview with Judith Karpova, Philadelphia, PA, July 30, 2000; Shin'ya Ono, "You Do Need a Weatherman," in Judith Clavir Albert and Stewart Edward Albert, *The Sixties Papers: Documents of a Rebellious Decade* (New York: Praeger Publishers, 1984), p. 258; Motor City SDS, "Break on Through to the Other Side," in Harold Jacobs, ed., *Weatherman* (Ramparts Press, 1970), p. 158; and Gitlin, *The Sixties*, pp. 384–401.

27. "Goldberg and Percy Assail SDS Rioting," *New York Times* (October 13, 1969); Dave Dellinger, "A New Stage of Struggle: Mayday and the Fall Offensive," *Liberation* (September 1971), p. 17; "Affinity Groups," *Berkeley Tribe* (May 29, 1970); The O.M. Collective, *The Organizer's Manual* (New York: Bantam Books, 1971), pp. 115–16. Although this manual wasn't published until 1971, it was largely written in the summer of 1970.

28. Jones interview; Scagliotti interview; telephone interview with John Froines, June 23, 2000.

29. Coffin interview; Froines interview.

30. "The Chess of Ending a War," *Time* (May 10, 1971); "Mayday: A Thousand Conspiracies," *Liberated Guardian* (May 20, 1971).

31. Joreen, "The Tyranny of Structurelessness," in Anne Koedt, Ellen Levine, and Anita Rapone, eds, *Radical Feminism* (New York: New York Times Books, 1973), pp. 285–99.

32. Interview with Perry Brass, New York City, February 4, 2000.

33. "What Is Gay Liberation Front?" undated leaflet, International Gay Information Center Archives, Ephemera Collection, New York Public Library; Donn Teal, *The Gay Militants* (New York: Stein and Day, 1971), p. 55; Edward Sagarin, "Behind the Gay Liberation Front," *The Realist* (May 6, 1970); Brass interview.

34. Telephone interview with Warren J. Blumenfeld, June 19, 2000; Toby Marotta, *The Politics of Homosexuality* (Boston: Houghton Mifflin Company, 1981), p. 92.

35. Arthur Evans, "How to Zap Straights," in Len Richmond and Gary Noguera, eds., *The Gay Liberation Book* (San Francisco: Ramparts Press, 1973), p. 112. On the founding and early activism of the Gay Activists Alliance, see Arthur Bell, *Dancing the Gay Lib Blues: A Year in the Homosexual Liberation Movement* (New York: Simon and Schuster, 1971).

36. Gay Mayday Tribe, "Off the Butch in S.E. Asia," undated leaflet, author's collection; "Mayday Is Gayday," *May Flowers*.

37. Angus Mackenzie, *Secrets: The CIA's War at Home* (Berkeley: University of California Press, 1997), p. 38; Scagliotti interview; "The Biggest Bust," *Newsweek* (May 17, 1971).

38. Brass interview; Scagliotti interview.

39. "Sexism in Peace City," *The Fifth Estate* (May 20–26, 1971); Videofreex Mayday footage. I am deeply grateful to Eileen Clancy for tracking down some of the surviving video footage from Mayday, and to Parry D. Teasdale for allowing me to view it. For an account of how it was shot, see his book, *Videofreex: America's First Pirate TV Station and the Catskills Collective That Turned It On* (Hensonville, NY: Black Dome Press, 1999). Some footage of Mayday 1971 is included in the 2015 documentary *Here Come the Videofreex*, directed by Jon Nealon and Jenny Raskin.

40. "Mayday: 12,000 Busts Can't Stop the People's Peace," *Liberation News Service* (May 8, 1971); "Everything You Need to Know," *Quicksilver Times* (April 30–May 13, 1971); Videofreex Mayday footage. For more on the takeover of the concert stage, see "May Day (1)," *off our backs* (May 27, 1971).

41. Cherríe Moraga and Gloria Anzaldúa, eds., *This Bridge Called My Back: Writings by Radical Women of Color* (New York: Kitchen Table: Women of Color Press, 1981), p. xv.

42. Bart Barnes and J.Y. Smith, "Campers Ousted, Still Planning to Snarl City Today," *Washington Post* (May 2, 1971).

43. Paul W. Valentine, "7,000 Arrested in Disruptions: New Obstructions Threatened Today," *Washington Post* (May 4, 1971); Mike Feinsilber, "Newly Released Nixon Tapes Show Anxiety Over Anti-War Protesters," *Detroit News* (October 18, 1997).

44. "Trouble Over Bridged Waters," *May Flowers*; "Mayday Tactics: Report from Washington, DC," *Northwest Passage* (May 24–June 6, 1971); "The Biggest Bust," *Newsweek*; "May Day Washington," *Berkeley Tribe* (May 14–21, 1971).

45. "The Biggest Bust," *Newsweek*; telephone interview with Ann Northrop, June 17, 2000; William H. Kuenning, *Free to Go: The Story of a Family's Involvement in the 1971 Mayday Activities in Washington* (Lombard, IL: Unicorn Publications, 1971), p. 16.

46. Brass interview; Coffin interview.

47. Sanford J. Ungar and Maurine Beasley, "Justify Arrests, Judge Orders Police: Total Sets a US Record," *Washington Post* (May 4, 1971); "Mayday Tactics: Report from Washington, DC," *Northwest Passage* (May 24–June 6, 1971).

48. Mariette, "Here We Are, We've Been Detained; Not a One of Us Has Been Arraigned," *off our backs* (May 27, 1971); Ivan C. Brandon, "Blacks Gave Protesters Food," *Washington Post* (May 6, 1971); "2,700 More Arrested in Protest: Crowd Seized at Justice," *Washington Post* (May 5, 1971); "May Day Washington," *Berkeley Tribe* (May 14–21, 1971).

49. Stokely Carmichael, "What We Want," *New York Review of Books* (September 22, 1966).

50. Interview with Kai Lumumba Barrow, New York, NY, September 20, 2000; interview with Terry Marshall, Brooklyn, NY, June 13, 2015.
51. Interview with Rev. Osagyefo Sekou, San Francisco, CA, April 6, 2015.
52. "Mayday in Atlanta," *Space City!* (August 31, 1971); "Mayday: A Thousand Conspiracies," *Liberated Guardian* (May 20, 1971); Joseph Lelyveld, "Status of the Movement: The 'Energy Levels' Are Low," *New York Times Magazine* (November 7, 1971); Scagliotti interview.
53. "Mayday," *Great Speckled Bird* (August 23, 1971); "Atlanta Mayday Conference," *Berkeley Tribe* (August 27, 1971); Carl Davidson, "Gays Dominate Mayday Meeting in Atlanta," *Guardian* (August 25, 1971).
54. "Mayday," *Great Speckled Bird* (August 23, 1971).
55. John Darnton, "Antiwar Protest Erupt Across US," *New York Times* (May 10, 1972); Linda Charlton, "Antiwar Protests Rise Here and Across the Country," *New York Times* (May 11, 1972); John Darnton, "Hundreds Are Arrested in Antiwar Demonstrations," *New York Times* (May 11, 1972); "Roving Bands of Godless Anarchists," *Up Against the Bulkhead* (May 1972); "Chicago Groups React to War Escalation," *The Torch* (May 15, 1972); "We Fight Beside the NLF," *The Augur* (May 20–June 3, 1972); "Protests Sweep Nation as Response to Nixon's War Escalation Grows," *Liberation News Service* (May 13, 1972), p. 19; telephone interview with Leslie Cagan, March 22, 2016.
56. Frank Hammer, "The Impact of Mayday," *Liberated Guardian* (July 1971).

2   SMALL CHANGE

1. Roberta Lynch, "Cynicism—An American Way of Life Afflicting Working Class and the Left," *In These Times* (March 2–8, 1977)
2. Berger, *Outlaws of America*, p. 242; on the party-building left, see Max Elbaum, *Revolution in the Air: Sixties Radicals Turn to Lenin, Mao, and Che* (New York and London: Verso Books, 2006).
3. Bo Burlingham, "They've All Gone to Look for America: A Veteran of the '60s Searches Out the Activists of Today," *Mother Jones* (May/June 2001, originally published in the February/March 1976 issue). On Burlingham's political background, see Bo Burlingham, "Paranoia in Power," *Harper's* (October 1974).
4. Interview with Ed Hedemann, New York, NY, November 10, 1999.
5. Interview with Leslie Cagan, New York, NY, November 3, 1999; Paul L. Montgomery, "End-of-War Rally Brings Out 50,000," *New York Times* (May 12, 1975).
6. Betty Medsger, *The Burglary: The Discovery of J. Edgar Hoover's Secret FBI* (New York: Alfred A. Knopf, 2014), p. 168; FBI memorandum, May 27,

1968, reprinted in Ward Churchill and Jim Vander Wall, *The COINTEL-PRO Papers: Documents from the FBI's Secret Wars Against Dissent in the United States* (Boston: South End Press, 1990), p. 181. Also see Tim Weiner, *Enemies: A History of the FBI* (New York: Random House, 2012), especially pp. 264–336.

7. Richard Aoki's role as a likely FBI informant has generated substantial controversy among both activists and scholars. On his arming of the Panthers, see Joshua Bloom and Waldo E. Martin, Jr., *Black Against Empire: The History and Politics of the Black Panther Party* (Berkeley: University of California Press, 2013), pp. 47–8. The initial disclosures were made by Seth Rosenfeld in his book *Subversives: The FBI's War on Student Radicals and Reagan's Rise to Power* (New York: Farrar, Straus and Giroux, 2012), pp. 418–35. Additional evidence came from files released after the book's publication; see Seth Rosenfeld, "FBI Files Reveal New Details About Informant Who Armed the Black Panthers," *Center for Investigative Reporting* (September 7, 2012). cironline.org, and Seth Rosenfeld, "New FBI Files Show Wide Range of Black Panther Informant's Activities," *Reveal* (June 9, 2015), revealnews.org. Many of Aoki's former friends and associates have raised questions about Rosenfeld's claims, as have numerous scholars. See especially Donna Murch, "Countering Subversion: Black Panther Scholarship, Popular History, and the Richard Aoki Controversy," *Perspectives on History: The Newsmagazine of the American Historical Association* (October 2012), historians.org.

8. Betty Medsger provides a vivid description of the street fair in *The Burglary*, pp. 189–90.

9. Carole Anne Douglas, "What If the Revolution Isn't Tomorrow?" *off our backs* (September 1977).

10. Ruth A. Eblen and William R. Eblen, eds., *The Encyclopedia of the Environment* (Boston: Houghton Mifflin, 1994), p. 702. On door-to-door canvassing, see Harry C. Boyte, Heather Booth, and Steve Max, *Citizen Action and the New Populism* (Philadelphia: Temple University Press, 1986), pp. 68–83. They trace the birth of the canvassing technique to 1971, when Marc Anderson—inspired in part by the "Appeal Army" used to sell the early-twentieth-century populist newspaper *An Appeal to Reason*—employed it on behalf of Citizens for a Better Environment in Chicago. Anderson describes canvassing as "selling social change door to door, the way you sell encyclopedias." On radical municipalism, see W.J. Conroy, *Challenging the Boundaries of Reform: Socialism in Burlington* (Philadelphia: Temple University Press, 1990); Bruce Dancis, "Community and Electoral Politics: An Interview with Mike Rotkin and Bruce Van Allen," *Socialist Review* No. 47 (September–October 1979), pp. 101–18; David Moberg, "The Santa Monica Story: From Rent Control to Municipal Power," *In*

These Times (January 12–18, 1983); David Moberg, "Surf City Socialism," *In These Times* (January 26–February 1, 1983); David Moberg, "Burlington Loves Bernie," *In These Times* (March 23–29, 1983); and Kevin J. Kelley, "Berkeley: A 'Zone of Control,'" *Guardian* (October 2, 1985). On community organizing, see Gary Delgado, "Taking It to the Streets: Community Organizing and National Politics," *Socialist Review* No. 63/64 (May–August, 1982), pp. 49–84.

11. See, for example, Clayborne Carson, "The Hollow Prize: Black Power After Ten Years," *The Nation* (August 14, 1976); Manning Marable, "Black Nationalism in the 1970s: Through the Prism of Race and Class," *Socialist Review* No. 50–51 (March–June 1980), pp. 57–108. On the increase in black elected officials, see "Gain Found in Number of Blacks in Office," *New York Times*, December 24, 1977.

12. On the Funding Exchange, see Kathleen Teltsch, "Founded by Idealists, Group Thrives on Need," *New York Times* (January 30, 1990) and Ellen Neuborne, "The Young and Wealthy Take Hands-On Approach to Philanthropy," *USA Today* (June 26, 1990). On the Public Media Center, see Kim Foltz, "Advertising Agency with a Cause," *New York Times* (May 21, 1990); Nell Bernstein, "Selling the Cause: Advertising in the Public Interest," *Nuclear Times* (Spring 1992); and Michael J. Ybarra, "Public Media Goes for Jugular to Push Causes," *Wall Street Journal* (September 7, 1990). On the Center for Third World Organizing, see Don Oldenburg, "Widening the Volunteer Base," *Washington Post* (July 1, 1991). On the Socialist Scholars Conference, see John Trinkl, "Survivors in Search of a Revival," *Guardian* (April 20, 1983). Technically, the 1983 Socialist Scholars Conference was not the first; there had been an earlier series of such conferences from 1965 to 1970.

13. Interview with Carol Seajay, San Francisco, February 28, 1994; "Gay Press Gathers for First Time," *Gay Community News* (February 28, 1976); Janis Kelly, "Conference of Women in Print," *off our backs* (November 1976); June Arnold, "Feminist Presses and Feminist Politics," *Quest*, Vol. III, No. 1 (Summer, 1976).

14. June Arnold, "A Severed Head," *Plexus* (July 1976); telephone interview with Ed Hermance, February 2, 1994.

15. Paul W. Valentine, "Causes Vary, Demonstrations Go On," *Washington Post* (August 21, 1978).

16. Andrew Kopkind, "What to Do Till the Movement Arrives," *Working Papers* (January–February 1978); Alicia Garza is quoted in Julia Wong, "As Ferguson 'Weekend of Resistance' Begins, Organizers Weigh How to Turn a Moment into a Movement," *In These Times* (October 10, 2014).

17. See, for example, Ruth Franklin, "A Literary Glass Ceiling?" *The New Republic* (February 7, 2011), newrepublic.com; Nathan Schneider explores

the question of how anarchist organizing helped revive socialist politics in *Thank You, Anarchy: Notes from the Occupy Apocalypse* (Berkeley and Los Angeles: University of California Press, 2013).

18. Interview with Barbara Smith, Albany, NY, August 5, 2016. More background on Smith's experiences with CORE can be found in an interview with scholar Barbara Ransby included in Alethia Jones and Virginia Eubanks, eds., *Ain't Gonna Let Nobody Turn Me Around: Forty Years of Movement Building with Barbara Smith* (Albany, NY: State University of New York Press, 2014), pp. 21–6.

19. On the history and activism of the Combahee River Collective, see Dutchess Harris, "'All of Who I Am in the Same Place': The Combahee River Collective," *Womanist Theory and Research* Vol 3.1 (1999) and Kimberly Springer, *Living for the Revolution: Black Feminist Organizations, 1968–1980* (Durham and London: Duke University Press, 2005); also see "Why Did They Die? A Document of Black Feminism," *Radical America* (November-December 1979); Smith interview.

20. The Combahee River Collective, "A Black Feminist Statement," in Zillah Eisenstein, ed., *Capitalist Patriarchy and the Case for Socialist Feminism* (New York: Monthly Review Press, 1978), pp. 362–72. The manifesto was reprinted in numerous influential anthologies of the 1980s including Moraga and Anzaldúa, eds., *This Bridge Called My Back* and Barbara Smith, ed., *Home Girls: A Black Feminist Anthology* (New York: Kitchen Table: Women of Color Press, 1983). The ways that Combahee's work inspired the notion of intersectionality, a term coined in 1989 by scholar and activist Kimberlé Crenshaw, are discussed in Jones and Eubanks, eds., *Ain't Gonna Let Nobody Turn Me Around*, pp. 52–7.

21. The quotation is from the Clamshell Alliance Founding Statement, printed—among other places—in *We Can Stop the Seabrook Nuclear Plant: Occupier's Handbook* (1977), archived at the Swarthmore College Peace Collection. On the founding of the Clamshell Alliance, see Barbara Epstein's important and influential *Political Protest and Cultural Revolution: Nonviolent Direct Action in the 1970s and 1980s* (Berkeley and Los Angeles: University of California Press, 1991), pp. 9–10, 63–8. Also see Anna Gyorgy and Friends, *No Nukes: Everyone's Guide to Nuclear Power* (Boston: South End Press, 1979), pp. 386–402.

22. Nan Robertson, "German and French Citizens Join in a Watch on the Rhine Against Pollution," *New York Times* (April 9, 1975); Paul Kemezis, "West German Farmers' Resistance Forces Review of Plans for Nuclear Power Plant," *New York Times* (August 28, 1975). Also see Christian Joppke, *Mobilizing Against Nuclear Energy: A Comparison of Germany and the United States* (Berkeley and Los Angeles: University of California Press, 1993), pp. 97–101.

23. The Rennie Cushing interview is on page 13 of the transcript from footage shot for a 1978 documentary about the beginnings of the Seabrook fight, *The Last Resort*, produced by Green Mountain Post Films. I am deeply grateful to Charles Light of Green Mountain Post Films for lending me this transcript. In retrospect, maple and corn seem like utterly inappropriate plantings for a coastal wetland, but the ecology movement was after all still in its infancy.

24. *Last Resort* transcript, pp. 99, 123.

25. Quoted in Sheryl Crown, "Hell No, We Won't Glow: Seabrook, April 1977, Nonviolent Occupation of a Nuclear Power Site," undated pamphlet, author's collection, p. 41.

26. On the internal fight to address racism as part of the 1979 Wall Street mobilization, see Tony Vellela, *New Voices: Student Political Activism in the '80s and '90s* (Boston, MA: South Press, 1988), p. 36; *Up Against the Wall Street Journal Training Handbook* (1979), author's collection, p. 26.

27. Telephone interview with Sukie Rice, May 2, 2002.

28. Elizabeth Boardman passed away in 1996; her role in introducing consensus decision-making to the Clamshell Alliance is reported by Epstein, *Political Protest and Cultural Revolution*, p. 64, and was confirmed by my interview with Sukie Rice. Brinton is quoted in A. Paul Hare, "Group Decision by Consensus: Reaching Unity in the Society of Friends," *Sociological Inquiry* Vol. 43, No. 1 (1973), pp. 75–84, which is also the source of the Hare quote.

29. Rice interview; Marty Jezer, "Learning from the Past to Meet the Future," *WIN* (June 16–23, 1977); interview with Ynestra King, New York City, June 25, 2001.

30. *Seabrook '78: A Handbook for the Occupation/Restoration Beginning June 24* (1978), author's collection, p. 13.

31. On Movement for a New Society, see Edward B. Fiske, "Quaker Commune is Seeking Nonviolent Social Change," *New York Times* (April 6, 1972); the Rice quotation is from the *Last Resort* transcript, p. 97; King interview.

32. *Seabrook '78*, p. 16.

33. Joanne Sheehan, "Tracing Our History: Affinity Groups and Nonviolent Action at Seabrook," *Peace News* (May 1996).

34. A thorough treatment of prefigurative radicalism can be found in Epstein's *Political Protest and Cultural Revolution*, especially pp. 83–91. Also see Polletta, *Freedom Is an Endless Meeting*, especially pp. 6–7; and, for a critical take written in the aftermath of Occupy Wall Street, Jonathan M. Smucker, "Can Prefigurative Politics Replace Political Strategy?" *Berkeley Journal of Sociology* (October 7, 2014). The IWW preamble is quoted in Joyce L. Kornbluh, "Industrial Workers of the World," in Mari Jo Buhle, Paul Buhle, and Dan Georgakas, eds., *Encyclopedia of the American Left* (New York and London: Garland Publishing 1990).

35. *Last Resort* transcript, p. 157; Clamshell Nonviolence Preparation and ODAM! (Outreach, Demonstrations, Actions and Marches) Committees packet, Swarthmore Peace Collection; Starhawk, *Dreaming the Dark: Magic, Sex & Politics* (Boston: Beacon Press, 1982), pp. 114–15.

36. King interview; Dave Drolet, "A Gay Clam at Seabrook," *WIN* (June 16 and 23, 1977).

37. Ed Hedemann, "Successes and Problems," *WIN* (June 16 and 23, 1977).

38. Hard Rain, "Direct Action Occupation; The Orange Proposal; Clams for Democracy Statements," photocopied packet, private achive of Dennis Fox, pp. 5, 11.

39. Gary Nielson, "Surrender at Seabrook," *Hartford Advocate* (June 21, 1978).

40. Telephone interview with Billy Nessen, May 6, 2002.

41. *Let's Shut Down Seabrook! Handbook for Oct. 6, 1979 Direct Action Occupation* (1979), author's collection, p. 9; Michael Knight, "Antinuclear Protest Bogs Down in Mud," *New York Times* (October 7, 1979); Associated Press, "Protesters Retreat at A-Plant Site," *Milwaukee Journal* (October 7, 1979); interview with Rudy Perkins, Brookline, MA, December 17, 2000.

42. Tacie Dejanikus and Stella Dawson, "Women's Pentagon Action," *off our backs* (January 1981). Other accounts of the event include Susan Pines, "Women's Pentagon Action," *WRL News* (January–February 1981); and "Talk of the Town: Demonstration," *New Yorker* (December 8, 1980).

43. The statement is reprinted in Charlene Spretnak, ed., *Politics of Women's Spirituality: Essays on the Rise of Spiritual Power within the Feminist Movement* (Garden City, NY: Anchor Books, 1982), pp. 455–7.

44. Pam McAllister, ed., *Reweaving the Web of Life: Feminism and Nonviolence* (Philadelphia: New Society Publishers, 1982); Gina Foglia and Dorit Wolffberg, "Spiritual Dimensions of Feminist Anti-Nuclear Activism," in Spretnak, ed., *The Politics of Women's Spirituality*, p. 460.

45. Sandra G. Boodman, "A '60s-Style Protest," *Washington Post* (November 18, 1980).

46. Dejanikus and Dawson, "Women's Pentagon Action."

47. "150 Arrested at Pentagon in Protest by 1,300 Women," *New York Times* (November 18, 1980); Boodman, "A '60s-Style Protest"; Amanda Claiborne and Dorothy Martin, "Women's Pentagon Action," *Resist* (December 1980–January 1981); King interview; Pines, "Women's Pentagon Action," *WRL News*.

48. Amanda Claiborne and Dorothy Martin, "Women's Pentagon Action," *Resist* (December 1980–January 1981).

49. Sarah Schulman, "Women's Action Criticized," *Womanews* (February 1981).

50. Associated Press, "Sixty-Two Protesters Arrested at Pentagon," *New York Times* (November 17, 1981); King interview.

51. Inteview with Leslie Cagan, New York, NY, February 3, 2000.

52. Francis X. Clines, "A Fledgling Protest Movement Gathers Steam," *New York Times* (August 5, 1985); "Protest Chronology," *Washington Post* (November 27, 1985); Karlyn Barker, "Antiapartheid Movement to Mark Anniversary," *Washington Post* (November 27, 1985); Krissah Thompson, "On Mandela Day, DC Founders of Free South Africa Movement Look Back," *Washington Post* (July 17, 2013).

53. Peter Grier, "Randall Robinson: Man Behind Anti-Apartheid Protests," *Christian Science Monitor* (February 4, 1985).

54. Interview with Kai Lumumba Barrow, New York, NY, September 20, 2000.

55. Michelle Alexander, *The New Jim Crow: Mass Incarceration in the Age of Colorblindness* (New York: The New Press, 2012), pp. 46–52; Ehrlichman is quoted in Dan Baum, "Legalize It All," *Harper's Magazine* (April 2016); Justice Policy Institute, "The Punishing Decade: Prison and Jail Estimates at the Millennium," Justice Policy Institute (May 2000), justicepolicy.org; Nathan James, "The Federal Prison Population Buildup: Overview, Policy Changes, Issues, and Options," Congressional Research Service (April 15, 2014), fas.org.

56. Quoted in Stephen Duncombe, "Lessons from Anti-Apartheid Organizing: Building the Student Movement," *The Mobilizer* (Fall 1985).

57. Tony Vellela, *New Voices: Student Political Activism in the '80s and '90s* (Boston: South End Press, 1988), pp. 24–7.

58. Vellela, *New Voices*, p. 87.

59. Interview with Howard Pinderhughes, San Francisco, CA, July 10, 2001.

60. Telephone interview with Pedro Noguera, July 3, 2001. In a document entitled "October 6th: Words of the People," from the files of CDAS organizer Rudy Perkins, Billy Nessen wrote of the occupation attempt, "We took that step. We took it together in the rain and the cold, shivering and hypothermic, under club and mace, through the Seabrook marshes. And instead of falling, WE SOARED." The quote describing CAA comes from Anne Edwards and William A. Ryan, "Unlike Old Times at Berkeley," *Guardian* (May 1, 1985). On the tensions between UPC and CAA, also see Melissa Crabbe, "Anti-Apartheid Forces Join But Cultures, Tactics Differ," *Daily Californian* (April 29, 1986); and Sumi Cho and Robert Westley, "Historicizing Critical Race Theory's Cutting Edge: Key Movements that Performed the Theory," in Francisco Valdes, Jerome McCristal Culp, and Angela P. Harris, eds., *Crossroads, Directions, and a New Critical Race Theory* (Philadelphia: Temple University Press, 2002), pp. 37–8. On sexual assault at Occupy Wall Street, see Tamara A. Lomax, "Occupy Rape Culture," *Feminist Wire* (November 5, 2011), thefeministwire.com.

61. *From Soweto to Berkeley* (1988), directed by Richard C. Bock.

62. *From Soweto to Berkeley*; Pinderhughes interview.

63. Pinderhughes interview; *From Soweto to Berkeley*; Cynthia Gorney, "Echoes of the '60s, A Cause for the '80s: On the Nation's Campuses, Apartheid Protests," *Washington Post* (April 20, 1985).

64. "Apartheid Protest Ends at Berkeley as Last 35 Depart," *Los Angeles Times* (May 23, 1985).

65. Bradford Martin, *The Other Eighties: A Secret History of America in the Age of Reagan* (New York: Hill and Wang, 2011), pp. 57–8.

66. Pinderhughes interview; *From Soweto to Berkeley;* Michael Taylor and Jaxon Van Derbeken, "Riot on UC Campus – 91 Arrested," *San Francisco Chronicle* (April 4, 1986); Lonn Johnston, "Violent Brawl Injures 29 at UC Berkeley," *Los Angeles Times* (April 4, 1986).

67. Martin, *The Other Eighties*, p. 65. Also see Jon Wiener, "Students, Stocks and Shanties," *The Nation* (October 11 1986); "Mandela's 1990 Speech in Oakland: 'We Cannot Turn Back'," *East Bay Times,* eastbaytimes.com.

68. Interview with Sean Carter, Washington, DC, February 3, 2001. The two women were not oblivious to the racial dynamics of the arrest, it should be noted: as Zahara Heckscher, the activist then known as Joanie, recalled, "We showed up to court, and Robin and I are in grubby jeans, t-shirts— just our usual messy activist style. And Ray and Sean are both wearing suits and ties and looking very, very proper. So Robin looks at me and she says, 'Well, I guess Joan and I are just wearing our white-skin privilege.'" Interview with Zahara Heckscher, Washington, DC, February 4, 2001.

69. Ken Brown, "Anti-Apartheid Protests Waning, Students Fight Racism on Campus," *United Press International* (May 23, 1988); Vellala, *New Voices*, pp. 83–117; Jeff Chang, *Who We Be: The Colorization of America* (New York: St. Martin's Press, 2014), pp. 115–19; Matthew Countryman, "Lessons of the Divestment Drive," *The Nation* (March 26, 1988).

3   IN YOUR FACE

1. This section draws on L.A. Kauffman, "On the Floor … And Out the Door: At the Democrats' Unity Fest," *SF Weekly* (July 22, 1991).

2. On the labor and gay marches, see Peter Dworkin and Gary E. Swan, "Labor's Big Show of Strength," *San Francisco Chronicle* (July 16, 1984); Randy Shilts and Katy Butler, "100,000 Join Gays Marching in Support of Democrats," *San Francisco Chronicle* (July 16, 1984); Jim Ryan, "National March for Lesbian/Gay Rights: 100,000 Deliver Petition to Democrats," *Gay Community News* (July 28, 1984).

3. "Rebel Earthquake Shakes S.F.," *Overthrow* (December 1984–January 1985); David Solnit, "Voting with Your Feet at the Altar of the Electoral Ritual," *San Francisco Music Calendar* (July 1984). Other noteworthy

accounts of the 1984 protests include Leslie Guevarra and Seth Rosenfeld, "Onlookers Jeer as 100 'War Chest' Demonstrators Arrested," *San Francisco Examiner* (July 16, 1984); Peter Page and Randy Shilts, "Punk Rocker Protest—84 Arrests," *San Francisco Chronicle* (July 17, 1984); "Protest of 'War Industries,'" *San Francisco Chronicle* (July 19, 1984); Edward Iwate and Bill Wallace, "Hundreds Arrested in Two S.F. Demonstrations," *San Francisco Chronicle* (July 20, 1984); Kevin J. Kelley and Joyce Stoller, "Activism and Affirmation," *The Guardian* (July 25, 1984); Erika Munk, "The Show of Violence," *Village Voice* (July 31, 1984); Joyce Stoller and Bill Allen, "500 Arrested in San Francisco Convention," *The Guardian* (August 8, 1984); and Kent Jolly, "Convention '84," *Maximum RocknRoll* (August 1984).

4. Gary Roush, "Convention Crackdown Greets San Francisco Demonstrators," *It's About Times* (August–September 1984). Publicly available accounts of the relationship between CISPES and the Fuerzas Populares de Liberación (FPL) tend to be vague on the exact nature of the collaboration; one of the frankest descriptions can be found in Libby Cooper, "The Salvadoran Labor Movement and Development," *Guild Practitioner* No. 54 (1997), p. 246. Hennessy is quoted in John Smith, "'Model Peaceful Demos': Your Actions Are Being Monitored," *Welcome to San Francisco—Bound Together Newsletter* No. 6 (Late July 1984). On LAG's decline, see Epstein, *Political Protest and Cultural Revolution*, p. 153.

5. David Solnit, "I Was There ... 1984 Warchest Tours II," posted at FoundSF, foundsf.org.

6. The Stop the City quotation is from Rupert Morris, "Anarchists Plan Repeat of Protest to Stop City," *The Times* (March 31, 1984); also see Rupert Morris, "400 Held on London Day of Protests," *The Times* (March 30, 1984); "'Stop the City' Disrupts UK Banks, Stock Market," *Overthrow* (August–September 1984); and the April–May 1984 issue of *Maximum RockNRoll*, which reprints an unattributed, undated news report about the protest. On Rock Against Racism, see "Rock Against Racism Movement Explodes in US," *High Times* (June 1979). RAR in England was a creation of the Socialist Workers Party; see David Widgery, *Beating Time: Riot'n'Race'n'Rock'n'Roll* (London: Chatto & Windus, 1986) and Simon Frith and John Street, "Rock Against Racism and Red Wedge: From Music to Politics, From Politics to Music," in Reebee Garofalo, ed., *Rockin' the Boat: Mass Music and Mass Movements* (Boston: South End Press, 1992), pp. 67–80. In the United States, RAR began as a project of the Yippies, who had embraced punk rock in the late 1970s and early 1980s. The Yippie newspaper, *Overthrow*, published regular reports on RAR concerts from 1979 onward. On *Maximum RockNRoll*, see Jeff Goldthorpe, "Interview with *Maximum RockNRoll*," *Radical America* Vol. 18, No. 6 (November–December 1984), pp. 9–24.

7. Jim Martin, *1984: The Summer of Hate* (Fort Bragg, CA: Flatland, 1989), pp. 67–78; *The Democratic National Convention Handbook 1984: What Is Democracy Anyway?* (1984).

8. Solnit, "Voting with Your Feet."

9. "Rebel Earthquake Shakes S.F.," *Overthrow* (December 1984–January 1985); *The Democratic National Convention Handbook 1984*. Jello Biafra is quoted in "Convention Capers," *Overthrow* (December 1984–January 1985).

10. On "loser culture" and its relationship to radical politics, see Stephen Duncombe, *Notes from Underground: Zines and the Politics of Alternative Culture* (London and New York: Verso, 1997).

11. On the founding of the National Right to Life Committee, see James Risen and Judy L. Thomas, *Wrath of Angels: The American Abortion War* (New York: Basic Books, 1998), pp. 19–20. On Focus on the Family, see William Martin, *With God on Our Side: The Rise of the Religious Right in America* (New York: Broadway Books, 1996), pp. 343–9. Anita Bryant, *The Anita Bryant Story: The Survival of Our Nation's Families and the Threat of Militant Homosexuality* (Old Tappan, NJ: Fleming H. Revell Company, 1977); Mark Thompson, "20 Years Ago: Hate Turns Deadly," *The Advocate* (December 9, 1997). For a historical overview of the religious right, see Martin, *With God on Our Side*, and Sara Diamond, *Roads to Dominion: Right-Wing Movements and Political Power in the United States* (New York and London: The Guilford Press, 1995). The notion of "politics in a new key" is borrowed from Carl E. Schorske's classic *Fin-de-Siècle Vienna: Politics and Culture* (New York: Vintage Books, 1981). The best history of Operation Rescue is Risen and Thomas, *Wrath of Angels: The American Abortion War*; for an account by a supporter of the movement, see Philip F. Lawler, *Operation Rescue: A Challenge to the Nation's Conscience* (Huntington, IN: Our Sunday Visitor Publishing, 1992). On anti-abortion activism before the advent of Operation Rescue, see Kristin Luker, *Abortion and the Politics of Motherhood* (Berkeley and Los Angeles: University of California Press, 1984) On the contrasts between the Moral Majority and the Christian Coalition, see Erin Saberi, "From Moral Majority to Organized Minority: Tactics of the Religious Right," *Christian Century* (August 11, 1993); William Martin, *With God on Our Side: The Rise of the Religious Right in America* (New York: Broadway Books, 1996), especially pp. 200–5, 229–32, and 270–1. On the Wise Use movement, see David Helvarg, *The War Against the Greens: The "Wise-Use" Movement, the New Right, and Anti-Environmental Violence* (San Francisco: Sierra Club Books, 1994).

12. Militants within the labor movement had also proposed blockading the bridges over the Potomac and the National Airport as part of the

demonstration, but the proposals went nowhere: on this and many other occasions, labor leadership was resolutely opposed to any form of direct action. Joseph A. McCartin, *Collision Course: Ronald Reagan, the Air Traffic Controllers, and the Strike That Changed America* (Oxford and New York: Oxford University Press, 2011), p. 318; Timothy J. Minchin, "Together We Shall Be Heard: Exploring the 1981 'Solidarity Day' Mass March," *Labor: Studies in Working-Class History of the Americas*, Vol. 12, Issue 3 (2015). For an account of the 1982 anti-nuclear mobilization, see Paul L. Montgomery, "Throngs Fill Manhattan to Protest Nuclear Weapons," *New York Times* (June 12, 1982).

13. The FBI was particularly focused on trying to prove that CISPES was controlled by the Communist Party USA. There certainly were CPUSA members involved in the organization, but it wasn't the dominant political influence; the FBI was quite ineptly barking up the wrong tree. Ross Gelbspan, *Break-ins, Death Threats, and the FBI: The Covert War Against the Central American Movement* (Boston: South End Press, 1991); telephone interview with Diane Greene Lent, May 15, 2016; Van Gosse, "CISPES: Radical, Pragmatic, and Successful," *Crossroads* (Spring 1994). Also see Bradford A. Martin, *The Other Eighties: A Secret History of America in the Age of Reagan* (New York: Hill and Wang, 2011), pp. 25–44.

14. Ken Butigan, Terry Messman-Rucker, and Marie Pastrick, eds., *¡Basta! No Mandate for War: A Pledge of Resistance Handbook* (Philadelphia: New Society Publishers, 1986); interview with Lisa Fithian, Washington, DC, January 23, 2000; Christian Smith, *Resisting Reagan: The US Central America Peace Movement* (Chicago and London: University of Chicago Press, 1996), pp. 80–6; "Ten Arrested in Central America Policy Protest," *United Press International* (December 17, 1988); Kathy Bodovitz, "Navy Train Severs Concord Protester's Leg," *San Francisco Chronicle* (September 2, 1987); Paul Glickman, "Furor Over Maiming of Protester," *Inter Press Service* (September 3, 1987). On Vietnam-era blockades at the Concord Naval Weapons Station, see "21 Seized in Coast Protest," *New York Times* (August 9, 1966), and "Marines Fight Coast Rally," *New York Times* (August 18, 1966).

15. Jonathan A. Bennett, "Rainbow Coalition Activists Getting Stop Signal," *Guardian* (October 12, 1988); Leslie Cagan, "Rainbow Realignment," *Z Magazine* (May 1989); Connie Hogarth, "Jackson Calls Rainbow to Action," *Guardian* (May 23, 1990); Thomas B. Edsall, "Jackson's Bid to Build Coalition Falters," *Washington Post* (August 15, 1991).

16. Ben A. Franklin, "Diverse Groups Mobilize for a Weekend of Protests in Capital," *New York Times* (April 20, 1985); Karlyn Barker, "More than 300 Arrested in White House Protest," *Washington Post* (April 23, 1985); interview with Leslie Cagan, New York City, February 3, 2000.

17. Matthew L. Wald, "Amy Carter Is Acquitted Over Protest," *New York Times* (April 16, 1987).

18. David Dyson, "Labor Takes the Field," *CrossRoads* (April 1994), archived at nathannewman.org. Most of the details about the internal workings of this mobilization come from an extraordinarily frank post-action report: Beverly Bickel, Philip Brenner, and William LeoGrande, *Challenging the Reagan Doctrine: A Summation of the April 25th Mobilization* (Washington, DC: Foreign Policy Education Fund, October 1987). Leslie Cagan, who coordinated the massive 1982 anti-nuclear protest in New York and the more modest 1985 multi-issue mobilization, was staff coordinator of this event as well.

19. The full text of Lane Kirkland's letter is archived at archive.org/stream/ executivecouncil87520afl2/executivecouncil87520afl2_djvu.txt; Albert Shanker, "Learning the Lessons of the '30s: Avoiding the 'Wrong Crowd,'" paid advertorial, *New York Times* (April 19, 1987); Jeane Kirkpatrick, "Another Popular Front," *Washington Post* (April 27, 1987); on the *Washington Times* allegation, see "2-Day Protest Planned on US Policy Abroad," *New York Times* (April 25, 1987).

20. *Challenging the Reagan Doctrine,* p. 14. Also see David L. Hostetter, *Movement Matters: American Antiapartheid Politics and the Rise of Multicultural Politics* (New York and London: Routledge, 2006), pp. 133–4.

21. *Challenging the Reagan Doctrine,* pp. 22, 53.

22. Wayne King, "Thousands Protest US Policy in Central America," *New York Times* (April 26, 1987).

23. Interview with Lisa Fithian, Austin, TX, March 18, 2015; John F. Harris, "Protesters Meet Police at the Gates of the CIA," *Washington Post* (April 28, 1987); Lee Hockstader, "560 Arrested at C.I.A. Headquarters," *Washington Post* (April 28, 1987); John E. Smith and Peter Baker, "561 Seized in Protest at CIA Headquarters," *Washington Times* (April 28, 1987); telephone interview with Tom Swan, May 6, 2016; Bernard Weinraub, "Hundreds Arrested at CIA in Protest on Foreign Policy," *New York Times* (April 28, 1987). Also see Vellela, *New Voices,* pp. 127–31, and "Nonviolent Civil Disobedience at CIA Headquarters, Langley, Virginia, Monday, April 27, 1987," organizing manual, private archive of Lisa Fithian.

24. "557 Arrested in Peaceful Protest at CIA," *Baltimore Sun* (April 28, 1987); Hockstader, "560 Arrested at C.I.A. Headquarters."

25. "National Student Convention '88 Registration Packet," author's collection; L.A. Kauffman, "Emerging from the Shadow of the Sixties," *Socialist Review* 90/4, pp. 11–12; "Vania del Borgo and Maria Margaronis, "Beyond the Fragments," *The Nation* (March 26, 1988)

26. The members of the advisory board were listed in the "National Student Convention '88 Registration Packet"; the figures on conference

demographics come from Barbara Haber, "Piscataway Stalemate: Sixties Myths Derail Student Radicals," *Propaganda Review* (Summer 1988), p. 23.

27. Christine Kelly, "Opening Plenary Speech," *Zeta Magazine* (March 1988); Angela Parker, "Homogenous Group Does Not Make a Unified Student Left," *The Guardian* (March 23, 1988).

28. Interview with Ray Davis, Kent, OH, May 5, 1990; Michael Albert and Lydia Sargent, "Conference Report," *Zeta Magazine* (March 1988); Del Borgo and Margonis, "Beyond the Fragments."

29. Dave Foreman, "Earth First!" *The Progressive* (October 1981), pp. 39–42. On the difficult political climate that environmentalists of the time faced, see "Hard Times Come to Environmentalists," *US News and World Report* (March 10, 1980); Murray Bookchin, "The Selling of the Ecology Movement," *WIN* (September 15, 1980).

30. Dave Foreman, "Violence and Earth First!" *Earth First! Newsletter*, Vol. II, No. 4 (March 20, 1982); Edward Abbey, *The Monkey Wrench Gang* (New York: Avon Books, 1975); the quotations are from p. 70.

31. On how Arizona's Eco-Raiders inspired Earth First!, see Susan Zakin, *Coyotes and Town Dogs: Earth First! and the Environmental Movement* (New York: Viking Penguin, 1993), pp. 59–60. Also see Tom Miller, "Lurkers on the Corporate Threshold," *Rolling Stone* (August 29, 1974). On the Fox, see: "The Fox," *Newsweek* (October 5, 1970); "The Kane County Pimpernel," *Time* (October 5, 1970); "The Fox Strikes Again," *Newsweek* (January 11, 1971); Georgia Straight, "The Eco-Guerrillas Are Coming," *Harry* (April 24–May 7, 1971); Mike Royko, "Fox Populi," *Esquire* (March 1972); Sally Wagner, "'The Fox' Tells Pollution Foes to Inform Public on Issues," *Chicago Tribune* (March 15, 1972); "Ecology's Fox Plans a Slyer Approach," *Los Angeles Times* (March 15, 1972); Sally Jones, "'Fox's' Hibernation Ends in Pollution Raid," *Chicago Tribune* (March 15, 1973); Sally Jones, "Kane County's Elusive Fox Broadens His Pollution War," *Chicago Tribune* (March 18, 1973). On the billboard bandits, see "6 Seized for Axing Billboards," *Detroit Free Press* (March 7, 1971); "The Billboard Caper," *Time* (March 22, 1971); Tom Nugent, "Phantoms Strike Again and More Billboards Fall," *Detroit Free Press* (April 8, 1971); Gene Goltz, "Billboard Falls ... Axmen Boast," *Detroit Free Press* (April 10, 1971); Julie Morris, "Advertisers Vow to Restore Billboards Axed by Vandals," *Detroit Free Press* (April 13, 1971); Cindy Felong, "A Tale of Giant-Slayers," *The Fifth Estate* (April 15–21, 1971); "Sign Cutters Flee, Newsmen Seized," *Detroit Free Press* (April 17, 1971); Larry Adcock, "Farm-Posses Hunt Billboard Bandits," *Detroit Free Press* (April 21, 1971); "Michigan Youths Fell Billboards," *The New York Times* (April 25, 1971); "Billboard Battle Is Joined," *Freedom News* (April 1971); "The 'True' Adventures of Billie Board," *Ann Arbor Argus* (June 1971). The Eco-Raider quotation is from James Steinberg,

"Vandalism, Assaults, Bombs Threaten Construction Sites," *Arizona Daily Star* (September 7, 1973). Also see Mark Ochs and Steve Karp, "Eco-Raiders: No Deposit, No Return," and Randy Holdridge, "Stalking the Wild Eco-Raider," *New Times* (November 8, 1972); Ken Burton, "Eco-Raiders' Efforts Called Total Failure by Builder," *Arizona Daily Star* (September 12, 1973); "4 Held in 'Eco-Raider' Case," *Arizona Daily Star* (September 19, 1973); Tom Miller, "Hey Maw, They Says They Caught Dem Fierce Ol' Ecoraiders," *New Times* (September 26, 1973); and Tom Miller, "What Is the Sound of One Billboard Falling?" *Berkeley Barb* (November 8–14, 1974).

32. "An Ecology Contest Aimed at Business," *Business Week* (April 17, 1971), p. 40; Myra MacPherson, "An Award for 'Ecotage,'" *Washington Post* (January 26, 1972); "6 'Eco-Commandos' Honored: Antipollution Efforts Don't Go to Waste," *Los Angeles Times* (January 27, 1972); Sam Love and David Obst, eds., *Ecotage!* (New York: Simon & Schuster, 1971) Love is quoted in MacPherson, "An Award for 'Ecotage,'" and in "Ecotage," *Newsweek* (August 23, 1971), p. 50.

33. Stewart McBride, "The Real Monkey Wrench Gang," *Outside* (December 1982–January 1983); Christopher Manes, *Green Rage: Radical Environmentalism and the Unmaking of Civilization* (Boston: Little, Brown and Company, 1990); Dave Foreman, *Confessions of an Eco-Warrior* (New York: Harmony Books, 1991); Zakin, *Coyotes and Town Dogs*. The Judi Bari quotation is from Judi Bari, *Timber Wars* (Monroe, ME: Common Courage Press, 1994), p. 41–2; the Earth First! tactics cited here are recounted in "Vandals Force Closing of New Golf Course," *New York Times* (August 11, 1991); Jim Robbins, "Saboteurs for a Better Environment," *New York Times* (July 9, 1989); and Christopher Manes, *Green Rage: Radical Environmentalism and the Unmaking of Civilization* (Boston: Little, Brown and Company, 1990), p. 104. The pro–tree spiking quotation is from Dave Foreman and Bill Haywood, eds., *Ecodefense: A Field Guide to Monkeywrenching*, Third Edition (Chico, CA: Abbzug Press, 1993), p. 18. Also see "Spike Those Trees!" *Earth First!* (May 1, 1985). On the injured mill worker, see Dale Champion, "Tree Sabotage Claims Its First Bloody Victim," *San Francisco Chronicle* (May 15, 1987); Peter Page, "More Spiked Trees Discovered in Mendocino Forest Areas," *San Francisco Chronicle* (June 11, 1987); Eric Brazil, "Tree Spiking in Mendocino Splinters All Sides," *San Francisco Examiner* (June 21, 1987). The most prominent Earth First!er to denounce the practice was Judi Bari; see her two-part series on "The Secret History of Tree-Spiking," reprinted in Bari, *Timber Wars*, pp. 264–82. Earth First!ers vehemently insisted they were not responsible for the incident. Radical environmentalists who spiked trees, they said, always notified the timber companies about what they had done (anonymously); otherwise, the tactic

would have little or no effect on logging operations. Moreover, the forest where the logger was injured was second growth, while Earth First!ers at that time concentrated their energies on old-growth forests exclusively. On the monkeywrenching convictions, see Karen Pickett, "Four of AZ 5 Get Maximum Jail Time," *Earth First!* (November 1, 1991).

34. See Karl and Dona Sturmanis, *The Greenpeace Book* (Vancouver: Orca Sound Publications, 1978); Robert Hunter, *To Save a Whale: The Voyages of Greenpeace* (San Francisco: Chronicle Books, 1978); Robert Hunter, *Warriors of the Rainbow: A Chronicle of the Greenpeace Movement* (New York: Holt, Rinehart and Winston, 1979), especially pp. 149–235 and 248–96; Michael Brown and John May, *The Greenpeace Story* (London: Dorling Kindersley, 1989), especially pp. 32–52; and Rik Scarce, *Eco-Warriors: Understanding the Radical Environmental Movement* (Chicago: The Noble Press, 1990), pp. 47–56. On Plowshares, see Arthur J. Laffin and Anne Montgomery, eds., *Swords into Plowshares: Nonviolent Direct Action for Disarmament* (San Francisco: Harper & Row, 1987); Ann Morrissett Davidon, "Warheads into Plowshares," and Philip Berrigan, "Why We Seized the Hammer," *The Progressive* (May 1981); Michael Diamond, "The Trial of the Plowshares 8," *WIN* (May 1, 1981); Frank Panopoulos, "The Strategy of Plowshares," *The Nonviolent Activist* (June 1986).

35. Deborah B. Gould has extensively explored the emotional landscape of AIDS activism in *Moving Politics: Emotion and ACT UP's Fight Against AIDS* (Chicago and London: The University of Chicago Press, 2009). Buck Young quoted in Joe Drape, "Green Panthers," *Atlanta Journal and Constitution* (June 24, 1990). Aldyn McKean is quoted in "Why We Get Arrested," an undated ACT UP/NY document compiled in the wake of a major 1991 action at Grand Central Station.

36. The AIDS-themed zine *Diseased Pariah News* was published from 1990 to 1999.

37. Centers for Disease Control, "Estimates of New HIV Infections in the United States," cdc.gov. The protests that followed the Supreme Court ruling in *Bowers* v. *Hardwick* presaged the public anger that would soon mark gay and lesbian activism. See Marc Sandalow, "S.F. Gays, Lesbians Vow to Fight: Sodomy Ruling Stirs Protest," *San Francisco Chronicle* (July 1, 1986); Kevin Flynn and Timothy Clifford, "Angry Gays Block Village Streets," *New York Newsday* (July 2, 1986); Tim McDarrah and Gene Ruffini, "Angry Gay Army Storms Through the Village," *New York Post* (July 2, 1986); William G. Blair, "City's Homosexuals Protest High Court Sodomy Ruling," *New York Times* (July 3, 1986); Anne-Christine d'Adesky, "Gays on Two Coasts Protest Supreme Court Sodomy Ruling," *New York Native* (July 14, 1986); Charles Linebarger, "Court Protest Takes Anger to the Streets," *Bay Area Reporter* (July 24, 1986); Tommi Avicolli, "Sodomites

and Friends Protest Supreme Court," *Philadelphia Gay News* (July 25–31, 1986); and "Hundreds Protest Supreme Court Sodomy Ruling," *New York Times* (August 12 1986). On setbacks. see Robert B. Gunnison, "State AIDS Bias Bill Vetoed Again," *San Francisco Chronicle* (October 1, 1986); James Strong and Manuel Galvan, "Gay-Rights Ordinance Fails," *Chicago Tribune* (July 30, 1986); on the actions by the Vatican, see Charles W. Bell, "The New Outcasts," *New York Daily News* (February 15, 1987).William F. Buckley, "Identify All the Carriers," *New York Times* (March 18, 1986); "Don't Panic, Yet, Over AIDS," *New York Times* (November 7, 1986). Also see *"New York Times* Allows Word 'Gay,'" *San Francisco Sentinel* (July 3, 1987).

38. On Citizens for Medical Justice, see David M. Lowe, "Activists Stage State Sit-In: AIDS at Duke's Door," *San Francisco Sentinel* (September 26, 1986); Charles Linebarger, "8 Protesters Arrested at Duke's Door," *Bay Area Reporter* (October 2, 1986); David M. Lowe, "Beyond the Sit-In: Sitting Down to Take a Stand," *San Francisco Sentinel* (October 10, 1986). On the Lavender Hill Mob, see Marty Robinson, "The Lavender Hill Mob Zaps the Cardinal," *New York Native* (November 17, 1986); Jean Elizabeth Glass, "Lavender Hill Mob Zaps D'Amato," *New York Native* (December 8, 1986); "Mob Zaps Grant," *New York Native* (December 22, 1986); and Mitchel Halberstadt, "Bringing Back the Zap: The Lavender Hill Mob is Reviving Early Gay Liberation Activist Tactics," *New York Native* (December 22, 1986). In 1987, the group also published several issues of a newsletter entitled the *Lavender Hill News*, which covered these and later actions.The Bill Bahlman quotation is from Dave Walter, "In Depth: CDC AIDS Conference," *The Advocate* (March 31, 1987); also see Darrell Yates Rist, "Antibody Testing Wars," *New York Native* (March 16, 1987).

39. The t-shirt is described in Sally Chew, "What's Going Down with ACT UP?" *Out* (October/November 1993); Cleve Jones is quoted in Deb Price, "Soldiers of Misfortune," *Detroit News* (November 19, 1990); Vito Russo, "Why We Fight," *Village Voice* (October 25, 1988); interview with Zoe Leonard, New York City, May 3, 1992; "How ACT UP Was Born," undated flier, Marty Robinson Papers, Lesbian and Gay Community Services Center Archive, New York City. Kramer's galvanizing speech is reprinted as "The Beginning of ACTing UP," in Larry Kramer, *Reports from the Holocaust: The Story of an AIDS Activist* (New York: St. Martin's Press, 1994). Also see Mike Salinas, "Kramer, Mob, Others Call for Traffic Blockade," *New York Native* (March 30, 1987) and Marty Robinson, "Acting Up," *New York Native* (April 6, 1987).

40. On ACT UP tactics, see Charles Babington, "AIDS Activists Throw Ashes at White House," *Washington Post* (October 12, 1992); Simon Watney, "Political Funeral," *Village Voice* (October 20, 1992); Diane Curtis, "Protest

Closes Gate Bridge," *San Francisco Chronicle* (February 1, 1989); "'Stop AIDS or Else,' Say Golden Gate Blockaders," *Guardian* (February 15, 1989). On props and visuals, see Guy Trebay, "The War at Home," *Village Voice* (February 5, 1991); the smoke bombs were used at the October 1988 FDA action. For an excellent discussion of ACT UP's use of graphics, including reproductions of many early posters, see Douglas Crimp and Adam Rolston, *AIDS Demo Graphics* (Seattle: Bay Press, 1990), which also includes a chronology and description of ACT UP/NY and national actions up through the December 1989 Stop the Church protest. A less detailed but more geographically inclusive list covering ACT UP's entire first decade of existence can be found in Jesse Heiwa Loving, "All in Good Time," *POZ* (March 1997). My figure on the number of ACT UP chapters comes from the "ACT UP Genl and Misc" folder in the ACT UP papers archived at the New York Public Library; my list of chapters is drawn from this source and from Jesse Heiwa Loving, "ACTing UP All Over," *POZ* (March 1997). On the Wall Street demo, see Frances McMorris, "Gays Protest Lack of Drugs to Wage War Against AIDS," *Daily News* (March 25, 1987); Peter Freiberg, "New York Demonstrators Demand Release of New AIDS Drug," *The Advocate* (April 28, 1987). On the FDA action, see Kiki Mason, "FDA: The Demo of the Year," *New York Native* (October 24, 1988); Dan Bellm, "Storming the FDA," *Village Voice* (October 25, 1988); Jon David Aloisi-Nalley, "Creative Anger Over AIDS," *Guardian* (October 26, 1988); and Rick Harding, "Gay Direct Action Comes of Age," *The Advocate* (November 21, 1988). On the *CBS Evening News* disruption, see "AIDS Action Disrupts News," *Daily News* (January 22, 1991). On the Stop the Church demo, see Jason DeParle, "111 Held in St. Patrick's AIDS Protest," *New York Times* (December 11, 1989); Andrew Miller, "AIDS/Abortion Rights Demo Halts High Mass at St. Pat's," *OutWeek* (December 24, 1989); John Hammond, "Civil Disobedience Flap Obscures Legitimate Issues: Community Responses to ACT UP Demonstration at Cathedral," *New York Native* (December 25, 1989); and Chris Bull, "Mass Action: A Raucous Disruption at St. Patrick's Cathedral Divides New York Gays," *The Advocate* (January 16, 1990).

41. Interview with David Crane, New York, NY, February 13, 2000; interview with Mike Spiegel, New York, NY, July 17, 2000; "National News Summary: Milwaukee," *Outlines* (April 1990); "National News Summary: Des Moines," *Outlines* (July 1991); Chris Nealon, "Shoe Store Chain Acquiesces to ACT UP," *Gay Community News* (July 21–27, 1991); Jesse Heiwa Loving, "ACTing UP All Over," *POZ* (March 1997).

42. See the ACT UP/NY Women & AIDS Book Group, *Women, AIDS & Activism* (Boston, MA: South End Press, 1992). Noteworthy discussions of the role of lesbians in AIDS activism include Sarah Schulman, *My*

American History: Lesbian and Gay Life in the Reagan/Bush Years (New York and London: Routledge, 1994), especially pp. 11–12, 120–4, and 216–19; Denise Kulp, "On Working with My Brothers: Why a Lesbian Does AIDS Work," *off our backs* (August–September 1988); Jackie Winnow, "Lesbians Working on AIDS: Assessing the Impact on Health Care for Women," *OUT/ LOOK* (Summer 1989); Risa Denenberg, "Lesbian AIDS Activists: What Are We Doing?" *OutWeek* (October 15, 1989); Eva Yaa Asantewaa, "Sister to Brother: Women of Color on Coming Together with Men," *OutWeek* (April 4, 1990); Amy Hamilton, "Women in AIDS Activism," *on our backs* (November 1991); and Ruth L. Schwartz, "New Alliances, Strange Bedfellows: Lesbians, Gay Men, and AIDS," in Arlene Stein, ed., *Sisters, Sexperts, Queers: Beyond the Lesbian Nation* (New York: Plume, 1993), pp. 230–44.

43. Interview with Maxine Wolfe, New York, NY, July 30, 1992; Holly Metz, "The Progressive Interview: Sarah Schulman," *The Progressive* (October 1994); *The Lesbian Avenger Handbook: A Handy Guide to Homemade Revolution* (New York: The Lesbian Avengers, 1993), p. 8. Extensive excerpts from this handbook can be found in Schulman, *My American History*, pp. 289–312.

44. ACT UP Oral History Project interview with Amy Bauer, March 7, 2004, actuporalhistory.org, p. 16. Rafsky wrote a powerful op-ed not long before his death from AIDS: Robert Rafsky, "A Better Life for Having Acted Up," *New York Times* (April 19, 1992); Michelangelo Signorile, *Queer in America: Sex, the Media, and the Closets of Power* (New York: Random House 1993), pp. 36–52; interview with David Norton, Seattle, WA, September 24, 1992.

45. ACT UP Oral History Project interview with Alexandra Juhasz, January 13 2003, actuporalhistory.org; Signorile, *Queer in America*, p. 15.

46. Cynthia Crossen, "Shock Troops: AIDS Activist Group Harasses and Provokes to Make its Point," *Wall Street Journal* (December 7, 1989); interview with David Crane, New York City, September 12, 2000.

47. The chants are captured in David France's 2012 documentary film *How to Survive a Plague*; Vito Russo is quoted in David France, "ACT UP Fires Up," *Village Voice* (May 3, 1988).

48. ACT UP Oral History Project interview with Elias Guerrero, March 17, 2004, actuporalhistory.org, p. 18; ACT UP Oral History Project interview with Kendall Thomas, May 3, 2003, actuporalhistory.org, p. 13.

49. ACT UP Oral History Project interview with Robert Vazquez-Pacheco, December 14, 2002, actuporalhistory.org, p. 13.

50. ACT UP Oral History Project interview with Kendall Thomas, p. 12; ACT UP Oral History Project interview with Lei Chou, May 5, 2003, actuporalhistory.org, p. 20.

51. ACT UP Oral History Project interview with Ron Medley, December 28,

2003, actuporalhistory.org, pp. 15–16; interview with Cathy Chang, New York City, May 10, 1992.

52. ACT UP Oral History Project interview with Kendall Thomas, pp. 11–12.

53. On the ACT UP/San Francisco split, see Tim Kingston, "Acting Up Is Hard to Do," *San Francisco Bay Times* (October 1990); on the broader tensions within the movement, see Victoria Brownworth, "Lesbians Press for More Attention to their Health Concerns," *The Advocate* (October 23, 1990); Natasha Gray, "Bored with the Boys: Cracks in the Queer Coalition," *NYQ* (April 26, 1992); and Chew, "What's Going Down with ACT UP?" *OUT* (November 1993).

54. All quotations concerning the San Francisco split are from Kingston, "Acting Up Is Hard to Do."

55. Kingston, "Acting Up Is Hard to Do."

56. These tensions are explored in depth in Steven Epstein's incisive *Impure Science: AIDS, Activism, and the Politics of Knowledge* (Berkeley: University of California Press, 1996); Harrington is quoted on p. 233. Also see Anne-Christine d'Adesky, "Empowerment or Co-optation? AIDS Activists," *The Nation* (February 11, 1991); Andrew Jacobs, "ACT UP Splits over Drug Trial," *NYQ* (December 15, 1991); interviews with Maxine Wolfe, New York, NY, July 11, 1992 and July 20, 1992.

57. See Emily Bass, "How to Survive a Footnote: AIDS Activism in the 'After' Years," *n+1* (Fall 2015).

58. Telephone interview with René Francisco Poitevin, October 11, 2000; interview with Tracy Morgan, New York City, July 17, 1992. On Queer Nation, see Deborah Schwartz, "'Queers Bash Back,'" *Gay Community News* (June 24–30, 1990); Carrie Wofford, "Queer Nation: 'We're Here, We're Fabulous,'" *The Guardian* (November 14, 1990); and Linnea Due, "Loud and Queer," *East Bay Express* (February 13, 1991).

59. The quotations are from Scarce, *Eco-Warriors*, pp. 91–2.

60. Interview with Mac Scott, Washington, DC, April 12, 2000; Judi Bari, *Timber Wars* (Common Courage Press, 1994), p. 220; interview with Ramin Karimpour, Shawnee National Forest, IL, October 19, 1992.

61. Bari, *Timber Wars*, p. 219; on Bari's work with the Pledge of Resistance, see Christine Keyser, "In Support of Mother(Earth)hood: A Conversation with Earth First! Activist Judi Bari," *On the Issues* (Summer 1991).

62. "Mississippi Summer in the Redwoods, 'Freedom Riders Needed to Save the Forest,'" *Anderson Valley Advertiser* (April 25, 1990).

63. Judi Bari, *Earth First! and Timber Workers* (Willits, CA: Rainy Day Women Press, 2000); Mark A. Stein: "'Redwood Summer': It Was Guerrilla Warfare," *Los Angeles Times* (September 2, 1990).

64. Howie Wolke, "Focus on Wilderness," *Earth First!* (September 22, 1990). Also see Eric Brazil, "Earth First! Faces an Identity Crisis: 'Monkey-Wrenchers'"

Fear FBI, Hippies," *San Francisco Examiner* (June 25, 1989); Karen Pickett, "Breaking Up or Breaking Apart?" *Earth First!* (November 1, 1990); Bill Devall, "An Open Letter to Earth First!ers," *Earth First!* (December 21, 1990); Bill Weinberg, "Earth First! Confronts Political Diversity," *Guardian* (January 16, 1991). On the Minnesota campaign, see Mary Losure, *Our Way or the Highway: Inside the Minnehaha Free State* (Minneapolis and London: University of Minnesota Press, 2002).

65. *The Lesbian Avenger Handbook,* pp. 45–7.

66. Lesbian Avengers, "Dyke Manifesto," 1993, author's collection.

67. Dyke March, Washington, DC, April 24, 1993, author's notes.

68. Telephone interview with Rachel Pepper, April 14, 1993.

69. On the Queens action, see Schulman, *My American History,* pp. 279–82; Elaine Herscher, "Lesbian Avengers Deliver a High-Attitude Message," *Houston Chronicle* (June 26, 1994); Paul Leavitt, "Gay Activists at School," *USA Today* (February 17, 1994).

70. Telephone interview with Annette Gaudino, April 13, 1993.

71. Interview with Elizabeth Meister, New York City, September 29, 2000; Sara Pursley, "Gay Politics in the Heartland: With the Lesbian Avengers in Idaho," *The Nation* (January 23, 1995); Lesbian Avengers, *Out Against the Right: An Organizing Handbook,* author's collection.

72. Meister interview; telephone interview with Eileen Clancy, October 18, 2000.

73. *Out Against the Right*; Clancy interview.

74. Rick Harding, "New York ACT UP's 'Freedom Ride' Jeered in Florida," *The Advocate* (October 10, 1988).

75. Barbara Smith, "Blacks and Gays: Healing the Great Divide," reprinted in Jones and Eubanks, eds., *Ain't Gonna Let Nobody Turn Me Around,* p. 181; Smith interview; Kelly Cogswell, *Eating Fire: My Life as a Lesbian Avenger* (Minneapolis: University of Minnesota Press, 2014), pp. 73–6; Schulman, *My American History,* pp. 313–19; telephone interview with Elizabeth Meister, September 8, 2016.

76. The *Southern Illinoisan* quotation is from August 22, 1990; Karimpour interview; Pollard is quoted in Dave Walter, "Does Civil Disobedience Still Work?" *The Advocate* (November 20, 1990).

4   TURNED UP

1. N.R. Kleinfeld, "Rush Hour Protest Causes Gridlock," *New York Times* (April 26, 1995); Tomio Geron, "APA Activism, New York Style: The Confrontational Tactics of the Coalition on Anti-Asian Violence Are Controversial, But Effective," *AsianWeek* (April 5, 1996); Andrew Hsiao and

Karen Houppert, "Birth of a Movement? Behind the Rush Hour Revolt," *Village Voice* (May 9, 1995); Esther Kaplan, "This City Is Ours," in Benjamin Shepard and Ronald Hayduk, eds., *From ACT UP to the WTO: Urban Protest and Community Building in the Era of Globalization* (London and New York: Verso Books, 2002), pp. 41–51.

2. The call to action is quoted in Karl Grossman, "From Toxic Racism to Environmental Justice," *E* (May/June 1992); Paul Ruffins, "Defining a Movement and a Community," *forward motion/CROSSROADS* (April 1992); Dana Alston, ed., *We Speak for Ourselves: Social Justice, Race, and Environment* (The Panos Institute, December 1990). Also see Robert D. Bullard, ed., *Confronting Environmental Racism: Voices from the Grassroots* (Boston: South End Press, 1993).

3. Manuel Callahan, "Zapatismo Beyond Chiapas," in David Solnit, ed., *Globalize Liberation: How to Uproot the System and Build a Better World* (San Francisco: City Lights Books, 2004), p. 228; Eric Sawyer, "An ACT UP Founder 'Acts Up' for Africa's Access to AIDS," in Shepard and Hayduk, eds., *From ACT UP to the WTO*, pp. 88–102; Bass, "How to Survive a Footnote: AIDS Activism in the 'After' Years"; Tony Davis, "Last Line of Defense: Civil Disobedience and Protest Slow Down 'Lawless Logging,'" *High Country News* (September 2, 1996); Liza Featherstone, *Students Against Sweatshops: The Making of a Movement* (London and New York: Verso Books, 2002). Active Resistance conference packet (1996), private archive of David Solnit; David Solnit, "Art and Revolution Convergence," *Reclaiming Quarterly* (No. 69, Winter 1997/98); Ruckus Society history, ruckus.org.

4. This section draws from L.A. Kauffman, "Who Are Those Masked Anarchists?" in Eddie Yuen, George Katsiaficas, and Daniel Burton Rose, eds., *The Battle of Seattle: The New Challenge to Capitalist Globalization* (New York: Soft Skull Press, 2001), pp. 125–9. Interview with Cloud, Willamette National Forest, May 26, 1998; Tony Davis, "Last Line of Defense: Civil Disobedience and Protest Slow Down "Lawless Logging,"" *High Country News* (September 2, 1996); Hakim Bey, *TAZ: The Temporary Autonomous Zone, Ontological Anarchy, Poetic Terrorism* (New York: Autonomedia, 1991).

5. Kathy Hedberg, "Waiting for the "Party," Earth First! Protesters Have Set Up Roadblocks on Controversial Cove-Mallard Timber Sale Area," *Lewiston Morning Tribune* (July 3, 1996); *Earth First! Direct Action Manual*, first edition, 1997, author's collection.

6. Maria L. La Ganga, "Police Sued Over Use of Pepper Spray on Protesters," *Los Angeles Times* (October 31, 1997); "An Assault with Pepper Spray," *New York Times* (November 4, 1997); interview with John Bowling, Seattle, November 27, 1999. A federal court ruled in 2005, in *Lundberg* v. *County*

of Humboldt, that the direct application of pepper spray to the eyes of the protesters was an excessive use of force and a violation of their constitutional rights.

7. "Worldwide Resistance Round-Up Inspired by Peoples' Global Action," Bulletin 5, February 2000, UK Edition, private archive of David Solnit. Also see Sophie Style, "Peoples' Global Action," in Eddie Yuen, Daniel Burton-Rose, and George Katsiaficas, eds., *Confronting Capitalism: Dispatches from a Global Movement* (Brooklyn: Soft Skull Press, 2014), pp. 215–21; "Carnival Against Capitalism," *The Progressive* (August 1999). Because of an aggressive police response, the New York action barely got off the ground; see Stephen Duncombe, "Stepping Off the Sidewalk: Reclaim the Streets/NYC," in Shepard and Hayduk, eds., *From ACT UP to the WTO,* pp. 224–5.

8. Correspondence from San Francisco Art and Revolution Collective, February 20, 1999, private archive of David Solnit; "Shut Down the WTO—Mass Nonviolent Direct Action—Action Packet," (1999), author's collection.

9. Interview with Brad Will, New York City, June 28, 2000.

10. Lesley J. Wood, *Crisis and Control: The Militarization of Protest Policing* (London: Pluto Press, 2014), pp. 25–7; interview with Yarrow Rain King, Seattle, November 30, 1999; Starhawk, "How We Really Shut Down the WTO," in Shepard and Hayduk, eds., *From ACT UP to the WTO,* pp. 52–6.

11. Telephone interview with Lisa Fithian, May 31, 2001; interview with Lisa Fithian, Washington, DC, January 23, 2000; interview with David Solnit, Washington, DC, January 22, 2000. See also Liz Highleyman, "Radical Queers or Queer Radicals? Queer Activism and the Global Justice Movement," in Shepard and Hayduk, eds., *From ACT UP to the WTO,* pp. 106–20.

12. For an excellent history and overview of recent anarchist organizing, see Chris Dixon, *Another Politics: Talking Across Today's Transformative Movements* (Oakland: University of California Press, 2014), especially pp. 41–5.

13. Chris Crass, "Shutting Down the WTO and Opening Up a World of Possibilities," in Stephanie Guilloud, ed., *Voices from the WTO: An Anthology of Writings from the People Who Shut Down the World Trade Organization,* undated booklet, author's collection, pp. 49–50.

14. On the rise of mass incarceration under Clinton, see Alexander, *The New Jim Crow,* especially pp. 56–8, and Keeanga-Yamahtta Taylor, *From #BlackLivesMatter to Black Liberation* (Chicago, IL: Haymarket Books, 2016), especially pp. 100–2 and 119–21; the quotation is from page 102. Suzy Subways, "A Culture of Resistance: Lessons Learned from the Student Liberation Action Movement," *Upping the Anti,* Issue 8, uppingtheanti.org; "Our History," Ella Baker Center for Human Rights,

ellabakercenter.org; "The History of Critical Resistance," *Social Justice*, Vol. 27, No. 3 (Fall 2000), pp. 6–10.

15. On the protests following the killing of Amadou Diallo, see "Response Time: A *City Limits* Roundtable," *City Limits* (June 1999); Dan Barry, "Daily Protesters in Handcuffs Keep Focus on Diallo Killing," *New York Times* (March 19, 1999); telephone interview with Richie Perez, March 23, 2000.

16. Elizabeth Betita Martinez, "Where Was the Color in Seattle? Looking for Reasons Why the Great Battle Was So White," *ColorLines*, colorlines.org, (March 10, 2000).

17. Interview with Jia Ching Chen, San Francisco, November 27, 2000; interview with Mac Scott, Washington, DC, April 12, 2000.

18. Martinez, "Where Was the Color in Seattle?"; interview with Sandra Barros, New York City, September 19, 2000; Andrew Hsiao, "Color Blind," *Village Voice* (July 18, 2000); interview with Kai Lumumba Barrow.

19. New York City Direct Action Network brochure, circa 2000, author's collection.

20. Hsiao, "Color Blind"; Colin Rajah, "Globalism and Race at A16 in DC," *ColorLines*, colorlines.org (October 10, 2000).

21. "Thousands Protest Acquittal of Police Officers Who Killed Amadou Diallo," *Democracy Now* (February 28, 2000); William K. Rashbaum, "The Diallo Case: The Protests; Marchers Protest Diallo Verdict, Taunting Police Along the Way," *New York Times* (February 27, 2000); Lakeisha Mcghee, "Don't Push Me 'Cause I'm Close to the Edge—Youth Use Hip-Hop Music to Fight Prop. 21," *Pacific News Service* (March 1, 2000).

22. Justino Aguila, "175 Held After Protest of Youth Crime Initiative," *San Francisco Examiner* (March 9, 2000); Davey D., "Third Eye Fights Back Against Prop. 21," *Hip Hop and Politics* (February 4, 2000), daveyd.com; Angela Ards, "Organizing the Hip-Hop Generation," *The Nation* (July 26/ August 2, 1999); Robin Templeton, "No Power Like the Youth," *Alternet* (March 10, 2000); interview with Edget Betru, San Francisco, November 27, 2000.

23. Interview with Jia Ching Chen.

24. Interview with Kai Lumumba Barrow; interview with Jia Ching Chen.

25. *Philadelphia Direct Action Handbook* (2000), author's collection.

26. Linda K. Harris, Craig R. McCoy, and Thomas Ginsberg, "State Police Infiltrated Protest Groups, Documents Show," *Philly.com* (September 7, 2000), articles.philly.com; Kris Hermes, *Crashing the Party: Legacies and Lessons from the RNC 2000* (Oakland, CA: PM Press, 2015), pp. 49–66; Francis X. Clines, "Demonstrators Nearly Steal the Spotlight at Convention," *New York Times* (August 2, 2000).

27. Wood, *Crisis and Control*, pp. 26–7; Hermes, *Crashing the Party*, pp. 37–8.

28. Interview with Sandra Barros; interview with Kai Lumumba Barrow; Suzy Subways, "We Shut the City Down: Six Former Student Action Liberation Movement (SLAM) Organizers Reflect on the Mass Direct Actions Against the 2000 RNC in Philadelphia," SLAM! Herstory Project (December 2, 2010), slamherstory.wordpress.com.

29. Interview with Lesley Wood, New York City, September 6, 2000.

30. Jodi Wilgoren, "Campuses Split Over Afghanistan," *New York Times* (October 15, 2001); Al Baker, "Huge Police Presence is Readied for World Economic Forum," *New York Times* (January 29, 2002).

31. For details on the mobilizing effort that led up to the February 15 protest, see an interview conducted by Benjamin Shepard: L.A. Kauffman, "A Short Personal History of the Global Justice Movement," in Eddie Yuen, Daniel Burton-Rose, and George Katskificas, eds., *Confronting Capitalism: Dispatches from a Global Movement* (Brooklyn, NY: Soft Skull Press, 2004), pp. 375–89; the list of the 793 cities worldwide that participated in the February 15, 2003 global day of action is archived at web.archive.org/web/20030801135105/unitedforpeace.org/article.php?id=725.

32. Richard W. Stevenson, "Antiwar Protests Fail to Sway Bush on Iraq," *New York Times* (February 19, 2003).

33. Rose Arce, "About 100 Arrested at Protest Outside Manhattan Investment House," CNN.com (April 7, 2003), edition.cnn.com.

34. ACLU press release, "Police Trampled Civil Rights During 2003 Free Trade Protests in Miami, ACLU Charges," aclu.org (November 15, 2005).

35. "Declaration of the Occupation of New York City," (2011), occupywallstreet.net. For detailed histories of the Occupy movement see David Graeber, *The Democracy Project: A History, a Crisis, a Movement* (New York: Spiegel and Grau, 2013); Michael A. Gould-Wartofsky, *The Occupiers: The Making of the 99 Percent Movement* (New York: Oxford University Press, 2015); Schneider, *Thank You, Anarchy;* and the 2015 documentary film by director and Occupy activist Marisa Holmes, *All Day All Week: An Occupy Wall Street Story.*

36. Marina Sitrin, "One No, Many Yeses," in Astra Taylor and Keith Gessen, eds., *Occupy! Scenes from Occupied America* (New York and London: Verso, 2011), p. 8.

37. Adrienne Maree Brown, "From Liberty Plaza; Let It Breathe," in Amy Schrager Lang and Daniel Lang/Levitsky, *Dreaming in Public: Building the Occupy Movement* (Oxford: New Internationalist Publications, 2012), p. 80.

38. On the informal behind-the-scenes leadership that emerged at OWS, see Gould-Wartofsky, *The Occupiers*, especially pp. 122–5.

39. For details on the evictions, see Gould-Wartofsky, *The Occupiers*, pp. 136–7 and 223.

40. Manissa Maharawal, "Standing Up," in Taylor and Gessen, eds, *Occupy!*, pp. 35–40.

41. Trymaine Lee, "Trayvon Martin's Family Calls For Arrest Of Man Who Police Say Confessed To Shooting," *Huffington Post* (March 8, 2012), huffingtonpost.com; Trymaine Lee, "Trayvon Martin Case Salts Old Wounds and Racial Tension," *Huffington Post* (March 14, 2012), huffingtonpost. com; Eric Deggans, "Trayvon Martin Updated: Story Is Now More Covered Than Presidential Race," *Tampa Bay Times* (March 30, 2012), tampabay. com; Ryan Devereaux, "Trayvon Martin's Parents Speak at New York March: 'Our Son Is Your Son'," *Guardian* (March 22, 2012), theguardian. com.

42. Interview with Alicia Garza, New York City, December 8, 2014; an edited version of this interview was published as "A Love Note to Our Folks," *n+1* (January 20, 2015), nplusonemag.com; also see Alicia Garza, "A Herstory of the #BlackLivesMatter Movement," *Feminist Wire* (October 7, 2014), thefeministwire.com.

43. Sarah Jaffe, "Young Activists Occupy Florida Capitol, Demand Justice for Trayvon," *In These Times* web only (July 25, 2013), inthesetimes.com; Kathleen McGrory, "Protesters at Florida Capitol: We Stay Until We Win," *Miami Herald* (July 23, 2013), miamiherald.com; Bill Quigley, "Dream Defenders Florida Take Over Enters Week Four," *Huffington Post* (August 6, 2013), huffingtonpost.com; Barbara Liston, "Dream Defenders, a New Generation, Fights for Civil Rights in Florida," Reuters (October 24, 2013), huffingtonpost.com; Mychal Denzel Smith, "How Trayvon Martin's Death Launched a New Generation of Black Activism," *The Nation* (August 27, 2014).

44. Matt Apuzzo, "Ferguson Police Routinely Violate Rights of Blacks, Justice Dept. Finds," *New York Times* (March 3, 2015); Wilson Andrews, Alicia Desantis, and Josh Keller, "Justice Department's Report on the Ferguson Police Department," *New York Times* (March 4, 2015).

45. Julie Bosman and Emma G. Fitzsimmons, "Grief and Protests Follow Shooting of a Teenager," *New York Times* (August 10, 2014); Johnetta Elzie's tweet is reproduced in "#Ferguson," a Storify created by DeRay Mckesson, storify.com/deray/ferguson-beginning; the *St. Louis Post Dispatch* tweet is quoted in Max Lewontin, "#Ferguson: How Twitter Helped Empower Ordinary Citizens," *Christian Science Monitor* (January 24, 2016), csmonitor.com. The tweet reflected the original headline on the story, which was later edited to replace the phrase "mob reaction" with "angry crowd." Niraj Chokshi, "Militarized Police in Ferguson Unsettles Some; Pentagon Gives Cities Equipment," *Washington Post* (August 14, 2014); Lyle Jeremy Rubin, "A Former Marine Explains All the Weapons of War Being Used by Police in Ferguson," *The Nation* (August 20, 2014).

46. Interview with Kayla Reed, St. Louis, MO, May 27, 2015.

47. Interview with Maurice Moe Mitchell, New York City, June 21, 2016; interview with Kayla Reed.

48. For a timeline of events in and around Ferguson, see Emily Brown, "Timeline: Michael Brown Shooting in Ferguson, MO," *USA Today* (August 10, 215), usatoday.com; interview with Derek Laney, St. Louis, MO, May 28, 2015; interview with Osagyefo Sekou, San Francisco, CA, April 6, 2015; Mitchell interview; Wesley Lowery, "The QuikTrip Gas Station, Protesters' Staging Ground, Is Now Silent," *Washington Post* (August 19, 2014) About two dozen additional businesses on West Florissant were burned in late November after a grand jury decided not to indict Darren Wilson for the killing of Mike Brown.

49. Julie Bosman, "Lack of Leadership and a Generational Split Hinder Protests in Ferguson," *New York Times* (August 16, 2014); interview with Cherrell Brown, New York City, June 8, 2015; interview with Maurice Moe Mitchell.

50. Interview with Kayla Reed. On the Organization for Black Struggle, see "A Very Brief History of OBS," obs-stl.org; also see a series of talks by OBS leader Montague Simmons, "An In-Depth Look at the Ferguson Eruption: Organization for Black Struggle Leader Lays It Out," freedomroad.org. Jeff Ordower of MORE is quoted in Jesse Bogan, "ACORN's Setbacks Force Local Office to Call It Quits," *St. Louis Post-Dispatch* (March 19, 2010), stltoday.com. On MORE's support for Occupy, see Manuel Valdes, "Occupy Wall Street Protesters Spotlight Home Foreclosures," Associated Press (December 7, 2011), stltoday.com; on tensions with MORE within the larger Ferguson movement, see Stephen Deere, "Ferguson Protesters Disagree Who Should Receive Donations," *St. Louis Post-Dispatch* (June 4, 2015), stltoday.com.

51. Interview with Michael McPhearson, St. Louis, MO, May 27, 2015.

52. Interview with Terry Marshall; interview with Maurice Moe Mitchell; for the "Vision for Black Lives," see policy.m4bl.org.

53. Interview with Osagyefo Sekou; telephone interview with Julia Ho, August 2, 2016.

54. Darnell L. Moore and Patrisse Cullors, "5 Ways to Never Forget Ferguson —and Deliver Real Justice for Mike Brown," *Guardian* (September 4, 2014); Akiba Solomon, "Get On the Bus: Inside the Black Life Matters "Freedom Ride" to Ferguson," *ColorLines* (September 5, 2014), colorlines.com; interview with Barbara Smith.

55. Interview with Alicia Garza; Kristin Braswell, "Ferguson Forward: 'Black Lives Matter' Brings Heartbroken Helping Hands to St. Louis," *Ebony* (September 2, 2014), ebony.com; Solomon, "Get on the Bus."

56. Interview with Maurice Moe Mitchell; the quotes from the Ferguson

October website are taken from the version archived at web.archive.org/web/20141005233336/fergusonoctober.com/about; Donna Murch, "Historicizing Ferguson: Police Violence, Domestic Warfare, and the Genesis of a National Movement Against State-Sanctioned Violence," *New Politics* No. 59 (Summer 2015), newpol.org.

57. Interview with Maurice Moe Mitchell; Liz Fields and Alice Speri, "St. Louis Protesters Arrested in Weekend of Mass Civil Disobedience," *Vice News* (October 12, 2014), news.vice.com; Wesley Lowery and Arelis R. Hernandez, "In Ferguson, Coordinated Acts of Disobedience as Protests Evolve," *Washington Post* (October 13, 2014); Rachel Lippman, Jason Rosenbaum, Dale Singer, and Durrie Bouscaren, "Ferguson October Day Four: Dozens of Arrests During 'Day of Civil Disobedience,'" St. Louis Public Radio (October 13, 2014), news.stlpublicradio.org; Dave Zirin, "#Ferguson-October Comes to Monday Night Football," *The Nation* (October 14, 2014).; interview with Julia Ho. For more on the tension between local and national organizers in Ferguson, see Sarah Kendzior, "Ferguson in Focus: How the Tragedy of a Police Shooting Became a National Industry," *The Common Reader* (October 30, 2015), commonreader.wustl.edu.

58. Josmar Trujillo, "Forgetting Ferguson: Mainstream Media Move On from a Movement," Fairness and Accuracy in Reporting (December 1, 2014), fair.org/extra/forgetting-ferguson; Alyssa Figueroa, "Meet the Badass Activist Collective Bringing Direct Action Back to Black Communities," *Alternet* (February 11, 2015), alternet.org.

Index